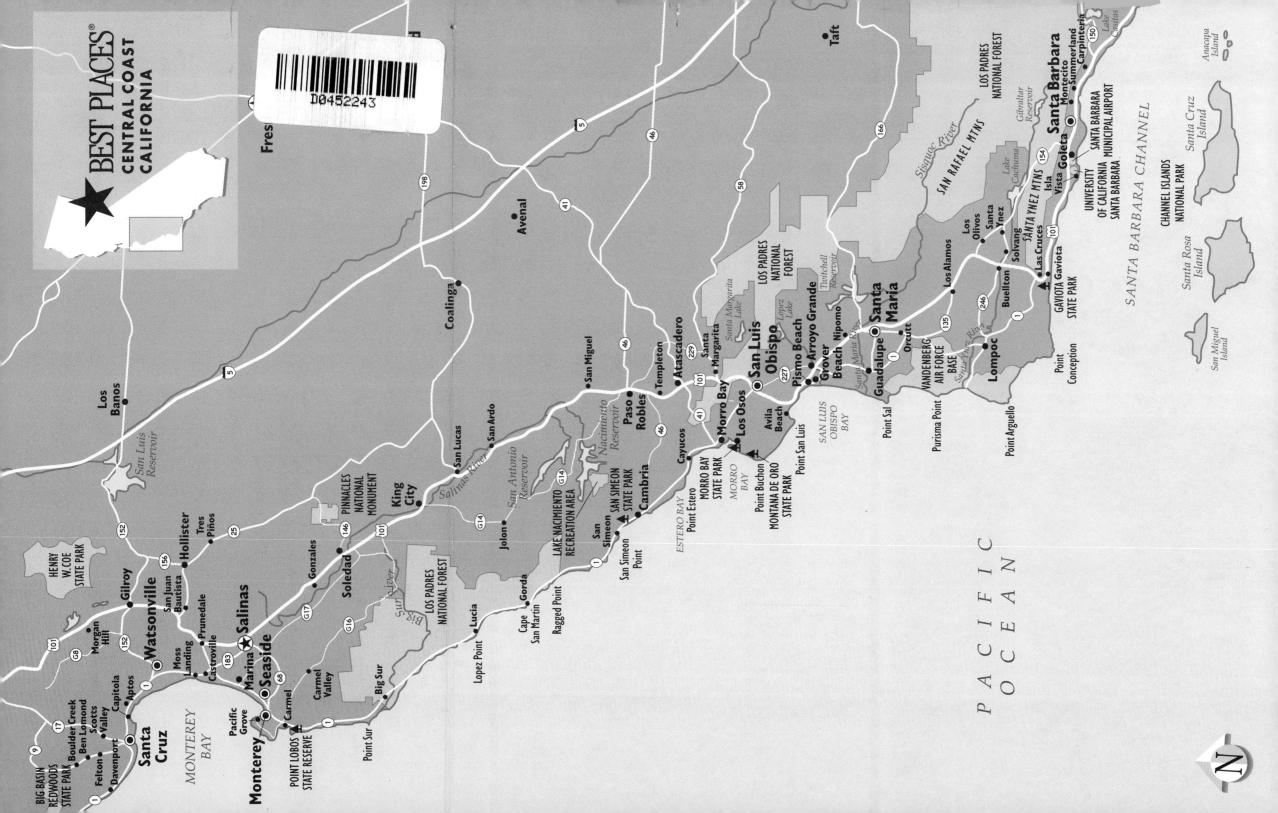

BEST PLACES®
CENTRAL COAST CALIFORNIA

D0452243

Taft

Santa Barbara
Summerland
Carpinteria

150

Lake
Casitas

Anacapa
Island

Los Padres National Forest

Sisquoc River

San Rafael Mtns

Gibraltar Reservoir

SAN RAFAEL MTNS

Santa Barbara
Municipal Airport

Montecito

UNIVERSITY OF CALIFORNIA
SANTA BARBARA

Goleta
Isla Vista

Santa Cruz
Island

5

46

58

166

Avenal

41

Los Padres National Forest

Santa Margarita Lake

Santa Margarita

Atascadero

Santa Ynez Mtns

Los Olivos
Santa Ynez

Solvang
Buellton

Las Cruces

GAVIOTA STATE PARK
Gaviota

CHANNEL ISLANDS NATIONAL PARK

Santa Rosa Island

SANTA BARBARA CHANNEL

Coalinga

San Miguel

Templeton

46

Paso Robles

101

Morro Bay

San Luis Obispo

227

Pismo Beach
Grover Beach

Arroyo Grande
Nipomo

Santa Maria

Los Alamos

135

246

Lompoc

Point Sal

San Miguel Island

5

San Lucas

San Ardo

Nacimiento Reservoir

G14

Salinas River

San Antonio Reservoir

LAKE NACIMIENTO RECREATION AREA

Cayucos

Morro Bay
Los Osos

Avila Beach

Point San Luis

SAN LUIS OBISPO BAY

Guadalupe

Orcutt

VANDENBERG AIR FORCE BASE

Purisima Point

Point Arguello

Los Banos

San Luis Reservoir

King City

Jolon

San Simeon

SAN SIMEON STATE PARK

Cambria

San Simeon Point

ESTERO BAY

Point Estero

MORRO BAY STATE PARK

MORRO BAY

MONTANA DE ORO STATE PARK

Point Buchon

Point Conception

HENRY W. COE STATE PARK

152

Hollister
Tres Piños

25

156

PINNACLES NATIONAL MONUMENT

146

101

Gonzales

Soledad

G14

Big Sur River

LOS PADRES NATIONAL FOREST

Lopez Point

Cape San Martin

Ragged Point

Santa Maria River

101

Gilroy

Morgan Hill

G8

152

Watsonville

Moss Landing
Castroville

Prunedale

San Juan Bautista

Marina
Seaside

Salinas

183

Carmel Valley

G17

G16

68

Lucia

Pacific Grove
Monterey

Carmel

POINT LOBOS STATE RESERVE

Big Sur

Point Sur

MONTEREY BAY

9

17

Felton
Davenport

Boulder Creek
Ben Lomond

Scotts Valley

Capitola
Aptos

Santa Cruz

BIG BASIN REDWOODS STATE PARK

1

PACIFIC OCEAN

N

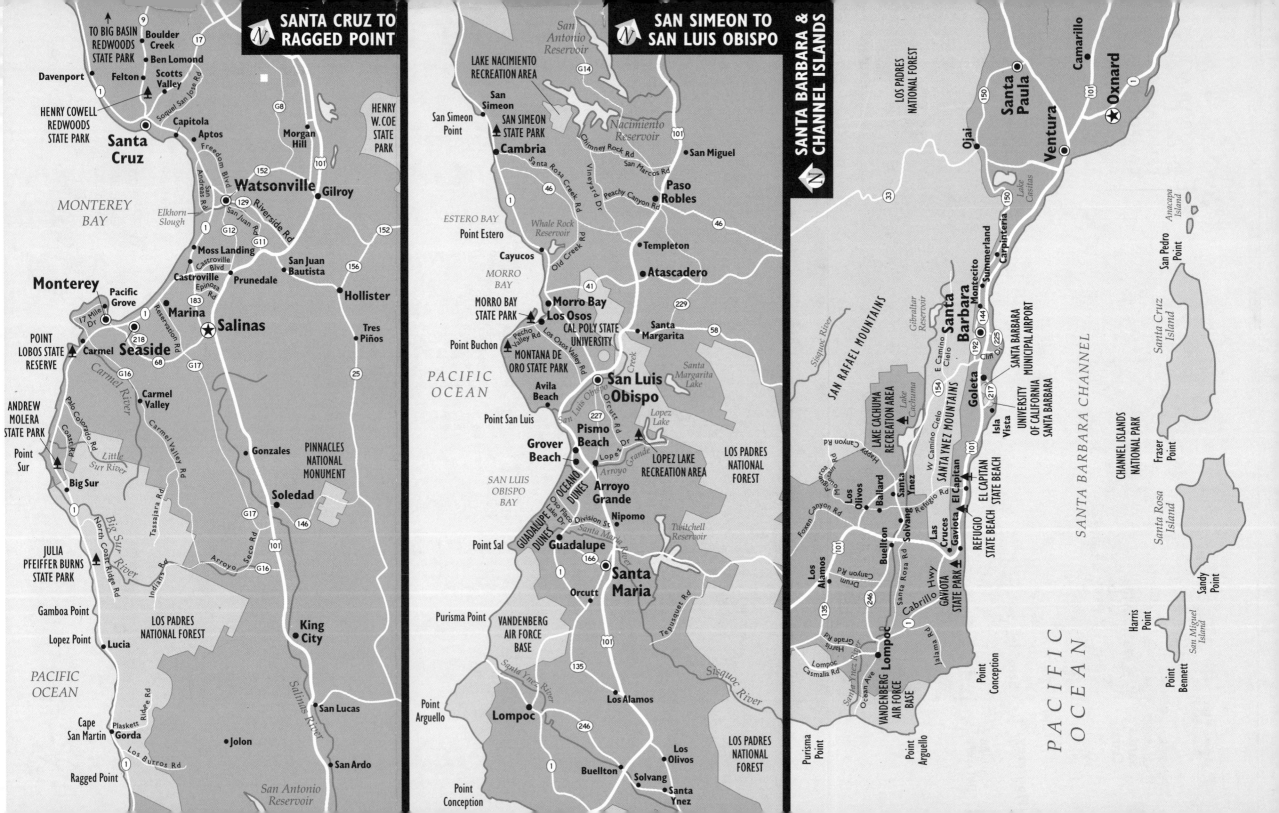

Praise for Best Places® Guidebooks

"Best Places *covers must-see portions of the West Coast . . . with style and authority. In-the-know locals offer thorough info on restaurants, lodgings, and the sights.*"
—NATIONAL GEOGRAPHIC TRAVELER

"Best Places *are the best regional restaurant and guide books in America.*"
—THE SEATTLE TIMES

". . . *travelers swear by the recommendations in the* Best Places *guidebooks . . .* "
—SUNSET MAGAZINE

"*Known for their frank yet chatty tone . . .* "
—PUBLISHERS WEEKLY

"Best Places San Francisco *has frank assessments of restaurants and accommodations . . .* "
—THE SEATTLE TIMES

"Best Places Northern California *is great fun to read even if you're not going anywhere.*"
—SAN FRANCISCO CHRONICLE

"Best Places Southern California *is just about all the inspiration you need to start planning your next road trip or summer vacation with the kids.*"
—THE FRESNO BEE

"Best Places Southern California *and* Best Places San Diego *are quite good, and any traveler to the area would do well to pick one up.*"
—LIBRARY JOURNAL

"*Eat, surf, and shop like a local with this insider's guide,* Best Places San Diego.*"
—AMERICAN WAY

"*For travel collections covering the Northwest, the* Best Places *series takes precedence over all similar guides.*"
—BOOKLIST

"*The best guide to Seattle is the locally published* Best Places Seattle . . . "
—MONEY MAGAZINE

TRUST THE LOCALS

COMPLETELY INDEPENDENT
— No advertisers
— No sponsors
— No favors

EVERY PLACE STAR-RATED & RECOMMENDED

★★★★	The very best in the region
★★★	Distinguished; many outstanding features
★★	Excellent; some wonderful qualities
★	A good place
NO STARS	Worth knowing about, if nearby

BEST PLACES®
DESTINATIONS

CENTRAL
CALIFORNIA COAST
FROM SANTA CRUZ TO SANTA BARBARA

1ST EDITION

EDITED BY JUDITH BABCOCK WYLIE

SASQUATCH BOOKS
SEATTLE

Printed in the United States of America
Distributed by Publishers Group West
First edition
09 08 07 06 05 04 03   5 4 3 2

Series editor: Kate Rogers
Project editor: Laura Gronewold
Cover design: Nancy Gellos
Cover photo: Getty One/John Wang
Foldout map: GreenEye Design
Interior design adaptation: Fay Bartels, Kate Basart, Millie Beard
Interior composition: Justine Matthies and Jenny Wilkson

ISBN: 1-57061-324-9
ISSN: 1538-7801

SASQUATCH BOOKS
119 South Main Street, Suite 400
Seattle, WA 98104
(206)467-4300
books@sasquatchbooks.com
www.sasquatchbooks.com

Special Sales

Best Places guidebooks are available at special discounts on bulk purchases for corporate, club, or organization sales promotions, premiums, and gifts. Special editions, including personalized covers, excerpts of existing guides, and corporate imprints, can be created in large quantities for specific needs. For more information, contact your local bookseller or Special Sales, Best Places Guidebooks, 119 South Main Street, Suite 400, Seattle, WA 98104, 800/775-0817.

CONTENTS

Acknowledgments, vii
About Best Places® Guidebooks, viii
How to Use This Book, viii

THE SANTA BARBARA COAST

THE CHANNEL ISLANDS

ACKNOWLEDGMENTS

My thanks to Frank W. Wylie for his encouragement, insight, and culinary talents at midnight. Thanks also to Fearless the cat who kept the keyboard warm.

I am grateful to live in one of the most beautiful places in the world, from its dramatic seaside cliffs to its soaring seabirds to its charming cottage inns. But one of the best things about the Central Coast of California is its genuinely friendly residents. Dozens of people kindly answered the questions of a stranger, took time to chat, and even walked along to show me hidden gems. I know they will be as friendly and welcoming to you the reader when you travel here. Their suggestions, tips, and favorites helped me find and include many treasures that have not appeared in print before.

Anyone who writes and edits a Best Places guidebook is able to draw on the other fine books in the series as resources. This book has especially benefited from the work of Matthew R. Poole, *Best Places Northern California Coast;* Linda Watanabe McFerrin, *Best Places Northern California;* Erika Lenkert, *Best Places Southern California;* Ed Zieralski, *Inside Out Southern California;* and Dennis J. Oliver, *Inside Out Northern California.*

In each region one person stood out as the most helpful and informed source. Thank you, Ranee Ruble of Santa Cruz County, Julie Armstrong of Monterey County, Susan Carvalho of San Luis Obispo County, Koleen Hamblin of Santa Barbara County, and Malei Jessee Weir of Ventura County. This is a richer book for your time and ideas.

—*Judith Babcock Wylie*

ABOUT BEST PLACES GUIDEBOOKS

Best Places Central California Coast is part of the Best Places guidebook series, which means it's written by and for locals, who enjoy getting out and exploring the region. When making our recommendations, we seek out establishments of good quality and good value, places that are independently owned, run by lively individuals, touched with local history, or sparked by fun and interesting decor. **Every place listed is recommended.**

Best Places guidebooks, which have been published continuously since 1975, represent one of the most respected regional travel series in the country. Each guide is written completely independently: no advertisers, no sponsors, no favors. Our reviewers know their territory, work incognito, and seek out the very best a city or region has to offer. We provide tough, candid reports and describe the true strengths, foibles, and unique characteristics of each establishment listed.

Note: Readers are advised that the reviews in this edition are based on information available at press time and are subject to change. The editors welcome information conveyed by users of this book, as long as they have no financial connection with the establishment concerned. A report form is provided at the end of the book, and feedback is also welcome via email: books@SasquatchBooks.com.

HOW TO USE THIS BOOK

RECOMMENDED RESTAURANTS AND LODGINGS

At the end of each town section you'll find restaurants and lodgings recommended by our Best Places editors.

Rating System Restaurants and lodgings are rated on a scale of zero to four stars (with half stars in between), based on uniqueness, loyalty of local clientele, performance measured against the establishment's goals, excellence of cooking, cleanliness, value, and professionalism of service. Reviews are listed alphabetically, and every place is recommended.

★★★★	The very best in the city
★★★	Distinguished, many outstanding features
★★	Excellent; some wonderful qualities
★	A good place
(*no stars*)	Worth knowing about, if nearby

 Watch for this symbol throughout the book, indicating those restaurants and lodgings that feature a coastal or water view.

Price Range Prices for restaurants are based primarily on dinner for two, including dessert, tax, and tip (no alcohol). Prices for lodgings are based on peak season rates for one night's lodging for two people (i.e., double occupancy). Peak season is typically Memorial Day to Labor Day; off-season rates vary but can sometimes be significantly less. Call ahead to verify, as all prices are subject to change.

$$$$	Very expensive (more than $200 for one night's lodging for two)
$$$	Expensive (more than $100 for dinner for two; between $150 and $200 for one night's lodging for two)
$$	Moderate (between $40 and $100 for dinner for two; between $100 and $150 for one night's lodging for two)
$	Inexpensive (less than $40 for dinner for two; less than $100 for one night's lodging for two)

Addresses and Phone Numbers Every attempt has been made to provide accurate information on an establishment's location and phone number, but it's always a good idea to call ahead and confirm.

Checks and Credit Cards Many establishments that accept checks also require a major credit card for identification. Note that some places accept only local checks. Credit cards are abbreviated in this book as follows: American Express (AE); Carte Blanche (CB); Diners Club (DC); Discover (DIS); Japanese credit card (JCB); Master-Card (MC); Visa (V).

Email and Web Site Addresses Email and web site addresses for establishments have been included where available. Please note that the web is a fluid and evolving medium, and that web pages are often "under construction" or, as with all time-sensitive information, may no longer be valid.

Directions Throughout the book, basic directions are provided with each restaurant and lodging. Whenever possible, call ahead to confirm hours and location.

Bed-and-Breakfasts Many B&Bs have a two-night minimum-stay requirement during the peak season, and several do not welcome children. Ask about a B&B's policies before you make your reservation.

Pets Most establishments do not allow pets; call ahead to verify, however, as some budget places do.

Index All restaurants, lodgings, town names, and major tourist attractions are listed alphabetically at the back of the book.

Reader Reports At the end of the book is a report form. We receive hundreds of reports from readers suggesting new places or agreeing or disagreeing with our assessments. They greatly help in our evaluations, and we encourage you to respond.

ACTIVITIES

Each town throughout this area has a variety of activities and attractions from which to choose. For quick and easy reference, we've created basic symbols to represent them, with full details immediately following. Watch for these symbols:

 Architecture and historical sites

 Arts and crafts, galleries

 Beaches, water recreation

 Bicycling

 Bird-watching, wildlife viewing

 Boating

 Camping

 Entertainment

 Fishing

 Food and drinks

 Golf

 Gourmet food, cooking

 Hikes and walks

 Horseback riding

 Kayaking and canoeing

 Kid-friendly, family activities

 Lighthouses

 Local produce, farmers markets

 Museums and memorials

 Parks, wilderness areas, recreation

 Seals, sea lions, other marine wildlife

 Shops: clothing, books, antiques

 Spas and salons

 Views, scenic driving tours, attractions

 Wineries, wine touring, wine tasting

THE SANTA CRUZ COAST

Located in a charmed zone between the redwoods and the sea, the Santa Cruz coast defines the term mellow. The weather is mild, if a bit foggy in the mornings, and locals are relaxed and friendly. Former clusters of summer cabins have evolved into mountain villages such as Felton, and there are also grand Victorian houses, built by sea captains, in downtown Santa Cruz. Mountain trails, wide beaches, small farms, lagoons studded with egrets and herons, and great views of the ocean are cherished by area residents, who have to be the most outdoor-focused population on the planet. Anyone who likes to hike, bike, sail, surf, windsurf, kayak, or fish will feel at home here. Driving down Highway 1, you may have to brake for surfers to cross the road to the water, and just try to keep your eyes on the road as the shockingly bright colors of windsurfers' sails draw your eye offshore, particularly at Waddell Creek. Even the rows of brussels sprouts lead your gaze down to the ocean. More than 100 years ago San Franciscans summered here, and the community is comfortable and easy with the tourism that brings in a large part of its livelihood. The Santa Cruz Beach Boardwalk, opened in 1907, still draws fans to its Great Dipper roller coaster and historic Looff Carousel. Come in off-season if you can; crowds are down and the beaches will be all yours. And what beaches! They appear in the most unlikely places—under cliffs, at the end of agricultural dirt roads, through groves of Monterey pines, and beyond rolling sand dunes.

The Santa Cruz County Conference & Visitors Council offers a useful Traveler's Guide and also has a referral service for lodgings. Walk in at 1211 Ocean Street, call 831/425-1234 or 800/833-3494, or search their web site at www.santa cruzca.org.

Thanks to the university, which opened here in 1965, the area is wide open to ideas and eccentricities. It's hard to shock anyone in Santa Cruz: fuchsia hair, nose rings, people living their lives in costumes, and poets declaiming their work on the street are just part of the scenery. The music scene is incredibly rich, with clubs featuring blues, jazz, rock, and world music every night of the week. More than 2,000 artists in the county work in studios tucked away from view, and many are open to the public during Open Studios each October. Famous and not-so-famous writers live here and can be seen chatting in coffee shops or tapping their laptops. Don't be surprised at the "Meat Is Murder" bumper stickers. This is the land of tofu burgers and veggie scrambles; organic is a way of life.

DAVENPORT

About 10 miles north of Santa Cruz on Highway 1 is the former whaling and lumber-shipping town of Davenport. Check out the simple and classic 1912 church made by residents out of cement from the local cement plant, whose smokestacks loom north of town. At the Whale City Bakery, Bar & Grill (490 Hwy 1; 831/423-9803; open daily 6am–5pm) you can get a low-fat carrot muffin or a 7-inch-wide go-for-broke cinnamon roll for the road—and be sure to opt for a cup of Steve's Smooth French coffee, a local fave. You can also order a sandwich or other snack to take across the highway for whale watching or an impromptu picnic underneath the cliff-side group of cypress trees called Sunset Grove, overlooking the water. This is the point where gray whales pass closest to shore in their twice-yearly migration along the coast.

ACTIVITIES

Davenport Landing Beach. Located just north of the town of Davenport, this is an easily accessible beach for picnicking and watching windsurfers. Turn seaward at Davenport Landing Road by the old wooden farmhouse, wind to the left, and come to a small parking area just above the sandy beach. There is also a wheelchair-accessible ramp down to the water's edge.

See a Hidden Glass Studio. Follow Coast Road by the south side of the New Davenport Cash Store & Restaurant, and at the bottom of the hill, the third house on your left is a bungalow housing Lundberg Studios Art Glass (121 Old Coast Rd, Davenport; 831/423-2532; 10am–5:30pm every day). The shop is fun to browse for the artists' signature World Weights—globe-shaped paperweights with deep blue hues and luminescent accents, which appear in many museums. There are also scent bottles, glass vases, and lamps. Don't forget to see the garage in the back, where items with slight flaws and "after hours" pieces created in practice sessions can be had for less.

Whales and Watercolors. Walk down the street that runs alongside the Whale City Bakery and you can't miss the Whale Hedge Studio (51 Ocean; 831/458-3119), because the hedge is pruned in the shape of a whale. Watercolorist Bill Fravel displays his scenic coastal watercolors inside and also offers free maps of Davenport. On Sundays the amiable Fravel welcomes everyone to a free informal demonstration of watercolor techniques between 10 and 11am.

The Perfect Beach. Just a few years ago it used to be a secret, this pristine gold-sand beach south of Davenport. Now there's not only a new parking lot, but a bus stop as well. No matter—it still remains the finest public beach between Santa Cruz and San Francisco, a postcard expanse of sand sheltered from wind and road noise by high bluffs. During high surf the waves put on quite a show smashing into the rocks. It's located exactly 1 mile south of Davenport on Highway 1. Park in the long, skinny lot across from Bonny Doon Road, walk over the railroad levee, down the steep path cut in the cliffs, and you'll find one of the most beautiful secluded beaches in California.

RESTAURANTS

NEW DAVENPORT CASH STORE RESTAURANT ★★

This perfect laid-back Northern California restaurant and bar has a new chef, Anthony Dias, who has redesigned the menu to feature California coastal cuisine including local seafood such as tuna, mahimahi, and salmon; salads; and light sandwiches. Something else new: from 4:30 to 9pm you can sit at the sleek copper bar on wooden barstools made by local craftsman Bud Bogle and order from a bar menu including steamer clams and mussels, potstickers, and fried calamari. The bar, just inside the entry, is an easy place to meet locals. The restaurant's ceilings are high, with heavy wood beams, and the concrete walls are hung with textiles from Afghanistan, Asia, Guatemala, and Mexico. Guests sit at simple wooden tables and chairs, plus an old church pew here and there. Have a glass of local Bonny Doon Vineyard's Big House Red, made just up the road. After ordering your meal, get up and browse the fabulous gift shop, stocked with exotic international goods—everything from folk art from all over the world to artisan-made earrings to important African carvings to Ethiopian silver jewelry. *1 Davenport Ave, Davenport; 831/426-4122 or 800/870-1817; $; AE, MC, V; no checks; breakfast, lunch, dinner every day; full bar; no reservations; inn@swanton.com; www. swanton.com; on Davenport Ave right off Hwy 1.*

LODGINGS

NEW DAVENPORT BED & BREAKFAST INN ★★

This pretty, rustic spot has a simple charm befitting this laid-back region of the coast. Artist-owners Bruce and Marsha McDougal, former potters who also own the restaurant on the first floor, have decorated no two rooms alike. Most have views of the ocean and decor that reflects the ethnic quality of the New Davenport Cash Store Restaurant (see review, above), folk art and crafts and American and European antiques. If you're not likely to be bothered by traffic sounds from Highway 1 or music drifting up from the restaurant below, opt for one of the eight rooms in the main building, where you can whale-watch from your room. All have private baths and open onto a narrow wooden porch commanding inspiring views of the ocean and cliffs; the grandest, Captain Davenport's Retreat, features two walls of windows framing the splendid vista. If it's peace and quiet you're after, forgo the view and settle down in one of the four slightly smaller rooms in the cottage. The room rate includes a full breakfast and a welcoming drink at the Cash Store. *31 Davenport Ave, Davenport; 831/425-1818 or 800/870-1817; $$; AE, MC, V; local checks only; inn@swanton.com; www.swanton. com; on Davenport Ave right off Hwy 1.*

SANTA CRUZ MOUNTAIN COMMUNITIES

Most of the small, woodsy towns that dot the Santa Cruz Mountains—Boulder Creek, Brookdale, Ben Lomond, and Felton—started as base camps for logging operations. By 1900 the redwoods were beginning to be logged out and the villages evolved into new roles as summer cabin communities or the sites of elegant summer hotel resorts. Most of the towns later developed into residential areas. They are all located on Highway 9 like buds on a twig.

BOULDER CREEK

The farthest north of the mountain towns, Boulder Creek is now the largest town along Highway 9, with the greatest variety of businesses. About a quarter mile south of downtown on Highway 9 is a green Gothic-style former church building built in 1885, now the town history museum. (Open Wed, Sat, and Sun, noon–3pm)

The Metro offers a shuttle service to Big Basin State Park on Saturdays and Sundays during most of the year. Shuttles leave at 8:30am from the Metro Center at 920 Pacific Avenue and take riders to the top of Big Basin. Riders can then hike the 10-mile trail to the beach or stay at Big Basin. Either way, buses appear for the return trip to Metro Center at 6:55pm; 831/425-8600.

ACTIVITIES

Hiking/Backpacking. With more than 100 miles of hiking trails, the redwood state parks northeast of Santa Cruz provide some of the best outdoor walking terrain anywhere in Northern California. The finest hikes in the Santa Cruz region are without question within Big Basin Redwoods State Park (21600 Big Basin Wy, Boulder Creek; 831/338-8860; www.bigbasin. org), not only because the forested canyons are cool and shady and gorgeous, but also because of the waterfalls; you'll be pinching yourself to make sure you aren't in a dream. Got half a day to kill? A great way to spend it is by trekking off to take a look at Berry Creek Falls in Big Basin along the Skyline-to-Sea Trail (moderate; about 12 miles round trip, depending on return route). The route eventually descends into Berry Canyon, an area of thick redwoods, tall ferns, and dark mosses 600 feet below. The 70-foot waterfall at the bottom is the first of four along Berry Creek Trail, which climbs to the 2,300-foot peak at Sunset Trail Camp. From the camp, it's a straight shot back to park headquarters. A shorter waterfall hike is along Sequoia Trail (easy; 1.5 miles round trip), a pleasant nature walk through redwood groves around Sempervirens Creek; this walk also begins at the park headquarters.

Stay in a Tent Cabin. Big Basin Redwoods State Park has 36 highly sought-after tent cabins nestled next to a creek in a grove of redwood trees and huckleberry bushes. You can rent one of these cabins (which sleep up to four comfortably) for about $49 a night from May to October or $35 a night from November to April, and four friends may camp out on the ground in front at no extra cost. Each cabin has wood floors and walls, a canvas roof, screened doors and windows, a wood-burning fireplace, and two double beds. A picnic table, storage cabinet, and grill are set up outside the door. There's no electricity in these units, so bring a propane lantern; also bring a sleeping bag, or rent bed linens ($10 for the duration of your stay) at the tent-cabin host site. Bathroom facilities (with coin-operated hot showers) and a laundry are in nearby buildings. Although Big Basin is 23 miles north of Santa Cruz, many people make the trek here and the cabins fill up fast. Reservations are required year-round; try to reserve at least two months in advance. (21600 Big Basin Way; off Big Basin Highway/Rte 236; 800/874-8368)

LODGINGS

BOULDER CREEK GOLF AND COUNTRY CLUB ★

Anyone looking for a leafy hideaway with all the amenities at a great value will love the Boulder Creek Golf and Country Club. Yes, there's an 18-hole golf course, but there are also tennis courts, hiking trails, a lake, and a swimming pool. It's also only a 30-minute drive from Santa Cruz, so you can still hit the beach. The redwood villa condos are handsome, with exposed beams, contemporary furniture, a full kitchen, a fireplace, a redwood deck, and cable TV. Prices are very reasonable, and even more so if you sign up for one of the golf, tennis, or basic packages, which all include lunches, cocktails, swimming, and tennis. There is a full bar, and the club's restaurant serves breakfast, lunch, and dinner. Reservations are recommended. *16901 Big Basin Hwy, Boulder Creek; 831/338-2111; $; AE, DIS, MC, V; checks OK; on Big Basin Hwy (Rte 236), west of Boulder Creek.*

BROOKDALE

Brookdale was home to several lumber mills starting in the 1870s, and later it was known as a summer resort for socialites. The town was laid out by James H. Logan, creator of the loganberry, and was known by several names until it changed its name to Brookdale in 1902. In 1923 it became famous for its Brookdale Lodge, built by the brilliant Dr. F. K. Camp, who created what became a world-renowned lodge that drew entertainers and politicians and eventually had three songs written about it. Dr. Camp was a teetotaler and not above sniffing his guests' drinks during prohibition and dumping them in the stream if he smelled alcohol.

RESTAURANTS

THE BROOKDALE LODGE ★★

Would you believe a restaurant with a brook running through it? The Brook Room at the Brookdale Lodge was built in the early 1920s and soon appeared in *Ripley's Believe It or Not* syndicated newspaper column as the only restaurant with a real stream, Clear Creek, running through it. It drew the rich and famous, and President Herbert Hoover liked to fish for trout off its interior bridge. Located in a rambling old pile of a rustic lodge in the redwoods, the Brook Room has a decor that is cuckoo clock run amok. Pink painted wood, rustic woods, white wrought-iron railings, live ferns, interior gables with shingles, rustic faux bridges, tables set on several levels, and the constant gurgle of the stream rushing from a rocky tunnel to its exit under the dance floor make this a place like no other. Amid all this is a pretty good formal restaurant with a new chef, William Bunker, who specializes in herb-crusted prime rib roasted for six hours in a special oven, grilled king salmon, and oak-wood-grilled top sirloin steak. *11570 Hwy 9, Brookdale; 831/338-6433; $$; AE, MC, V; no checks; dinner Wed–Sun, brunch Sun; full bar; reservations recommended on weekends; manager@brookdalelodge.com; brookdalelodge.com; on Hwy 9, north of Boulder Creek.*

BEN LOMOND

Ben Lomond was founded by a winery owner from Scotland, Robert Burns, who named the town in 1851 for the best winegrowing region in Scotland. Although *Ben* means mountain, Ben Lomond is actually at the base of a mountain. From the 1890s to the 1930s, large destination summer hotels were built for Bay Area families who would take the train down and spend the summer. The most famous hotel was the log cabin–style Rowardennan (which means "enchanted forest").

ACTIVITIES

Mountain Music. Henfling's Firehouse Tavern is a small, unpretentious tavern that serves simple yet good food. But its real claim to fame is the outstanding ongoing series of roots and traditional music performances that occur almost nightly. Called Henfling's International Folk Series, in a single week it might offer Tuvan throat singers, a marimba band, a bluegrass fiddle group, an Australian group that features both the bagpipe and the didgeridoo, a Hawaiian slack key guitar trio, and a Japanese blues band. Before each concert the tavern serves special regional dinners that reflect the theme of the music. If you listen to local nonprofit FM radio stations such as KUSP (88.9), KAZU (90.3), and the irreverent KPIG (107.5) while in town, you will likely hear musicians performing live in the studio the day of their appearance at Henfling's. You must be 21 or older to attend (call in advance for tickets), and be sure to come at least an hour early or you won't get a seat. (9450 Hwy 9, Ben Lomond; 831/335-1642; www.henflings.com; Mon–Fri 11am–midnight, Sat 8am–2am, Sun 8am–midnight)

RESTAURANTS

CIAO! BELLA! ★★

Ciao! Bella! is a restaurant with a sense of humor. You can tell by the mannequin legs wearing fishnet stockings and platform shoes sticking out of the ground by the entrance and the parking slot marked Reserved for Elvis. A Rapunzel-like sister mannequin leans out of a dormer above, letting down her hair, a perfect metaphor. This exuberant restaurant, nestled in a mountain redwood grove, features what owner Tad Morgan describes as "new California-Italian" cuisine. In addition to nightly specials, Ciao! Bella! serves up delectable pasta dishes, ranging from tutto mare (prawns, clams, calamari, and fresh fish sautéed in cream and white wine) to penne alla Napolentana (penne with tomatoes, basil, garlic, and mozzarella tossed in a marinara sauce). Secondi piatti include scampi as well as chicken with prosciutto, mozzarella, and spinach, topped with a sauce of basil, tomatoes, and garlic. Be sure to save room for the rich house-made desserts: zabaglione, tiramisu, and bread pudding. While the food is good, it's the racy entertainment by the staff that brings down the house—a cross between a musical revue and *The Full Monty. 9217 Hwy 9, Ben Lomond; 831/336-9221; $$; AE, DIS, MC, V; no checks; dinner every day; beer and wine; reservations recommended; just south of town.*

TYROLEAN RESTAURANT INN AND COTTAGES ★★

Although this is in a redwood forest, inside this cheery place feels like it might be tucked into the Black Forest. Bavarian beers and lagers are part of what draws people here, which explains why merry German drinking songs play on the sound system in this neat-as-a-pin Bavarian-style restaurant with its wood paneling and brick walls, cozy fireplace, and German mugs hanging over the bar. Hearty German fare is served, such as Wiener schnitzel, jager schnitzel (a pounded pork cutlet with creamy mushroom sauce), and schweinshaxe, similar to a ham hock, baked with beer sauce and served with dumplings and red cabbage—if you want this dish, phone ahead to reserve an order since it's quite popular. This restaurant is informal and fun, but not necessarily inexpensive. *9600 Hwy 9, Ben Lomond; 831/336-5188; $$; MC, V; checks OK; dinner Tues–Sun, brunch Sun; full bar; reservations recommended; www.tyrolean-inn.com; Hwy 9 at Mill St.*

LODGINGS

TYROLEAN RESTAURANT INN AND COTTAGES ★★

The Tyrolean Inn, nestled under the redwoods in Ben Lomond, has a fairy-tale setting and woodsy cottages that make you think Hansel and Gretel will step from behind a tree any minute. Dieter and Gabi Seider from Bavaria bought the inn not long ago and have been redecorating throughout. All cottages were recently redone, each appointed differently but keeping to a Bavarian theme, with new wallpapers and stenciling and solid pine furniture with a country feel. One cottage has sunflower-yellow walls and bright country colors in the curtains and spreads, including chairs with linen upholstery in a red flowered pattern. Cabins range from simple studios with no kitchens to deluxe two-bedrooms with a full kitchen. *9600 Hwy 9, Ben Lomond; 831/336-5188; $$; MC,V; checks OK; www.tyrolean-inn.com; Hwy 9 at Mill St.* &

FELTON

Felton began as a Gold Rush town between the 1850s and 1860s, when Isaac Felton found the "Golden Boulder" in a spot he called Gold Gulch. He promptly hauled the sparkling rock up to San Francisco and displayed it in a real estate office to lure people to Felton. After the boulder functioned as a lure, it was broken and melted down, yielding a large amount of gold and a fortune for Mr. Felton. Felton became the end point for logs coming from farther up the mountain, first arriving via a huge flume (constructed waterway), then later via railroad. In Felton the logs would be loaded onto another rail line for Santa Cruz and ships waiting in the harbor.

ACTIVITIES

Henry Cowell Redwoods State Park. There are few experiences as awe-inspiring as strolling beneath a cathedral of thousand-year-old redwoods at Henry Cowell Redwoods State Park in Felton. Only a few miles from downtown Santa Cruz on Highway 9 (from Mission St, take the Hwy 1 entrance, then turn north on River St/Hwy 9 at the first light and continue north), the 1,800-acre park has 20 miles of trails through thick, cool forests and golden meadows. Don't miss the easy walk called the Redwood Grove Trail, a wide, flat path that loops a tenth of a mile around an ancient stand of giant redwoods.

There are no organized tours, but you will often find roving docents on the loop trail to explain the area's natural history. Or pick up a self-guided trail brochure "Redwood Grove Nature Trail Guide," at the Nature Center for 25 cents. For more information call 831/335-7077 or 831/335-4598.

Not Heaven, but Close. For a cool dip in a secluded forest pool so perfect the locals call it the Garden of Eden, drive toward Felton on Highway 9 and look for the small unmarked Ox Road parking pull-out on the right, about 1½ miles south of the main entrance of Henry Cowell Redwoods State Park. Walk down the dirt road, which curves though the woods until it dead-ends at a railroad track, then turn right and walk half a mile along the side of the track (if you hear the Big Trees Railroad tourist train coming, wait until it passes) until you come to a marked trail on the left, leading down a short, steep embankment. Here the San Lorenzo River burbles over granite rocks, over shallow waterfalls, and into a deep calm pool shaded by oak and sycamores and bordered by two small sandy beaches. It's a beautiful spot.

The Best Park. One of the nicest small parks in the state is Felton Covered Bridge County Park at the corner of Graham Hill Road and Mt. Hermon Road. Just look for the life-size carved wooden ox at the entrance. Children love to play on the wooden and rope net playground equipment. If you walk down the path at the edge of the woods, you'll find it leads down behind the historic Felton Covered Bridge to a secluded small beach along the San Lorenzo River, shaded by the bridge looming overhead. (831/454-7956; www.scparks.com; open 8am to sunset)

Fees for most California state parks have been cut in half (from $6 to $3) in the last two years, and camping fees have also been reduced, in an effort by Governor Gray Davis to make parks accessible to all. Although it is the second smallest county in the state, Santa Cruz has more state parks than any of its other cousin counties.

A Beautiful Ride. People who know their way around a horse can arrange a private horseback ride that traces along the San Lorenzo River, winds through chaparral, and climbs up through towering redwoods in the Santa Cruz Mountains, on land set aside as an equestrian park. Redwood Riding Adventures is not a riding stable; the owner's horses are like family, so expect to be grilled on your riding experience—to participate, you should qualify as a serious or intermediate rider. You may be asked to take a riding lesson that lasts from 5 to 20 minutes to prove your horsemanship before being permitted to ride. Rides are private and by prearrangement only, so discuss their length and other expectations when you call. All this caution is worth the time, as the scenery on the trail makes for one of the best riding parks in the country. ($30 per hour for lessons and/or rides; call 831/335-1334 for an appointment and directions)

A Little Bit o' Scotland. As Toad said in *The Wind and the Willows*, there is "nothing quite so fine as messing around in boats," and Loch Lomond Reservoir is a perfect serene place to while away an afternoon paddling a flat-bottom rowboat, a canoe, or a quiet electric boat. As this is the drinking water reservoir for the city of Santa Cruz, no motorboats, no swimming, and no body contact with the water are permitted. So the place is peaceful and quiet for paddlers, hikers, or people who love to fish. Coast redwoods tower over you and the mountain lake is clear and still. Even on the busiest weekends there are few people here. Bring a lunch and row out to the island in the middle of the reservoir and picnic there. (On Sequoia Dr, about 5 miles from Felton; open Mar 1–Sept 15; call 831/335-7424 for information and driving directions)

Railroad in the Redwoods. Hop on the open-air historic Roaring Camp train for a 6-mile, 1½-hour round-trip excursion up the steepest narrow-gauge grades in North America. The steam-powered locomotive winds s-l-o-w-l-y through dense, cool redwood groves to the summit of Bear Mountain and back. Young kids love it, though older children can get a bit bored. A second train, called Big Trees and Pacific Railroad, offers an 8-mile ride through mountain tunnels and along ridges (with spectacular views of the San Lorenzo River) and past Victorian houses to the Santa Cruz Beach Boardwalk. Everyone loves this route. Both trains are located on Graham Hill Road off Highway 17 in Felton (follow the signs); the Big Trees Railroad can also be boarded at the east end of the Santa Cruz boardwalk. Call for specific departure times. The grounds at Roaring Camp often feature Civil War or Mountain Man reenactments, so check the schedule to see what's happening. (Roaring Camp: Trains run weekends Dec–Mar, every day the rest of the year; 831/335-4484. Big Trees and Pacific Railroad: Trains run weekends and holidays Sept–Nov, every day in summer; closed Dec–Apr; 831/335-4484; www.roaringcamp.com)

RESTAURANTS

THE COWBOY DINER

The Cowboy Diner is an unassuming diamond in the rough. It's in a drab corner building tucked into a small strip of businesses on Highway 9. The decor is Western-bar basic, decorated with a cardboard cutout of John Wayne and several still photographs from the Duke's most famous Westerns. There are also little plastic gunmen shooting it out on the counter, but the menu is very sophisticated: filet mignon crusted with black pepper and nestled in Gorgonzola cream sauce; Napoleon prawns between yam cakes, drizzled with honey-Dijon-caper sauce; and blackened New York steak with horseradish cranberry chutney. Live music is offered on Friday nights, with a "cheap beer" happy hour Monday through Friday from 4 to 6pm. *$–$$; 6155 Hwy 9, Felton; 831/335-2330; AE, V; checks OK; lunch, dinner every day; beer and wine; reservations recommended; on Hwy 9 near the Grocery Outlet.* &

THE EMPIRE GRILLE ★★

Skip Barnes opened this simple and elegant restaurant in the 125-year-old Kramer building, the oldest structure in town. Unlike the rest of Felton, which can still be a bit of a rough-and-tumble mountain town, this is an oasis of elegant calm. For lunch there's a great portobello mushroom sandwich, a blackened salmon Caesar salad, and other seafood dishes. In the evening there is also a big demand for steaks, rack of lamb, seafood, and pastas (the seafood pasta is the best seller). The hands-down favorite dessert is the bread pudding with rum-caramel sauce. The decor is muted, with linens and soft lighting. During the summer and on weekends the rest of the year, guests can catch the Big Trees and Pacific Railroad open-air train at the Santa Cruz Beach Boardwalk, get off at Felton, and walk here to have lunch. *6250 Hwy 9, Felton; 831/335-2127; $–$$; AE, DIS, MC, V; checks OK; breakfast, lunch, dinner every day; beer and wine; reservations recommended; empgrlle@pacbell.net; www.empgrille.com; on Hwy 9 in Felton.* &

SANTA CRUZ

Travelers sometimes bypass downtown Santa Cruz, because Highway 1 zigs around it on its way south. They are missing a jewel, as the downtown has sprung up triumphant since the devastating Loma Prieta earthquake in 1989 and reminds one of a small European village. The sidewalks are lively with cafes with outdoor seating, and the smell of gourmet coffee drifts out of the several boutique coffeehouses. Convenient city parking garages provide three free hours of parking. Victorian-inspired kiosks sell everything from flowers to tacos, and there are sculptures for people to pat and children to climb. Shops sell goods ranging from fine art and crafts to designer jewelry to

BOARDWALK PARTICULARS

Open:	Most weekends and holidays Jan–Nov; daily Memorial Day–Labor Day (call ahead in bad weather).
Closed:	December 1–25.
Hours:	Open at 11am in summer, noon in winter. Closing hours vary.
Admission:	Free.
Unlimited rides pass:	$23.95
Number of rides:	37
Information:	831/426-7433
Web:	www.beachboardwalk.com
Location:	400 Beach St, at the south end of Front St

On Friday nights in the summer, the Santa Cruz Beach Boardwalk offers free concerts by classic rock groups from the '60s, '70s, and '80s, such as the Shirelles and Sha Na Na. Concerts are at 6:30 and 8:30pm. Bring your blanket and sit on the sand to soak up the sounds.

tie-dyed clothes that would have been perfect at Woodstock. A nine-screen movie theater has revitalized the downtown after dark, and bookstores and coffee shops are open even at 10pm, as both the wan and the wealthy stroll from one to the other.

ACTIVITIES

 The Beach Boardwalk. For nearly a century, Santa Cruz has been synonymous with "beach and boardwalk," as if this seaside city of 50,000 exists solely to sustain what is now the only major beachside amusement park left on the Pacific Coast. Considering that the annual number of visitors to the Santa Cruz Beach Boardwalk is 62 times greater than the city's population, it's no surprise that Santa Cruz's other highlights are often overlooked. Ranked among the top amusement parks in the nation, with a higher attendance than either Marine World–Africa USA or Paramount's Great America, the privately owned amusement park has concentrated on improvements and security, and the boardwalk is truly safe and clean. Then there's the legendary Giant Dipper, considered by some to be the greatest roller coaster ever built, and the hand-carved horses of the Looff Carousel, the last bona fide brass ring merry-go-round in North America. Just strolling is free. Fees are charged per ride or you can buy a day pass. New rides and attractions include a 3D Fun House, where you wear 3D glasses and walk through space filled with optical illusions, and Ghost Busters, an interactive "dark ride" where you can zap ghosts with phasers as they zip by.

Pacific Avenue: Stroll, Shop, Sip. Peruvian flute music, Indonesian gamelan melodies, or an old Eagles tune crooned by a lone guitarist are all likely to hang in the air as you walk down Pacific Avenue browsing in shops and peeking in restaurants. Although the town lost more than 30 buildings in the 1989 Loma Prieta earthquake, it has come back better than ever with more than 250 shops and restaurants, sidewalk sculptures, benches, and new trees sporting white lights. Pacific Avenue can satisfy nearly every need. If hunger strikes, you can always stop for a bagel at the local branch of Noah's New York Bagels (1411 Pacific Ave; 831/454-9555); if you need a jolt, sip coffee at the Santa Cruz Coffee Roasting Company (1330 Pacific Ave; 831/459-0100); if your sweet tooth needs a fix, get an ice cream cone at Marinii's (1308 Pacific Ave; 831/423-3299). For more serious munchies, order a generous turkey, cheese, and avocado sandwich at Zoccoli's Delicatessen (1534 Pacific Ave; 831/423-1711) to take out, or a veggie sandwich at the deli counter of the New Leaf Community Market (1134 Pacific Ave; 831/425-1793). If retail therapy is what you need, you'll find stores that range from exotic to elegant to outrageous. Annieglass (just off Pacific Ave at 110 Cooper St; 831/427-4260) offers locally made art glass dinnerware, glasses, bowls, and other objects both useful and fanciful, and at the related shop across the street, Eyecandy at Annieglass, you'll find bright glass jewelry and accessories. Many Hands Gallery (1510 Pacific Ave; 831/429-8696) features artisan-made jewelry in metal, glass, and semiprecious stones, plus lovely scarves and vases. The Vault Gallery (1339 Pacific Ave; 831/426-3349) has very fine (and expensive) designer jewelry and clothes by Eileen Fisher. There's also a wet suit and watersports shop called O'Neill Downtown Surf Shop (corner of Pacific Ave and Cooper St; 831/469-4377), named for Jack O'Neill, the local hero who invented the wet suit that makes it possible to surf in the chilly waters off Santa Cruz.

Nearby, look for the Octagon Building on Cooper, an ornate, eight-sided Victorian brick edifice built in 1882 that has survived numerous quakes. Previously serving as the city's Hall of Records, it's now the gift shop for the adjacent McPherson Center for Art and History, which showcases 10,000 years of the area's past as well as contemporary art of the Pacific Rim (705 Front St at Cooper St; 831/429-1964; Tues–Sun 11am–5pm, Thurs till 7pm).

Santa Cruz has the only paperweight museum west of Chicago. Located at 123 Locust Street, the International Paperweight Society Museum hosts rotating exhibits of antique and contemporary paperweights, and also has a display on how they are made; open by appointment. 831/427-1177; www. TheGlass Gallery.com.

Book Nooks. Bookshop Santa Cruz (1520 Pacific Ave, near the entry to town; 831/423-0900) is the beating heart of the community, presided over by owner and former mayor Neal Coonerty. Go for browsing, author readings, book buying, flirting, and reading. There's a free do-it-yourself gift-wrapping area for prettifying your purchases. The shop is open until 11pm, and the later the hour, the more like a literary salon it becomes. There are newspapers from around the world, and scores of obscure alternative and literary magazines. Chocolate, a cafe, is tucked just inside the front door and offers sandwiches, sweet rolls, and cookies. It also features a cool-case full of Belgian-trained local chocolatier Richard Donnelly's astounding gourmet chocolates. An extensive children's department features politically correct books for kiddies. The thoughtful staff-written reviews attached to the shelves under recommended books are helpful for finding something you might like. Other bookstores in town include Gateways Books and Gifts (1531 Pacific Ave at Cathcart; 831/429-9600), which specializes in books on self-help, religion, meditation, and inspiration. Logos Books and Records (1117 Pacific Ave; 831/427-5100) has the best selection of used books as well as some new; Herland Women's Bookstore has women's and lesbian literature (1014 Cedar St; 831/429-6636), and the Literary Guillotine (204 Locust St; 831/457-1195) offers serious literary, political, and historical volumes. Borders Books, Music & Cafe (1200 Pacific Ave;

Downtown Santa Cruz has plenty of free parking; there are three parking garages and many surface lots that offer three hours of no-pay parking. But leave before your car turns into a pumpkin—those busy meter people mean business.

831/466-9644) is the newest and most controversial bookstore— it draws tourists and some residents, but many locals are fiercely loyal to the independent book shops.

 Boat Tours of the Bay. The view of the Santa Cruz coast from the water shouldn't be missed. Stagnaro Fishing Trips and Bay Tours has a one-hour tour of the bay at 3pm that cruises the harbor, swoops around the wharf, and passes by Seal Rock and back (831/427-2334; Sat–Sun year-round, weekdays in summer; $7 adults, $5 kids). For a more elegant tour, sign up for the *Chardonnay*, a 70-foot luxury yacht, which sails year-round on sunset, ecology, wine-tasting, and whale-watching tours (call 831/423-1213 for schedule and prices; www.chardonnay.com).

 Sea Kayaking. The best ride on the boardwalk isn't the Giant Dipper roller coaster, it's paddling a sea kayak along the Santa Cruz coast. Venture Quest Kayaking, located on the northeast end of the Santa Cruz Wharf, rents single and double kayaks for exploring the nearby cliffs and kelp beds where a multitude of sea otters, seals, sea lions, and other marine animals congregate. No experience is necessary, and all ages are welcome. Guided tours are also available; 831/427-2267.

 Surfing. Whatever your level of skill, if you already basically know how to surf, the Santa Cruz coast has numerous consistently good surfing spots, some small and at times shielded adequately enough from ocean breezes to be suitable for beginners. In general, the larger, wilder breaks occur at the northern reaches of the

LEARN TO SURF

If you've always wanted to skim over the waves hanging ten, it's not too late to learn. Club Ed Surf and Windsurf School, located on Cowell Beach in front of the West Coast Santa Cruz Hotel, offers lessons, rentals, and surf camps. Most days owner Ed Guzman and his staff teach a two-hour small group lesson for $80 that includes a wet suit, surfboard, and water booties. The class starts with yoga stretches on the surfboard on shore, and goes on to include how to read waves, how to position yourself on the board, how to paddle, and of course how to stand up and actually surf. Guzman has designed special surfboards that are extra wide and thick, so they catch waves well and are easy to stand up on, and he has taught wishful surfers from 4 years old up to 71 how to do it. Ed can also take paraplegics and quadriplegics out on his tandem board to experience the sensation of surfing. Open spring through fall (831/459-9283 or 800/287-7873; ed1@cruzio.com; www.club-ed.com).

coast, such as at Waddell Creek Beach just south of the San Mateo County line and the popular and infamous Steamer's Lane, north of the Santa Cruz beach and boardwalk area. Both of these spots are considered expert surf turf, with breaks in excess of 20 feet not unheard of—so don't jump in unless you're experienced enough to know how to blend in and adhere to the local surfers' pecking order. Fatal freak accidents involving experienced surfers have been tallied at both locations; both are flanked by rocky shores, and Waddell Beach (north of Davenport, 831/427-2288) has seen its share of sharks. A more suitable beginner's spot is Cowell Beach (just west of the wharf; 831/420-6014), a family surfing area where the breaks are small and tame enough for parents to bring their children. Pleasure Point Beach (E Cliff Dr and Pleasure Point Dr, Santa Cruz; 831/454-7956) is a popular surf spot south of the boardwalk, but conditions are often too rough for beginners.

From roughly Memorial Day to Labor Day, a free Santa Cruz Beach Shuttle runs a continuous loop to the Beach Boardwalk, wharf, and the main beach every 15 minutes from 12:15 to 9pm. The parking lot is at the Santa Cruz County Government Center, 701 Ocean Street. For information contact 800/833-3494 or www.santacruz ca.org.

Windsurfing. Santa Cruz is not easy for beginning board sailors because of the high winds and large breaks at many of the popular beaches. The inexperienced are better off watching and practicing elsewhere first. The Santa Cruz shores get both north and south swells, so be sure to check on conditions before venturing out. A good resource is the Surfrider Foundation Santa Cruz chapter web site, www.gate.cruzio.com/~surfride, which posts up-to-date surf condition reports. Also note that as with virtually all of the Northern California coast, the water off these beaches is downright chilly—don't venture in without a full wet suit.

Wine Touring. Santa Cruz has tasting rooms throughout the county. Downtown, Storrs Winery is in the Old Sash Mill (303 Potrero St, off River St; 831/458-5030) and offers handcrafted wines such as chardonnay, zinfandel, and merlot. It offers wine tastings Thursday to Monday, 12pm to 5pm. Hallcrest Vineyards and the Organic Wine Works are in the same location (379 Felton Empire Rd; 831/335-4441). Some of the wines there are organically grown and processed. You can taste wines and picnic on a sunny deck overlooking 52-year-old riesling vines, daily from 11am to 5:30pm. Bonny Doon Vineyard (10 Pine Flat Rd; 831/425-4518) has a charming wooden tasting room set on a redwood-shaded country road north of town. Here the specialty is Rhone/Italian varietals and blends—and the funniest wine labels in the county. They're open daily 11am to 5pm. The Roudon-Smith Winery (2364 Bean Creek Rd; 831/438-1244) is an unpretentious and friendly winery located 2.5 miles north of Scotts Valley Drive. They feature Estate Chardonnay, Merlot, Syrah, and Gewürztraminer in tastings Saturday only, 11am to 4:30 pm. Pick up

For three weekends every October, during Open Studios, roughly 250 artists, from potters to painters, open their studios, demonstrate their art, and sell their work. The sponsor is the Cultural Council of Santa Cruz County. The admission fee of $15 includes a colorful catalog/calendar featuring images from each artist and a map to help you find the studios (831/688-5399; www.ccscc.org).

a brochure/map listing all the Santa Cruz mountain wineries at any winery, or call the Santa Cruz Mountains Winegrowers Association (831/479-9463) for information.

Marine Laboratory. Secrets of the sea are revealed at the new Seymour Marine Discovery Center at the Joseph M. Long Marine Laboratory, a coastal research facility run partly by UC Santa Cruz. Children love the seawater table that allows visitors to handle—and learn about—sea stars, anemones, sea cucumbers, and other slimy marine life. Take the outdoor tour given at 1pm, 2pm, and 3pm each day to see the dolphin overlook and the marine mammal pool, where scientists study those creatures. Behind the gift shop are the skeletal remains of an 85-foot blue whale. With other exhibits visitors can play marine scientist and learn firsthand about how these researchers work. (From Hwy 1/Mission St in west Santa Cruz, turn south on Swift St, right on Delaware Ave, and proceed to the end; 831/459-3800 or 831/459-3799; Tues–Sat 10am–5pm, Sun noon–5pm; $5 adults, $3 seniors/students and ages 6–16; ages 5 and under free)

Music and Dancing. Santa Cruz is perfectly positioned to catch famous performers traveling between shows in Los Angeles and San Francisco. That's why for just a few dollars you can hear legendary blues or jazz performers in one of the city's more intimate venues. Artists love to play this town, both for the laid-back ambience and the sophistication of its audiences. The coolest blues are at Moe's Alley (1535 Commercial Wy; 831/479-1854; www.moesalley.com), featuring live music and dancing every night of the week. For traditional and modern jazz, the Kuumbwa Jazz Center (320 Cedar St; 831/427-2227), a nonprofit (and nonsmoking) landmark of 200 seats that's been around for the past two decades, presents jazz artists on Monday and Friday nights. Local rock, reggae, blues, and world-beat bands appear at the Catalyst (1011 Pacific Ave; 831/423-1336), which occasionally pulls in some big names, too; they also serve breakfast, lunch, and dinner. Rock, reggae, bluegrass, Hawaiian, and folk music find a venue at the cavernous Palookaville dance club (1133 Pacific Ave at Lincoln St; 831/454-0600), with its two bars and a restaurant serving dinner.

Bike Rental. Santa Cruz is a bicycler's heaven. The pedal-friendly downtown area is flat and wide (ditto the wharf and boardwalk), and the shoreline bike path along West Cliff Drive is sensational. The Bicycle Shop of Santa Cruz also rents everything from cruisers to mountain bikes (1325 Mission St; 831/454-0909;

www.BicycleShopSantaCruz.com). If you feel you might need a bit of a boost to get where you're going, try Electric Sierra Cycles (302 Pacific Ave; 831/425-1593; escuspd@attitude.com; www.electricrecbikes.com), which specializes in electric-assisted bikes, scooters, trikes, folding tandems, and regular pedal bikes.

 Surfing Museum. Within the small brick lighthouse building off West Cliff Drive is the Santa Cruz Surfing Museum, built in memory of Mark Abbott, a young local surfer who died doing what he loved most: surfing. Old photographs, a surfboard bitten by a shark, vintage boards, and piles of other memorabilia depict the history and evolution of surfing around the world (831/420-6289; every day but Tues noon–5pm).

In summer, a second tourist information office is set up in the beach area in a shack next to the Ideal Seafood restaurant, at the entry to the Municipal Wharf. It's open from 9am to 5pm.

After the tour, walk to the point's edge and watch the sea lions waddle around Seal Rock. Between the lighthouse and the boardwalk is that famous strip of the sea known as Steamers Lane, the summa cum laude California surfing spot (savvy surfers say this—not Southern California—is the most popular place to catch breaks in the state).

 Beach and Butterflies. At the north end of West Cliff Drive is Natural Bridges State Beach, named after archways carved into the rock formations here by the ocean waves (only one of the three original arches still stands). Popular with surfers, windsurfers, tide pool trekkers, and sunbathers, the beach does a brisk winter business as well: between October and February up to 200,000 monarch butterflies roost and mate in the nearby eucalyptus grove. Walk down the wide redwood walkway that descends to a platform on the floor of the grove. Look up. Those dead leaves you think you see hanging overhead will begin to flutter at the slightest ray of sun and turn into butterflies that swoop and delight. Skip the $6 parking fee at the West Cliff Drive entrance; park for free and walk in from Delaware Avenue. (just east of the entrance off Swanton Blvd; 831/423-4609)

 On the Wharf. There is more to this former working fishing wharf than touristy shops, fish markets, and pricey restaurants. See the remarkably tiny fishing boat the *Marcella* on the wharf near the Wharf Office. It is one of many actually used by Italian fishermen once based at the wharf, who ventured far out to sea to make a living fishing for salmon, cod, and halibut. Then walk to the end of the wharf and look down over protective railings for a bird's-eye view of barking sea lions lounging on struts under the wharf. Take your camera: there are a number of big savvy pelicans who will allow you to stand close and will even pose for a nibble of whatever you're eating. Next, stroll over to the Made in Santa Cruz shop, where jewelry, sculpture, paintings, scarves, glass vases, and handmade soaps created

The sailing yacht Chardonnay II offers "Taste of Santa Cruz" Cruises featuring local chefs from 3:30 to 5:30pm Sundays. Saturdays there are Brewmaster Cruises, with beer and pizza, from 4 to 6pm, and on Sundays from 10:30am to 12:30pm they serve brunch. Most cruises cost $39.50 per person; call 831/423-1213.

by local artists and artisans are featured. Favorite buys: lavender or lemon verbena soaps made by Bonny Doon Lavender Farm. Riva's Fish House, although a bit noisy, is a surprisingly inexpensive restaurant with good food—try the mussels (Bldg 31, Municipal Wharf; 831/429-1223). The night view of the boardwalk from the wharf is magical, as the lights of the Ferris wheel and the Giant Dipper reflect off the water and light up the night.

Coastal Walk. Santa Cruz's best attraction is the 2-mile walking-biking-jogging path along West Cliff Drive, which hugs the coast. Runners, jogging moms with strollers, walking seniors, surfers biking along grasping a surfboard, and lots of people walking their dogs all look happy to be there as they make their way on this paved trail from the wharf to Natural Bridges State Park. Along the way surfers paddle and surf, sea lions bark, and waves wink. The best time to visit is at sunset, when serious devotees of the drumming culture gather to drum down the sun on tribal drums, an eerie, only-in-Santa Cruz experience: there are so many passionate drummers here that the city enacted a "drum curfew" ordinance so downtown dwellers could get some sleep.

Boardwalk Bargains. Save a bundle at the boardwalk by visiting on "1907 Nights." Every summer after 5pm on Monday and Tuesday, the Santa Cruz Beach Boardwalk celebrates the year it opened by reducing its prices to 60 cents a ride (it's normally $1.80 to $3.60), and 60 cents buys a hot dog, a Pepsi, or cotton candy. Call 831/423-5590 for more information.

Farmers Market. Year-round on Wednesday afternoons from 2:30 to 6:30pm, the Downtown Farmers Market of Santa Cruz is set up at the corner of Cedar and Lincoln Streets, where small-operation farmers sell cut flowers, honey, vegetables from onions to cucumbers, fruits such as strawberries and apples, cheese, eggs, seafood, and olive oil. Bring your own bag, shop for great prices on organic produce, and enjoy the laid-back organic ambience of the whole scene.

Yacht Harbor. The Santa Cruz Harbor, also known as the yacht harbor, offers restaurants overlooking the harbor, whale watching tours in winter, a free water taxi service on summer weekends, and a Marine Sanctuary Center. It also features a 2-mile interpretive walk with stations that explain fishing, wildlife, and local history, as well as free docent-led tours of the harbor. (off 7th Ave; 831/475-6161)

RESTAURANTS

CASABLANCA RESTAURANT ★★

There's nothing very Moroccan about this boardwalk bastion of California-continental cuisine, except, perhaps, the palpable air of romance. Soft music fills the candlelit dining room and stars wink on the water outside the window—this is the sort of place where you get the urge to hold hands across the table. Chef Scott Cater has crafted a regional American menu with European accents. Starters include fried calamari with a spicy lime dipping sauce, clam chowder, and fried brie served with jalapeño jelly and toast rounds. Entrees range from grilled Hawaiian swordfish served on a bed of garlic-herb linguine to a cilantro-marinated chicken breast with garlic whipped potatoes and sun-dried tomato pesto. Local wines share a book-length wine list with selections from Italy, Germany, France, and Australia. *101 Main St, Santa Cruz; 831/426-9063; $$$; AE, DC, DIS, MC, V; no checks; dinner every day; full bar; reservations recommended; on Main St at Beach St, on the waterfront.*

CLOUDS DOWNTOWN ★

The mayor, city council members, musicians, artists, lawyers, and anyone who knows anyone gathers at the Clouds bar and restaurant for a drink after work, or meets there for dinner to catch up with friends. It's hip and happening, with so many patrons wearing chic black that you'll think you've slipped a few time zones and have landed in Manhattan. The bartenders are known for their martinis and lemon drops, the latter made of vodka, fresh lemon juice, and triple sec. You can graze for dinner on tapas or sushi, or have a real entree of filet mignon, salmon, or pasta. *110 Church St, Santa Cruz; 831/429-2000; $$; AE, MC, V; no checks; lunch, dinner every day; full bar; reservations recommended; on Church St downtown across from the Church St parking garage.* &

CROW'S NEST ★

This large, multilevel seaside restaurant offers a heated, glassed-in deck that's an uncommonly pleasant place to watch boats cruise in and out of Santa Cruz Harbor. The food at the Crow's Nest isn't exactly gourmet, but the steaks, seafood, chicken, and salads are competently prepared and tasty. The staff is friendly and efficient, and there's a bar area for drinks and light eats. The Crow's Nest continually wins local awards as having the best happy hour. Young mateys can

Those trim and friendly helpers wearing khakis and burgundy shirts who you see downtown are there to answer questions, give directions, and assist visitors. They are called Hospitality Guides and are trained and provided by the Downtown Association; 831/429-8433.

For a quick, inexpensive lunch, El Palomar, 831/425-7575, has a great taco bar across an inside hallway from its main restaurant at 1336 Pacific Avenue. Walk through the Santa Cruz Coffee Roasting Company to the back to find it. From 5pm to 8pm Monday through Thursday you can get $1.50 tacos or $2 burritos, plus draft beers or margaritas.

choose from a bargain-priced children's menu, then top off their meal with a little toy from the treasure chest. It's hard to think of a more relaxing and scenic place for a casual repast. On Thursday nights in the summer there are beach barbecues on the sand. *2218 E Cliff Dr, Santa Cruz; 831/476-4560; $$; AE, DC, DIS, MC, V; no checks; lunch, dinner every day; reservations recommended; full bar; on E Cliff Dr at the Santa Cruz Harbor.* &

EL PALOMAR ★★

El Palomar, Mexican restaurant extraordinaire, is a Santa Cruz institution. You have two choices: sit inside in the shadowy, dramatic dining room with a vaulted ceiling that was the lobby of a former '30s hotel, its beams painted in the Spanish manner and a huge mural depicting a Mexican waterfront village scene, or sit out in the happy, glassed-roof conservatory-patio, where the sun always seems to shine and you might squint and think you are in Mexico itself. If you need further convincing, have an Ultimate Margarita and munch on tortilla chips still warm from the oven. El Palomar is known for its seafood dishes, which are topped with exotic sauces, but traditional Mexican favorites such as burritos and tacos are also outstanding. *1336 Pacific Ave, Santa Cruz; 831/425-7575; $$; AE, DIS, MC, V; local checks only; lunch, dinner every day, brunch Sun; full bar; no reservations; on Pacific Ave near Soquel Ave.* &

GABRIELLA CAFE ★★

Downtown on Cedar Street is a small mission-style cottage with a tiny garden courtyard entry graced with cupid statues and ivy. Owner Paul Hocking named this romantic Mediterranean-inspired trattoria after his daughter Gabriella. Inside, the whitewashed walls are hung with art from local artists, and tables are draped with white linens, then covered with white paper; crayons are provided so you can doodle or write love poems over lunch. Flowers poke out of old olive oil bottles. The rooms are small, and the tables are small too, so you can't stretch out, but the ambience and food are worth it. The homemade focaccia is perfect, served with roasted garlic, caponata, or basil pesto. Chef Jim Denevan buys organic fruits and vegetables at the weekly farmers market. His menu offers such items as a crab and squash cakes appetizer with red pepper, red onion, and Meyer lemon aioli; a caprese salad with heirloom tomatoes, fresh mozzarella, fresh basil, and extra-virgin olive oil; and a daily-changing gnocchi special that might include a truffle version. Main courses include pan-roasted pork loin with peach compote and summer vegetable slaw, and chicken Gabriella, a sautéed chicken breast with a marinade of prunes, apricots, olives, capers, oregano, and olive oil. *910 Cedar St, Santa Cruz; 831/457-1677; $$; AE, V, M; local checks OK; lunch, dinner every day, brunch Sun; beer and wine; reservations recommended; www.gabriellacafe.com; on Cedar St between Locust and Church Sts.* &

GILDA'S ★

View An unpretentious family restaurant on the Municipal Wharf, Gilda's is owned by an old fishing dynasty family, the Stagnaros, and the restaurant's elegant silver-haired namesake, Gilda, still acts as hostess at lunch. The big open space has vinyl seating and laminated tables, and walls are hung with historic photographs of the wharf and its fishing families. There are terrific views of boats bobbing in the water, soaring pelicans dive-bombing for fish, and the lighthouse near Steamers Lane. Good quality and generous portions are the rule. You can bring large families or groups, as there are adjoining booths with removable partitions, and on Wednesdays Gilda's offers the best deal in town: a prime rib dinner for $7.95, including soup, vegetables, and potato. Low-priced specials are offered other nights too, including cioppino and spaghetti. All seafood, from sand dabs to calamari to salmon to halibut, is fresh, never frozen, and prices are reasonable, under $11 for dinners. Gilda's is not chic, but it has a warm personality, from host/bartender Robert Stagnaro's passion for playing Bing Crosby music to the warmth of his sons Dino and Malio. *Bldg 37, Municipal Wharf, Santa Cruz; 831/423-2010; $; AE, DC, DIS, MC, V; checks OK; breakfast, lunch, dinner every day; full bar; reservations recommended in summer only; midway along the Municipal Wharf.* &

O'MEI RESTAURANT ★★★

Named after a mountain in the Sichuan province of China, this gourmet Chinese restaurant is a wondrous little paradox tucked into a strip mall on the west side of town. Owner/chef Roger Grigsby is not Chinese, nor are any of his cooks, but his food caters less to American sensibilities than do most Chinese restaurants. A tray of creative appetizers is brought to each table for you to order from before dinner, including candied cashews that are addictive. Pushing the envelope of Chinese cuisine, O'mei offers tasty provincial curiosities such as litchi chicken, and its most popular dish is gang pung chicken—battered chicken with wood ear mushrooms, ginger, and cilantro, served with a sweet and slightly spicy sauce. They also serve an enchanting black sesame ice cream. Another plus: the limited but well-chosen wine list, with all wines available by the glass. O'mei is so popular with locals that it is smart to make reservations, and even so, you may wait a while to be seated, especially on weekends. *2316 Mission St, Santa Cruz;*

831/425-8458; $$; AE, MC, V; no checks; lunch Mon–Fri, dinner every day; beer and wine; reservations recommended; on Mission St near Fair Ave. ♿

OSWALD ★★

This small California-French bistro will remind you of Berkeley's celebrated Chez Panisse. The dining room has a spare, arty look, with bold still-life paintings on the brick and pale-yellow-painted walls, high ceilings, wooden banquettes, and a petite wrought-iron-railed balcony set with a couple of tables. Chef Domani Thomas offers a seasonal menu supplemented nightly by a roster of specials that takes good advantage of the best meats and veggies in the markets that day (organic whenever possible). Good options are the sherry steamed mussels with fried garlic and parsley; poached foie gras with port wine reduction and toasted hazelnuts; and a butter lettuce salad with citrus and creamy herb dressing. Entrees include the crispy and moist "chicken under a brick" served with sweet pepper and potato hash. There's always a very reasonably priced entree of carefully cooked vegetables for vegetarians. The dessert list includes a seasonal fruit choice, as well as chocolate soufflé, a classic crème brûlée, and a Basque almond custard torte. Sweet wines are recommended for each dessert—with the chocolate soufflé a 1987 Graham's Malvedos Vineyard Porto, with the crème brûlée the NV Broadbent Terrantez (40 to 50 years old). The servers are knowledgeable and solicitous, and the wine list features a good lineup of both California and French offerings. *1547 Pacific Ave, Santa Cruz; 831/423-7427; $$; AE, DC, MC, V; local checks OK; dinner Tues–Sun; beer and wine; reservations recommended; on Pacific Ave near Water St—use the parking lot on Cedar St and enter the restaurant through the courtyard.* ♿

RISTORANTE AVANTI ★★★

With its unassuming strip mall location, you'd never guess this is a fine restaurant, but it is. In keeping with the Santa Cruz lifestyle, Avanti prides itself on serving "the healthiest meal possible" (think fresh, organic produce and free-range chicken, veal, and lamb). The modern, casual decor, with Italian ceramics covering every inch of walls and shelves, provides a welcome setting for aromatic, seasonal dishes such as sweet squash ravioli with sage butter; lasagne primavera; spaghetti with wild mushroom and shallot duxelles; and orecchiette with salmon, Italian greens, mushrooms, and sun-dried tomatoes. The grilled lemon chicken and balsamic-vinegar-marinated lamb chops also demonstrate the kitchen's skillful and delicate touch, and you simply can't go wrong with the daily specials. Menu items change with the seasons, and anything with wild mushrooms is prepared with locally gathered varieties. The ample and reasonably priced wine list contains selections from California, Spain, and Italy. *1711 Mission St, Santa Cruz;*

831/427-0135; $$; AE, MC, V; local checks only; breakfast, lunch, dinner every day; beer and wine; reservations recommended; on Mission St near Bay. &

ZACHARY'S ★

Breakfast at Zachary's is a true Santa Cruz experience, with liberal-intellectual electricity in the air. The wait staff sport rad hair and not-so-discreet tattoos, the service runs the gamut from enthusiastic to indifferent, and the clientele ranges from young mothers with toddlers to poets stuck in the Beat era. But this is a crossroads of Santa Cruz culture, and long conversations on the Tao of bicycling and other abstruse topics will surely be going on at the next table. The breakfast menu offers generous portions of delicious items such as Mike's Mess (scrambled eggs with potatoes, cheese, sour cream, mushrooms, tomatoes, and bacon), and a spicy tofu scramble to die for, and the toast is made from wonderful breads they bake in-house. If you go on the weekend, expect a wait. *819 Pacific Ave, Santa Cruz; 831/427-0646; $; MC, V; checks OK; breakfast, lunch Tues–Sun; no alcohol; no reservations; downtown on Pacific Ave between Laurel and Maple Sts.* &

LODGINGS

THE ADOBE ON GREEN STREET ★★

Tucked away on a lovely old residential street, the four-room Adobe on Green Street is surrounded by desert plants, courtyards, and quiet spaces. It's an easy walk to shops and restaurants. Arts and Crafts–style mission furniture and American Indian blankets give it an organic feel, and world artifacts such as a bell brace from Nepal keep it interesting. Former hospice nurse Judith Hutchin-

A GOOD DAY IN SANTA CRUZ

9–10am:	**Breakfast at Zachary's.**
10am–noon:	**A stroll through Henry Cowell Redwoods State Park.**
Noon–1:30pm:	**Lunch at Gabriella Cafe.**
1:30–3:30pm:	**Shop along Pacific Avenue.**
3:30–5pm:	**Sea kayaking from the wharf.**
5–6:30pm:	**A walk along West Cliff Drive; watch surfers and hear drums.**
6:30–8pm:	**Dinner at O'mei Restaurant.**
8–10pm:	**Browse the boardwalk or take in a foreign movie at the Nickelodeon.**
10–11:30pm:	**Decaf mocha and a good read at Bookshop Santa Cruz.**

Foreign, experi-
mental, cult,
and art films all
show up at the
Nickelodeon
Theater, a town
treasure at 210
Lincoln Street;
831/426-7500.
It's the thinking
person's movie
house. Close to
dinner? Grab
a great burger
at Jack's Ham-
burgers on the
corner before you
get in line; 202
Lincoln Street;
831/423-4421.

son and her business partner Arnie Leff, an M.D., have created an unstressful, laid-back inn with Annie the border collie as chief greeter. In-room massage is available, and breakfast is served in the cheery breakfast room, which fills with light. The real star of the mornings is chef Andrea Tyra, who makes French toast out of her prizewinning bread pudding. All rooms have private baths. The Ohlone Room, named for an early native tribe, has white brick walls, a white quilt, a fireplace, a whirlpool tub in the bath, and a comfy wooden rocker. Adobe has been applied to most interior surfaces, forming charming arches and nooks. All rooms have cable TVs and VCRs, and there is a large library of videotapes. The inn is also the family home, so it is informal and a bit casual, and Judith says you may occasionally find her in her pjs. Every book may not be in place, but the inn is so restful, no guests seem to mind. *103 Green St, Santa Cruz; 831/469-9866 or 888/878-2789; $$–$$$; AE, DIS, MC, V; checks OK; www.adobeongreen.com; on Green St just off Mission St.* &

THE BABBLING BROOK INN ★★✦

The original building was a gristmill, and the 200-year-old working mill wheel still churns water from a creek that flows through the property from high above town. Ensconced in a fantastical garden with waterfalls, gazebos, and, of course, the babbling brook, Santa Cruz's oldest B&B offers 13 rooms, most named after famous artists. Recently bought by the Inns by the Sea group, the rooms and grounds have been upgraded and manicured to near perfection. The mauve-and-blue Van Gogh Room has a private deck, a fireplace, a beamed ceiling, and a whirlpool tub for two. Peach and ivory predominate in the Cézanne Room, with its generous bath and canopy bed. The blue-and-white Monet Room has a corner fireplace, a private deck, and a view of the waterfall and footbridge. Breakfast is served in the comfortable lobby, and wine and nibbles are also served there from 5:30 to 7:30pm. *1025 Laurel St, Santa Cruz; 831/427-2437 or 800/866-1131; $$–$$$; AE, DIS, MC, V; checks OK; www. cacoastalinns.com; on Laurel St near California St.* &.

THE CARMELITA COTTAGES ★

From the street you'd never guess that this gaggle of shaded whitewashed Victorian cottages is a hostel. Located a mere two blocks from the boardwalk in a quiet residential neighborhood on top of Beach Hill, the Carmelita Cottages consist of simple dormitory-style white clapboard cottages containing 2 to 15 beds or bunks. All paths lead to the large main house, which houses 15 and has three baths, a communal kitchen, and comfy common rooms. Prices are $17 (members) to $19 (nonmembers) per person for adults, and parking is free. There is also a couples' room with an upper and lower bunk, and a family room with a double lower bunk and a single upper. Rates are lower if you become a member of Hosteling International for $25 ($15 if you are over 54). A morning chore is appreciated, and lockout from rooms is 10am to 5pm, but the grounds are a state park, so you may enjoy them all day. *321 Main St, Santa Cruz; 831/423-8304; $; MC, V; checks OK via mailed reservations 10 days prior; info@hi-santacruz.org (no reservations via email); on Main St off Beach St, 2 blocks north of the wharf.* &

Santa Cruz is one of only two towns in the country that has what is informally known as a "lookism law." It ensures that no matter how large or small your size, or how oddly you look or dress, no one can discriminate against you by refusing you service or a job.

CLIFF CREST INN ★★

From its perch on Beach Hill high above the boardwalk, this antique-laden Victorian B&B has five highly decorated rooms. The more casual lobby and solarium/sitting room/ breakfast nook has a fireplace, antique furniture, and displays of old-time family photos from the original owners. Recently, Constantine Gehriger and Adriana Gehriger Gil bought the inn, spruced up the gardens and grounds, and have done some upgrading inside. The entire house has carved woodwork, bright square panes of stained glass, intriguing nooks, claw-footed tubs, and converted gaslight fixtures. The Empire Room downstairs has a four-poster king bed (all the rooms have four-posters) and a fireplace, and the Rose Room upstairs boasts bay views, a sitting area, and an Eastlake bed, with a private bath across the hall containing a claw-footed bathtub and a profusion of lace. Two other guest rooms have fireplaces, all the rooms are equipped with telephones, and TVs are available upon request. The complimentary full breakfast is served downstairs in the solarium or you can take it to your room. There is off-street parking, and you can walk to the wharf or boardwalk or to town. *407 Cliff St, Santa Cruz; 831/427-2609; $$$$; AE, DIS, MC, V; checks OK; info@cliffcrestbed andbreakfast.com; www.cliffcrestbedandbreakfast.com; on Cliff St near 3rd St.*

THE DARLING HOUSE—A BED-AND-BREAKFAST INN BY THE SEA ★★

Location, location, location. There are probably no better views in all of Santa Cruz than those you'll find at the Darling House, a Spanish Revival mansion built as a summer home for a Colorado cattle baron in 1910. From its vantage point a few yards from the water, you can see endless miles of gray-blue sea, boats, sea gulls, and the lights of faraway towns. On chilly days a fire crackles in the living room's glorious art deco fireplace. The downstairs has not been gentrified, and the beautiful Craftsman-style living room has carved oak pillars and beveled glass windows. Upstairs, the large Pacific Ocean Room is decorated like a sea captain's quarters, with a crown Victorian bed, a fireplace, and a telescope on the desk to spy ships at sea. Across the hall, the Chinese Room features an exotic canopied, carved, and gilded Chinese rosewood wedding bed. The cottage out back has a kitchenette, a wood-burning stove, and two bedrooms—each with a double bed, a claw-footed tub, and a kitchenette. Owners Darrell and Karen Darling have worked hard to preserve the house's beautiful woodwork and have outfitted all eight guest rooms with mostly American Victorian antiques; there are also fluffy robes in every closet. Karen's breakfasts include fresh fruit, homemade granola with walnuts, and oven-fresh breads and pastries. *314 W Cliff Dr, Santa Cruz; 831/458-1958 or 800/458-1958; $$$; AE, DIS, MC, V; checks OK; www. darlinghouse.com; on W Cliff Dr between the pier and the lighthouse.*

CAPITOLA-BY-THE-SEA

If you can't make it to Cannes or Capri this year, how about Capitola? The Mediterranean-style buildings, curved streets, white-sand beaches, outdoor cafes, and perpetually festive atmosphere seem more akin to the French or Italian Riviera than Monterey Bay. If you're staying on the coast for more than a day, and especially if you're around during the week, a visit to this ultraquaint hamlet is highly recommended. Park the car anywhere you can, feed the meter (bring quarters), spend an hour browsing the dozens of boutiques along the esplanade, then rest your bones at Zelda's sunny beachside patio with a pitcher of margaritas. As in any upscale beach town, the ambience is breezy and informal and you can go anywhere in a bathing suit with a cover-up.

ACTIVITIES

 Ocean Fishing. Even if you don't know an outboard from a Ouija board, the friendly staff at Capitola Boat & Bait have faith that you'll bring their fishing boats back in one piece. Around $65 (weekdays) to $75 (weekends) buys you a four-person boat for the day, including an outboard motor, fuel, safety equipment, anchor, oars, seat cushions, and free maps of the hot fishing spots. Fishing gear can also be rented and one-day licenses purchased, so there's no excuse not to brave the open ocean just for the halibut. (1400 Wharf Road, at the end of Capitola Wharf; 831/462-2208; every day 7am–4pm; closed Jan–mid-Feb)

Up a Creek with a Paddleboat. If your nautical thrills run to the more modest, hop on a paddleboat at Creektime Paddleboats (831/334-0043) and paddle

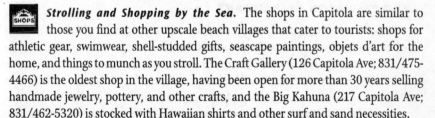

BEST BEACHES FOR

Walking your dog off-leash: *At It's Beach, near the lighthouse on West Cliff Drive, there's even a dispenser for free cleanup bags; 6am to 9am only.*

Romantic sunsets: *Bluffs of Seacliff State Beach; 201 State Park Drive, Aptos; 831/685-6500.*

Swimming au natural: *Red, White, and Blue Beach, Highway 1, 5 miles north of Santa Cruz (look for the red, white, and blue mailbox); 5021 Coast Road, Santa Cruz; 831/423-6332.*

Campfires: *Twin Lakes State Beach, Santa Cruz; East Cliff Drive at 7th Avenue; 831/429-2850 or 831/427-4869.*

Fishing: *Seacliff State Beach, 201 State Park Drive, Aptos; Rio Del Mar Blvd, Santa Cruz; 831/685-6500.*

Volleyball: *Main Beach, Santa Cruz, off Beach Street between the Boardwalk and the Wharf; 831/420-5270.*

Surfing: *Steamers Lane, Santa Cruz, off West Cliff Drive near lighthouse, across from Lighthouse Field. For information on surfing conditions at city beaches (summer only), call 831/420-6015.*

up Soquel Creek about a quarter mile as far as the Shadowbrook restaurant—past woodsy greenery, quacking ducks and geese, and a few lovely old homes—then paddle down again. It takes about half an hour, $7 per boat ($12 for an hour), and two willing foot-paddlers. Carole Kettmann opens for business at noon daily, and closes between 5 and 6pm, roughly between Memorial Day (when the city dams up the creek to form a lagoon) and Labor Day. Adults and kids all love it, and you don't even have to get wet. This is a longtime summer tradition for vacationing families in Capitola. (On the Esplanade in Capitola; look for the sandwich sign at the walkway between Margaritaville and the Paradise Grill, follow the walkway out to Creektime Paddleboat dock)

 Strolling and Shopping by the Sea. The shops in Capitola are similar to those you find at other upscale beach villages that cater to tourists: shops for athletic gear, swimwear, shell-studded gifts, seascape paintings, objets d'art for the home, and things to munch as you stroll. The Craft Gallery (126 Capitola Ave; 831/475-4466) is the oldest shop in the village, having been open for more than 30 years selling handmade jewelry, pottery, and other crafts, and the Big Kahuna (217 Capitola Ave; 831/462-5320) is stocked with Hawaiian shirts and other surf and sand necessities.

Begonia Festival. The coastal climate makes for lush, colorful begonias, a fact celebrated in September when the Begonia Festival takes over Capitola. One

Rather than driving in circles looking for an elusive parking space in Capitola, hop on the free Capitola Beach Shuttle, which runs every 20 minutes from 8am to 10pm. Park at the lot off McGregor Drive, near Highway 1 and Park Avenue. The shuttle stops at the Esplanade and Capitola Beach.

day is devoted to a sand sculpture contest, another to a fishing derby off Capitola Wharf and rowboat races, and another to the big event: a Nautical Parade, when begonia-covered barges float down Soquel Creek to the lagoon. If you don't want to stand along the route, get a lunch reservation at Shadowbrook Restaurant and sit near the windows so you can see them go by. Kids and families wave from their barges and prizes are given for the best "begonia'd" craft; call 831/476-3566. If you're in town another time of year and want to see beautiful begonias, go to Antonelli Brothers Begonia Gardens (2545 Capitola Rd; 831/475-5222), known for having some of the finest tuberous begonias in the world.

RESTAURANTS

GAYLE'S BAKERY & ROSTICCERIA ★★

Take a number and stand in line; it's worth the wait. A self-service bakery and deli, Gayle's offers numerous imaginative sandwiches, pastas, casseroles, roasted meats, salads, cheeses, appetizers, breads, and treats. The variety is staggering and the quality top-notch. There's a good selection of wine, beer, bottled water, and espresso drinks, too. Once you've fought your way to the counter, you'll have the makings of a first-class picnic to take to one of the nearby parks or beaches. Recent daily specials included carrot ginger soup and braised meatballs with red wine gravy. You can also eat your feast in the cafe's small dining area or on the heated patio. Gayle's web site lists hot items and specials to be offered the following day. *504 Bay Ave, Capitola; 831/462-1200; $; MC, V; checks OK; breakfast, lunch, dinner every day; beer and wine; no reservations; www.gayles.com; on Bay Ave by Capitola Ave.* &

SHADOWBROOK RESTAURANT ★★

Known for years as the most romantic restaurant in the county, Shadowbrook is everyone's favorite place for proposals, birthdays, and anniversaries: the fun starts with the ride aboard the tiny funicular that runs down through the ferny woods, past a waterfall, to the multistoried, woodsy restaurant bedecked in white lights. Now people are also beginning to come for the food on the seasonal California-Mediterranean menu. Starters might include the signature crab cakes, artichoke hearts with lime-cilantro sauce, or tender calamari strips served with a Creole rémoulade. Some of the more popular entrees are blackened lamb with roasted root vegetables, tender braised lamb shank, bacon-wrapped prawns with creamy polenta, and swordfish. Jack Daniels mud pie and New York–style cheesecake remain the most requested desserts. The best seats in the house are at the alfresco tables on the brickwork terraces, nestled romantically among rock gardens and rhododendrons. Management recently remodeled the entryway, allowing diners to eat in the informal bar area with a view of the waterfalls and gardens. *1750 Wharf Rd, Capitola; 813/475-1511; $$–$$$; AE, DC, DIS, MC, V; local checks only; lunch Mon–Fri (served only in the Rock Room Lounge), dinner every day, brunch Sun; full bar; reservations recommended; www.shadowbrook capitola.com; on Wharf Rd near the end of Capitola Rd.*

LODGINGS

THE INN AT DEPOT HILL ★★★

When Martha Stewart stayed here a few years ago, she enthused about the Delft Room, with its antique Dutch tile fireplace, feather bed decked out in white Belgian lace, and collectible Dutch blue and white porcelains. Located in a 1910-era former Southern Pacific train depot, the Inn at Depot Hill sits on a bluff overlooking Capitola, but its selection of rooms will take you around the world. Decorated with passionate attention to detail, the 12 guest rooms, lavishly designed to evoke international ports of call, seem to have sprung directly from the pages of *Architectural Digest*. The terra-cotta-walled Portofino Room, patterned after a coastal Italian villa, sports a stone cherub, ivy, frescoes, and a brick patio. No less charming is the Stratford-upon-Avon, a faux English cottage with a cozy window seat. The Railroad Baron Room has sumptuous red fabric walls, heavy gold silk drapes, and formal gilt mirrors. Every room has a TV and a VCR, a built-in stereo system, a gas fireplace, and a marble-appointed bathroom complete with a mini-TV and a coffee machine. In the morning, there's a buffet of pastries, cereal, and quiche, as well as a hot dish such as French toast or a spinach omelet. In the evening, you'll find sweets and wine in the downstairs parlor. You may also browse along the massive wall-length bookcase for a tome or videotape to borrow. *250 Monterey Ave, Capitola; 831/462-3376 or 800/572-2632; $$$$; AE, DIS, MC, V; checks OK; lodging@innatdepothillcom; www.innatdepothill.com; Monterey Ave near Park Ave, next to the railroad tracks.* &

APTOS

Most of Aptos's appeal is of the outdoor variety: beyond its handful of B&Bs, people come for the good hiking trails and state beaches and state parks. Aptos has little in the way of tourist entertainment, leaving that up to neighboring Capitola and Santa Cruz. The focus here is on quality lodgings in quiet surroundings. The only drawback is that the beaches are too far to walk to from town, but if you don't mind the short drive, Aptos is the ideal place for a peaceful vacation on the coast. Seacliff State Park Beach has picnic tables with shade covers and the infamous Concrete Ship, built by the Navy to sail the coast, but now permanently moored (it later became a dance hall) and looking very much like a concrete wharf. In the spring the local park in Aptos Village is home to a fun and funky blues festival.

ACTIVITIES

Redwood Trails. The Forest of Nisene Marks State Park is one of the largest parks in central California and also one of the least known. The entire forest was clear-cut less than a century ago; today, however, a solid canopy of mostly second-growth redwoods shades the 2½-mile dirt road leading to the trailhead, where more than 30 miles of trails disappear into the 10,000-acre forest. The most popular hiking trail is the Loma Prieta Grade, a 6-mile round trip past the wooden remnants of a turn-of-the-century lumber camp (not far from the epicenter of the 1989 Loma Prieta earthquake). Mountain bikers and leashed dogs are also welcome. (At the end of Aptos Creek Rd off Soquel Dr; 831/763-7062; open year-round; free)

RESTAURANTS

CAFE SPARROW ★★

Chef/owner Bob Montague and his wife, Julie, opened this quaint French Country restaurant in June 1989. Then along came the Loma Prieta earthquake on October 17th. Fortunately, the couple didn't throw in the towel, and their remodeled restaurant is now a gem of a dining spot and a magnet for local gourmets. Two dining rooms, decorated with country furniture and a tentlike expanse of French printed fabric, provide a romantic backdrop for Montague's spirited culinary creations. Lunch may include a croissant layered with shrimp in lemon, fresh dill, and crème fraîche, or a bowl of creamed spinach with a vinaigrette salad and bread. Dinner, however, is when Montague puts on the Ritz. Start with a pâté of fresh chicken livers seasoned with herbs and Cognac, or a fondue of white wine, herbs, and cheeses, served in a puff pastry with fresh fruits and vegetables. Then progress to such entrees as an Yvette salad—grilled chicken breast with pears topped with brie; or lamb chops in a rich red-wine and mint sauce. Favorite desserts are profiteroles—puff pastries filled with custard or vanilla ice cream and smothered in Ghirardelli chocolate sauce. The wine list is far-ranging and agreeably priced, and the service is amiable. *8042 Soquel Dr, Aptos; 831/688-6238; $$; MC, V; checks OK; lunch Mon–Sat, dinner every day, brunch Sun; beer and wine; no reservations; on Soquel Dr near Trout Gulch Rd.*

LODGINGS

THE BAYVIEW HOTEL ★★

This old-fashioned three-story inn sits in the tiny tree-shaded hamlet known as Aptos Village. Built in 1878 on former Spanish land-grant property, it is the oldest hotel on Monterey Bay, and the huge magnolia tree in front is one of the two oldest in the world. The inn has recently been redecorated, with additional antiques, and the result is stunning. Each of the 12 rooms has its own phone, bath, and a luxurious feather bed and feather comforter, resting in an ornately carved Renaissance Revival–style or Queen Anne–style bed. There are matching dressers and side tables, with antique paintings and prints on the walls. Pillowcases have the look of embroidered antique linens. Two rooms have fireplaces; Room 12, the Honeymoon Suite, has a fireplace, a big soaking tub, a glass three-sided shower, and a canopy bed draped with watered silk and lace. The Redwood Suite has two large bedrooms that share a bath, good for families or two couples. In the hall you'll find cut-glass decanters full of sherry for guests. The newly designed patios, courtyards, and gardens in the back are lit with Victorian-style streetlamps and look like pages from a gardening magazine. The hotel is a popular place for weddings, with its 100-year-old rosebush arches. A full breakfast is served to guests downstairs on tables dressed with white linens and gold candelabras. *8041 Soquel Dr, Aptos; 831/688-8654 or 800/422-9843; $$–$$$; AE, MC, V; checks OK; lodging@bayviewehotel.com; www.bayviewhotel.com; on Soquel Dr at Trout Gulch.*

HISTORIC SAND ROCK FARM ★★

The word "nestled" was made for this inn, positioned on a woodsy knoll under a grove of redwoods. It originally was a 1,000-acre ranch and winery built in the 1880s by a doctor's family, who also built the Craftsman-style shingled mansion in 1910 from virgin redwood growing on the site. Lynn Sheehan, formerly chef at several of San Francisco's finest restaurants, and her mother Kris Sheehan, who previously was innkeeper at the Wild Rose Inn in Sonoma, have teamed up to create this inn, bringing the home back to its original glory with European antiques and an obvious love for light, airy rooms. The living room features redwood box beams, leaded glass, and a mantel made of rare curly redwood. The Sun Porch suite, a large, open room in the lower wing of the house, has a private enclosed sunporch sitting area and access to a large outdoor hot tub. The Hidden Garden suite opens onto a rose garden framed by a stone wall. The Morning Glory room has rugs blooming with morning glories and faces east; as the sun rises, the Eastlake-style brass queen bed glows with reflected light. Thanks to Lynn's background as a culinary professional, breakfast is a gourmet delight, usually served outdoors on the redwood deck under the trees. There are many nooks, crannies, hidden gardens, and old winery buildings to explore at this historic country retreat. *6901 Freedom Blvd, Aptos; 831/688-8005; $$; AE, MC, V; no checks; www.sandrockfarm.com; on Freedom Blvd, ½ mile from Hwy 1.*

SEASCAPE RESORT ★★

View This attractive condo-resort complex on 64 cliff-side acres offers spacious accommodations and plenty of creature comforts. The 285 guest suites and villas are arranged in a cluster of three-story stucco buildings and are available in studio or one- or two-bedroom configurations. Each suite and beach villa is outfitted with identical beach-house-style furnishings in light colors of sand and blue and comes with a fireplace, a private balcony or patio, a TV, and a kitchenette. The studios are quite large, with minikitchens, and the one- and two-bedroom villas are larger still, with complete kitchens, sitting areas, and, in the two-bedroom units, washer-dryers. All rooms and villas have balconies or patios. Largely given over to corporate functions during the week, the complex turns into a haven for couples and families on the weekend. For a fee you can have the staff provide wood and build a private bonfire on the beach, or you can just buy a bundle of wood from the resort and do it yourself. A paved path leads down through a small canyon to the beautiful beach, and guests enjoy member privileges at a nearby PGA-rated golf course and the Seascape Sports Club, which offers tennis, swimming, and a fully equipped gym. The resort also provides 24-hour room service, a children's program during the summer, and a spa offering massage and beautician services. Fresh seafood is the specialty at Sanderlings, the resort's airy restaurant, which has just undergone a makeover, with curvy light wood dividers and a mega-aquarium. You can sit inside or on the patio; either way you'll see gorgeous ocean vistas. Rates come down in the winter months. *1 Seascape Resort Dr, Aptos; 831/688-6800 or 800/929-7727; $$$; AE, DC, MC, V; checks OK; www. seascaperesort.com; Seascape Resort Dr at Sumner Blvd.* &

RIO DEL MAR

Located on the ocean side of Highway 1 near Aptos, Rio Del Mar is a wide strip of welcoming sand, a jetty, and an upscale residential neighborhood now, but the palisades of Rio Del Mar were once the site of the first crop of sugar beets in California, planted by future sugar magnate Claus Spreckles.

RESTAURANTS

BITTERSWEET BISTRO ★★

Local gourmets love "the Bittersweet." And now, after a few years in its much larger location, it's still packing them in. This sleek restaurant and wine bar features a patio for dining alfresco and a stylish mahogany, lacquer, and black granite bar area. Chef/owner Thomas Vinolus is still at the kitchen's helm, creating appetizers such as grilled shrimp martini with mesclun and cocktail sauce or Monterey Bay calamari. Pasta offerings include seafood puttanesca and five-cheese ravioli. For a main course, order the oak-roasted pork tenderloin with apple Calvados jus; the fresh fish of the day in parchment paper over spinach, squash, tomatoes, and eggplant; or the Bittersweet paella. The seasonal menu also features a range of pizzas from the wood-fired oven. The pretty-as-a-picture desserts are scrumptious—lemon napoleon, ricotta cheesecake, and chocolate mousse in a florentine cookie cup, to name a few. That's no surprise, given that the chef's last gig involved whipping up pastries at Carmel's Casanova restaurant. The wine list is extensive and varied, with some interesting if pricey older vintages among its treasures. *787 Rio Del Mar Blvd, Rio Del Mar; 831/662-9799; $$–$$$; AE, MC, V; checks OK; late lunch 3pm–6pm, dinner every day; full bar; reservations recommended; www.bittersweetbistro.com; take Hwy 1 south of Santa Cruz to the Rio Del Mar exit.* &

WATSONVILLE

Watsonville is a lively agricultural community with a large Hispanic population, which explains why many signs are in both English and Spanish. Once known for its miles of apple orchards, it still grows some apples but now primarily produces row crops such as strawberries and vegetables. In the center of town is an old-fashioned park with a charming bandstand and plenty of benches for enjoying the passing scene. Mexican bakeries, restaurants, and boot shops reflect the tastes of its residents.

ACTIVITIES

 Down on the Farm. The Watsonville area is known for growing fruits and vegetables that are shipped all over the country. You can visit a real working farm and ranch at Gizdich Ranch (55 Peckham Rd; 831/722-1056) and pick whatever fruit is in season yourself, or buy some already picked. In June it's strawberries and olallieberries; in July, raspberries. In September and October, you can pick apples and on Saturday mornings watch the cider-making process. The bakery-deli in the apple barn offers awesome strawberry shortcake in the spring, boysenberry pies in the summer, and in the fall, sky-high apple pies. There's an antique shop for Mom to browse while the kids enjoy the play yard out back, with an old tractor and bales of hay. Any time of year guests are encouraged to take orchard walks, or walk up Peckham Road to the top of the hill to see the ocean. Gizdich Ranch is open every day, 9am to 5pm (Apr 2–Dec 31, closed Jan 1–Apr 1); pie shop is open all year. Check the web site at www.gizdichranch.com to see what is in season.

GILROY

Located on Highway 101 between Morgan Hill and Salinas, Gilroy was once a farming community known primarily for being the grower or processor of nearly 100 percent of this country's garlic. Now it also grows customers at its spreading collection of outlet malls.

ACTIVITIES

Garlic Mania and Beyond. Will Rogers called Gilroy the only town in America where you can marinate a steak just by hanging it out on the line—and, yes, when the wind's blowing in the right direction, the aroma from the area's garlic fields is just about that strong. So it only made sense that the people of Gilroy decided in 1979 to celebrate their odoriferous claim to fame with the now-famous Garlic Festival (408/842-1625; www.gilroygarlicfestival.com), held the last weekend in July. The three-day-long festivities attract throngs of people eager to try such oddities as garlic ice cream and garlic chocolate and to enter their own recipes in the Great Garlic Cook-off. To find out about Gilroy before the age of garlic, visit the Gilroy Historical Museum (5th and Church Sts; 408/848-0470). If bargain hunting, not garlic, happens to set your heart aflutter, be sure to stop at the newly expanded Gilroy Premium Outlets (Leavesley Rd; just east of Hwy 101; 408/847-4155), with 150 attractive outlets for big-name retailers.

Bonafante Gardens Theme Park. This newly opened and unusual 75-acre arboreal theme park on Hecker Pass Highway is the dream of former supermarket king Michael Bonfante, who is in love with trees. No wonder the park has 10,000 of them. It's also part flower show, part horticultural extravaganza, and part gentle family amusement park. The park features 25 one-of-a-kind "circus trees" planted and shaped in the 1920s by Axel Erlandson, a farmer who grew and intricately wove trees into fantastical shapes that still survive. The park also has 40 rides and attractions, highlighted by a 1927 Illions Supreme Carousel, two narrow-gauge steam trains, a 60-foot-tall greenhouse, a thrilling mine coaster ride, and several theme restaurants. The five unique gardens reflect California plants and history. Even the rides have California agricultural and historical angles: the Mushroom Swing is a 39-foot-tall ride that swings out in a circle, the Quicksilver Express mine coaster speeds through a replica of the historic New Almaden Mine, and the Garlic Twirl takes families for a spin inside 12 different garlic bulbs. Eat your heart out, Walt Disney. (3050 Hecker Pass Hwy; 408/840-7100; www.bonfantegardens.com)

SAN JUAN BAUTISTA

This sunny little town is home to one of the most beautifully restored missions in California, Mission San Juan Bautista, named for John the Baptist. With its pretty chapel and gardens, the mission sits on a broad plaza surrounded by other well-preserved Spanish colonial buildings. It may look familiar: this is where Alfred Hitchcock filmed the mission scenes in *Vertigo*. On Sunday mornings the bells still ring out calling the faithful to Mass at the mission, which was dedicated in 1792 and nearly destroyed in the 1906 quake. Locals later rebuilt it. Now doves murmur overhead and nest in the eaves, and the mission gardens blossom with prickly pear cactus, desert sage, and old roses. From behind the church, where mission-trained Indians are buried in graves with simple wood crosses, you can gaze out over the rich vegetables fields in the valley below. Several rooms in the mission are preserved, such as the library for the priests, full of old leather-bound books and maps. The town grew up around the mission, and for such a small village it has many programs, parades, and special historical events; for details contact the Chamber of Commerce (831/623-2454; www.san-juan-bautista.ca.us).

ACTIVITIES

Slip into a Time Warp at the State Historic Park. The sense of being in the past is particularly strong as you wander the houses and other colonial buildings in the State Historic Park surrounding the San Juan Bautista mission. Exterior signs are kept to a minimum, so every building you step into is a private discovery. Everywhere it looks as if the families, livery stable workers, Plaza Hotel patrons, and town fathers wandered off on a normal day and never returned. Tables are set for dinner, branding irons in the shed are ready for marking cattle, and the piano in the parlor of the Castro Breen Adobe appears ready to play old tunes.

At the old Plaza Hotel be sure to see the 12-minute slide show on the mission and town's history, which details how the town boomed during the Gold Rush, and shortly after became an important market where ranchers sold cattle and sheep to buyers from San Francisco and San Jose.

Across the plaza at Plaza Hall, once also home to the Zanetta family in the 1860s, you can see the family's parlor and personal items. Behind it is a barn and livery with carriages such as an 1890s mud wagon and a Corning Top Buggy from the early 1900s, sold through the Montgomery Ward catalog for $44.50. (For State Historic Park info: 831/623-4881; www.sjbshp.hollinet.com)

Theater Troupe. San Juan Bautista is the home of the world-famous political theater troupe El Teatro Campesino (705 4th St; 831/623-2444). Director Luis Valdez left the San Francisco Mime Troupe in the '60s to form this activist troupe composed of migrant farmworkers. The group puts on plays during the year and is most famous for its Christmas plays, *La Virgen del Tepeyac* and *La Pastorela*, presented in the mission.

Hike the Pinnacles. Hikers, rock climbers, bird-watchers, and other nature lovers will want to explore the volcanic spires, ravines, cliffs, and caves of Pinnacles National Monument (831/389-4485), a glorious 16,000-acre volcanic park located high in the hills above the Salinas Valley off Highway 101. The dark red contorted rock shapes and crumbling terraces sit on top of a still-active earthquake fault. If you can only stay a short while, visit the park's east side, which has the most dramatic rock formations and caves. Of the four self-guided trails the favorite (and the easiest) is Moses Spring Trail. Come in the spring when wildflowers are in bloom.

RESTAURANTS

FELIPE'S CALIFORNIA & MEXICAN CUISINE ★

One of several Mexican places on San Juan Bautista's main street, this crowded storefront restaurant serves all the standard Mexican fare—good chicken mole, pork burritos, and light, freshly made tortilla chips—but its Salvadoran dishes are what set it apart. Especially delicious are the handmade pupusas (fat corn tortillas stuffed with cheese) and the plátanos fritos (fried plantains) served on a bed of rich, nicely textured refried pinto beans. The Salvadoran entrees are served with an appropriately tangy pickled-cabbage dish called curtido. Felipe's also has several good Mexican beers. Don't leave without trying the fried ice cream, a house specialty. Vegetarians take note: Felipe's uses no lard. *313 3rd St, San Juan Bautista; 831/623-2161; $; MC, V; no checks; lunch, dinner Wed–Mon; beer and wine; no reservations; between Mariposa and Polk Sts.*

JARDINES DE SAN JUAN ★

On Third Street, walk around an old white clapboard house with green trim to the complex of cool shady gardens set with tables that is Jardines de San Juan. Red bricks, softly sprinkling fountains, and the sounds of guitar and mandolin music make it hard to leave. Try the local beer from the San Andreas Brewing Company and the crab and shrimp tostada, or the delicious enchiladas. For dessert they have a delicate flan and a chocolate mousse. This popular place fills up on weekends with large groups of friends and families, so come early in the lunch or dinner hour for the best service. *115 3rd St, San Juan Bautista; 831/623-*

4466; $; MC, V; checks OK; lunch, dinner every day; full bar; no reservations; on 3rd St between Washington and Franklin. ♿

TRES PINOS

If you blink, you'll miss Tres Pinos, located on Highway 25 south of Hollister. There is not much of a town, just an intersection; most people blast through here on the way to Pinnacles National Monument. It once was home to an agricultural community but now migrant workers are being replaced by high-tech commuters and well-off retirees who live in the new housing developments that have spread outward from Hollister.

RESTAURANTS

INN AT TRES PINOS ★★

This dark, romantic restaurant in a former bordello built in 1880 makes for a surprising find in the tiny town of Tres Pinos outside Hollister. "Keep it fresh and keep it simple" is owner Mike Howard's philosophy, a credo that executive chef Rob Stevens translates into a continental menu with an Italian accent. Popular dishes include filet mignon with green peppercorn sauce, Fettuccine Fantasia (chicken, artichoke hearts, sun-dried tomatoes, olives, herbs, and garlic with a white-wine and cream sauce), and calamari sautéed in chardonnay and butter. Rustic but surprisingly elegant, the inn wins high praise for its desserts, from New York–style cheesecake with fresh raspberries and mango to a Granny Smith apple crisp. *6991 Airline Hwy, Tres Pinos; 831/628-3320; $$$; AE, MC, V; local checks only; dinner Tues–Sun; full bar; reservations recommended; 5 miles south of Hollister.* ♿

MOSS LANDING

The fun and funky fishing village of Moss Landing, a 35-minute drive south of Santa Cruz on Highway 1, has a lot to offer: one of the state's largest commercial fishing fleets, nature tours, informal waterside restaurants, fresh fish, bird-watching, fishing, diving, and beachcombing. There are also hiking trails that lead to sand dunes, beaches, and the nearby wildlife reserve Elkhorn Slough (say "sloo"), a network of salt marshes and tidal flats. And mixed in among the boat repair and marine supply businesses are more than a dozen antique and collectibles stores offering everything from old saws to antique drop earrings. Don't worry about missing Moss Landing: it's right on Highway 1 across from the towering smokestacks of a power plant.

ACTIVITIES

Natural and Nautical. Nature lovers have long revered Moss Landing's Elkhorn Slough as a prime spot to study egrets, pelicans, cormorants, terns, great blue herons, and many other types of aquatic birds, not to mention packs of frolicking harbor seals and otters. One of the best ways to explore this scenic coastal wetland is to embark on an Elkhorn Slough Safari. Naturalist guides provide expert and enthusiastic commentary aboard a 26-foot-long pontoon; special activities (such as Bird Bingo) are provided for children; binoculars are available for rent; and coffee, soda, and cookies are served on the way back. The two-hour tours, which cost about $26 for adults, operate on a regular basis every day. Tours can also be arranged for groups of six or more (831/633-5555; www.elkhornslough.com). If you're more adventurous, the Kayak Connection (831/724-5692) gives three- and four-hour tours, including double kayaks and all equipment. First-timers are welcome, as instruction is gladly given. Three-hour tours are $40 per person, four-hour tours $48 per person. Four-hour rental only is $30 for single kayaks, $40 for doubles.

Hiking Trails along the Slough. To learn more about the Slough and its wildlife, turn onto Dolan Road from Highway 1, drive 3 miles, turn left on Elkhorn Road for 2 miles, and you'll come to the Elkhorn Slough Visitors Center of the Elkhorn Slough National Estuarine Research Reserve (1700 Elkhorn Rd; 831/728-2822). Browse the exhibits on bird life and the wetlands, and pick up a guide to the hiking trails, which depart from the visitor center to points all over the reserve. There are three loop trails, one less than a mile, the others over 2 miles, and all trails have points for you to stop and view birds and overlook the slough system.

Antique Shopping. Near Sandholdt Road and Highway 1, Moss Landing has a cluster of ramshackle old buildings that make up a charming village of 21 antique and collectibles shops. At the Caboose, Sherryle Goes packs hundreds of items from old toys to cat figurines into an old red caboose (831/684-1022). Fine antique jewelry and silver are sold at Potter Palmer Antiques by owners who dress as if they were going to tea with the Queen (weekends only; 831/649-4049). Yesterday's Books specializes in California and maritime history, children's books, and art books (831/633-8033).

RESTAURANTS

PHIL'S FISH MARKET ★★

Turn at the Whole Enchilada, keep driving inland on Sandholdt Road, over the short one-lane bridge and past fishing boats, and you'll come to Phil's Fish Market, a local institution owned by the eternally cheerful Phil DiGirolamo. It's much more than a fish market—a kind of community center, joke central, and indoor picnic spot as well as a restaurant and takeout place. And of course there are the fresh fish, lying in state on ice like sculptures in a museum. Beautiful fish, most of it caught that morning. If you like your fish still moving, there are banks of tanks full of undulating catfish, clunky lobsters, and mussels. Phil's most famous dish is cioppino-to-go, but he also offers lunch items including albacore salad and pizzas with shrimp and sun-dried tomatoes. For dinner there is fettuccine with lobster meat and bay scallops in saffron cream sauce or a blackened scallops Alfredo. Should you get addicted to Phil's grub, you can have his chowder base with clams and red potatoes (just add milk or cream) or his Lazy Man's cioppino shipped overnight in a frozen vacuum gel pack to any place in the country. Just open and heat! *7600 Sandholdt Rd, Moss Landing; 831/633-2152; $; AE, DC, DIS, MC, V; local checks only; lunch, dinner every day; beer and wine; no reservations; www.philsfishmarket.com; off Hwy 1 at the end of Sandholdt Rd.* &

THE WHOLE ENCHILADA ★

Fresh seafood is the focus of this upbeat restaurant on Highway 1 with gaily painted walls, folk-art decorations, and leather basket chairs that lend an engaging south-of-the-border ambience. You'll find the usual lineup of burritos, tacos, chiles rellenos, and enchiladas on the comprehensive menu, but go for one of the more exotic regional specialties, such as Oaxacan chicken mole, tamales, and garlic prawns. Have one of the fabulous Cadillac margaritas. Service is warm and efficient, and little touches like crayons and plastic mermaids clinging to the drink cups make this a place your kids will like, too. *7902 Hwy 1, Moss Landing; 831/633-3038; $$; AE, DC, DIS, MC, V; no checks; lunch, dinner every day; full bar; reservations recommended; www.wenchilada.com; on Hwy 1 at Moss Landing Rd* &

CASTROVILLE

Gilroy made history with garlic; Castroville chose the artichoke. The undisputed Artichoke Capital of the World, tiny Castroville celebrates its choke-hold on the artichoke market during the annual Artichoke Festival, held every third weekend in September. It's mostly small-town stuff: the crowning of the Artichoke Queen, a 10K run, artichoke cook-offs, and the Firefighters' Pancake breakfast. The town's most famous queen of the thistle was Marilyn Monroe. The best souvenir in town is the postcard with an (apparently) nude model lying in a sea of artichokes. If that's too racy for you, you can still get deep-fried artichokes at almost every quick-food place.

RESTAURANTS

LA SCUOLA ★★

This buonissimo Italian restaurant on the main street of Castroville is a real find. Tucked away in a tall schoolhouse that's more than a century old, it's an elegant little place serving up classic Italian staples such as veal parmigiana, lasagne, and chicken Toscana. The most popular appetizer is a giant artichoke (naturally), prepared five different ways. The fettuccine with fresh Manila clams is very good (the house-made pasta comes perfectly al dente and the fresh clams explode with flavor), as is roasted garlic chicken in a mushroom and white wine sauce. The vegetable side dishes are cooked just enough to bring out their flavor and color, and the buttery, oven-roasted potatoes are delicately crisp on the outside and creamy-smooth within. *10700 Merritt St, Castroville; 831/633-3200; $$; AE, DIS, MC, V; no checks; lunch Tues–Fri, dinner Tues–Sat; full bar; no reservations; at Preston Rd, downtown.* &

THE MONTEREY COAST

For the past 25 years, the Monterey coast has maintained a split personality. The handful of families who own most of the land south of Carmel—i.e., Big Sur—as well as environmental activists have tried to keep this rugged region as indigenous and unpopulated as possible. The coastline north from Carmel, however, is just the opposite, a high-income haven blanketed with expensive homes, hotels, and boutiques. Try to find free parking or affordable lodging on a summer weekend, and the difference becomes readily apparent.

Problems aside, no one can dispute that the Monterey coast is a land of superlatives. It has one of California's most renowned scenic thoroughfares (17-Mile Drive), a slew of internationally renowned golf courses, the most popular aquarium in the nation, and even one of the most famous ex-mayors in America (Clint Eastwood). Combine all this with truly incredible coastal vistas—particularly around Big Sur—and it's not hard to see why the Monterey coast's 7 million annual visitors don't mind paying a little to park.

MONTEREY

Monterey is really two towns: Old Monterey (the historic part, including colonial buildings and Fisherman's Wharf) and New Monterey, which hosts the Monterey Bay Aquarium and Cannery Row. If you're looking for the romantically gritty, working-class fishing village of John Steinbeck's novel *Cannery Row*, you won't find it here. Even though Monterey was the sardine capital of the Western Hemisphere during World War II, overfishing (among other factors) forced most of the canneries to close in the early '50s. Resigned to trawling for tourist dollars instead, the city converted its low-slung sardine factories along Cannery Row into a rather tacky array of boutiques, knickknack stores, yogurt shops, and—the Row's only saving grace—the world-famous Monterey Bay Aquarium. As you distance yourself from Cannery Row, however, you'll soon see that Monterey also has its share of pluses that help even the score: dazzling seacoast vistas, stately Victorian houses, wonderfully preserved historic architecture, and a number of quality lodgings and restaurants. More important, Monterey is only minutes away from Pacific Grove, Carmel, Pebble Beach, and Big Sur, which makes it a great place to set up base while exploring the innumerable attractions lining the Monterey coast.

Stop by the Monterey County Convention and Visitors Bureau (380 Alvarado St, near the intersection of Pacific St and Del Monte Ave; 831/649-1770) and pick up a free map and visitor's guide to Monterey or visit the web site at www.montereyinfo. org. As you enter town from the north, there is another visitor center at Lake El Estero at Franklin and Camino El Estero (831/649-1770). A third is located in the Maritime Museum at Custom House Plaza (831/649-1770).

STEINBECK COUNTRY

John Steinbeck's novel Cannery Row, *set amid the sardine canneries of Monterey in the 1940s, begins with the line "Cannery Row is a stink, a poem, a grating noise." This doesn't exactly hold true anymore; the smell left when the canneries closed down in the 1950s. However, a few of Cannery Row's monuments remain, most notably the Wing Chong Grocery, which now houses Alicia's Antiques (835 Cannery Row; 831/372-1423). Stand across the street to see its vintage facade and imagine the Chinese immigrants who lived upstairs in its 22 hotel rooms; inside, be sure to check out the Steinbeck memorabilia room and the collection of authentic Chinese lanterns. If you'd like a personal escort through Steinbeck country, Carol Robles & Associates (831/751-3666) offers tours, slide presentations, and lectures by appointment.*

One of the best places to get a feel for Steinbeck's life and work is at Salinas's fascinating National Steinbeck Center (1 Main St; 831/775-4720; www.steinbeck.org). Opened in 1998, the center contains a theater that shows a short biographical film, multimedia exhibits, and gallery with Steinbeck-themed art. This fun, family-oriented museum is no dusty shrine: kids (especially those who can read) will have a blast exploring the colorful interactive exhibits, which allow them to touch clothing and tools in a replica of the bunkhouse from Of Mice and Men, *smell the sardines at a Monterey cannery, and try washing laundry as the Joads did in* Grapes of Wrath. *If they get too rowdy, have them chill out in the refrigerated boxcar à la* East of Eden. *The on-site gift shop has a comprehensive collection of Steinbeck's works, and the museum's One Main Street Cafe offers breakfast and lunch with regionally inspired dishes such as Gilroy Garlic Fries, Chicken Castroville, and Tortilla Flat Black Bean Soup.*

—Christi Phillips

ACTIVITIES

The Monterey Sculpture Center. Just north of Monterey, between Moss Landing and Monterey, is the largest art foundry on the West Coast. Much of the bronze sculpture you see at high-end galleries in Carmel, Big Sur, and Monterey has been cast here. You can take a fascinating tour (call for reservations) and see the whole process of how a sculpture gets made. The process begins with artisans carving the clay for molds, other workers trimming the molds, and others pouring hot molten metal into the mold. After a few more steps the process ends with artisans applying patina finishes on each piece of sculpture. There is a gallery, and some pieces are available to buy at a discount. When you call, ask when they will be doing a pouring, as it is an impressive sight you don't want to miss. Afterward, stroll the 7-acre sculpture habitat complete with benches and a path that winds up a nearby knoll. (711 Neeson Rd, near the airport; 831/384-2100 or 831/384-1700)

Monterey Bay Aquarium. Monterey's top draw is the amazing Monterey Bay Aquarium, the largest and most popular aquarium in the nation. Formerly a boarded-up old sardine cannery, the 322,000-square-foot building features some 200 hundred galleries and exhibits—including one of the world's largest indoor glass-walled aquarium tanks—with more than 700 species, and more than 250,000 specimens of animals, plants, and birds found in Monterey Bay. One of the aquarium's main exhibits is a three-story, 335,000-gallon tank with clear acrylic walls that offers a stunning view of leopard sharks, sardines, anchovies, and other sea creatures swimming through a towering kelp forest. Even more impressive, however, is the Outer Bay, a million-gallon exhibit that showcases aquatic life living in the outer reaches of Monterey Bay. Schools of sharks, barracuda, yellowfin tuna, sea turtles, ocean sunfish, and bonito can be seen through one of the largest windows on earth: an acrylic panel 15 feet high, 13 inches thick, and 54 feet long that weighs 78,000 pounds.

During the years that Monterey was a sardine-canning capital, when a boat loaded with fish was spotted coming in, each factory blew its own unique horn signal, which called all workers to come can the sardines, sometimes even in the middle of the night.

Three other popular exhibits are the Outer Bay's jellyfish exhibit, the bat-ray petting pool (not to worry, their stingers have been clipped), and the two-story sea-otter tank, particularly at 10:30am, 1:30pm, and 3:30pm every day when the sea otters get to scarf down a mixture of clams, rock cod, and shrimp. In 1999, the Deep Sea exhibit opened with the largest collection of live deep-sea species in the world, many of which have never been part of an exhibit before.

The fairly recent Splash Zone exhibit is the first-ever children's museum inside an aquarium, with adorable midget-size South African penguins and child's-eye-level interactive exhibits for kids. Just opened in spring of 2002 is an exhibit called *Jellies: Living Art,* which includes live jellyfish as well as artists' interpretations of jellyfish, including paintings by David Hockney, marine-inspired blown glass objects by famous glass artist Dale Chihuly, and even art pieces made of neon.

Predictably, things get a little crowded on summer weekends; reservations are recommended in summer and on holidays. Tip: Go in the early afternoon—by 2pm the crowds have thinned out, and you will have a much easier time getting an unobstructed view of the exhibits. (886 Cannery Row; general information 831/648-4888; tickets 800/756-3737; www.montereybayaquarium.org; every day 10am–6pm, 9:30am–6pm summer and holidays)

Culinary Center of Monterey. This is a fabulous new facility like no other: a fantasyland for people who love to cook. Here you can take a one-evening class in specialties such as Tuscan Cooking from a master chef, then eat your creations outdoors on a deck with an ocean view. Chef/owner Mary Pagan wanted to share her love of the culinary arts with others and now she has, in a 10,000-square-foot facility on Cannery Row. A culinary retail shop for chefs and passionate cooks greets you as you walk in the door, with everything from a huge array of cookbooks to flexible plastic chopping boards to $365 sauté pans. Keep walking to find the two "hands on" dream kitchen-classrooms, one designed in a state-of-the-art ultra contemporary style and the other like a country French kitchen in Provence, with baskets and hanging copper pots. The classes are four- to five-hour experiences, and each participant gets to prepare every dish, so there is plenty to eat afterward on the deck, and also more to take back to your hotel for a late-evening snack. The center also has a gourmet deli and dining space (open daily) in case you want to sit down for lunch or dinner, plus breakfast on weekends (closed Mondays)—or you can pick up items for a picnic. They also have wine and beer by the glass or the bottle to enjoy outside with the view. (625 Cannery Row; 831/333-2133)

  Fisherman's Wharf. This former brawny working pier known as Municipal Wharf #1 (located in Monterey Harbor; 831/649-6554) once rang with the cries of drunken whalers and ships' crewmen slinging cattle hides into ships' holds, and was later a place for sardine boats to off-load their smelly cargo. It's now a honky-tonk gauntlet of tourist shops selling T-shirts, ice cream cones, and key chains in the shape of whales. At the very end of the wharf a few sightseeing and glass-bottom boats wait for customers, and there may be a few sea lions lounging about. To see a real working pier, look to your right in the near distance at gritty Municipal Wharf #2 (at Del Monte and Figueroa), with its cranes, crates, and rusty boats belonging to a few remaining fishing companies.

Historical Walking Tour. Kudos to the staff at the Monterey State Historic Park, who have recently created a sparkling new set of exhibits in historic Pacific House. Start here, because it will help you decide which other historic sites in Monterey to see. The three-dimensional nooks and roomlets each represent a different home or historic site and display objects, letters, and pieces of clothing used or worn there. If you want to take the whole 2-mile Path of History, a self-guided walking tour of the most important historic sites and well-preserved old buildings, pick up the "Path of History" brochure with a great map on the back. Remember, this city was thriving under Spanish and Mexican flags when San Francisco was still a crude village, so there are many beautiful places to see, including the Custom House, California's oldest public building (at the foot of Alvarado St, near Fisherman's Wharf), and

Colton Hall, where the California state constitution was written and signed in 1849 (on Pacific St between Madison and Jefferson Sts). Guided walking tours led by state park guides cost $5, which gains you admission to any part of the park all day. Get a tour schedule at Pacific House Museum on Custom House Plaza (831/649-7118) or one of the other historic buildings. Tours depart from the Stanton Center on the Custom House Plaza.

The Custom House in Monterey was a happening place where ship's captains often swapped sea tales. After Mexican independence, all ships had to stop in Monterey first to pay a high duty to Mexico on their goods before going on to other ports in Alta California.

Maritime History. Nautical history buffs should visit the Maritime Museum of Monterey, which houses ship models, whaling relics, and the two-story-high, 10,000-pound Fresnel lens, used for nearly 80 years at the Point Sur lighthouse to warn mariners away from the treacherous Big Sur coast. You can also see a life-size re-creation of a ship captain's cabin, manifests of goods shipped, maps, and ship models. A free orientation film on historic Old Monterey is shown in the lobby every 20 minutes, starting every day at 10:10am. (5 Custom House Plaza, in Stanton Center near Fisherman's Wharf; 831/373-2469)

Rent a Roadster. Ah-*ooga!!* If you have ever wanted to roar around in an open-air Model A Roadster, the Monterey Peninsula is a good place to do it, with its 17-Mile Drive and shore-hugging Ocean View Avenue in Pacific Grove. Rent-A-Roadster has three vintage types of replica roadsters: Model A's, a 1929 Mercedes, and a 1930 Ford Phaeton, plus two newer models just added: a 1997 Porsche Boxster and a 1966 Ford Cobra. All are full-time convertibles, with no tops. The usual rental is three hours, at $30 per hour; on weekdays the special rate is three hours for the price of two. (229 Cannery Row; 831/647-1929)

Shop & Go. Serious shoppers should stroll Alvarado Street, a pleasantly low-key, attractive downtown area with a good mix of art galleries, bookstores, and restaurants. The best time to go is during the hugely popular Old Monterey Farmer's Market and Marketplace, held Tuesday afternoons year-round from 4 to 8pm (4 to 7pm in the winter) on Alvarado Street between Pearl and Del Monte Streets. It's a real hoot, with more than 100 vegetable, fruits, and crafts vendors plus musicians and performers. Tantalizing smells of barbecue ribs and Thai specialties like chicken satay cooking on the outdoor grills will make you want to browse here for dinner. Don't forget to visit the special "bakery street," where bakeries and ethnic restaurants put up booths on a side street and sell pies, cakes, rolls, and savory items such as Greek spinach pie.

GOLF COUNTRY

The Monterey coast is golf country, hosting some of the most famous (and lucrative) tournaments in the world. While all of the following courses are open to the public, greens fees of up to $350 tend to keep the oceanside clubs rather exclusive. Not to worry, though—drive a little ways inland and the fees slice rather nicely.

Pebble Beach Golf Links: 6,799 yards, 18 holes, driving range, greens fee $375 (nonguests, with cart); 800/654-9300.

The Links at Spanish Bay: 6,820 yards, 18 holes, greens fee $235 (nonguests); 800/654-9300.

Spyglass Hill Golf Course: 6,859 yards, 18 holes, driving range, greens fee $275 (nonguests); 800/654-9300.

Laguna Seca Golf Course: 5,711 yards, 18 holes, greens fee $65; 831/373-3701.

Bayonet/Blackhorse Golf Course (Seaside/Monterey): 7,017 and 7,009 yards, 18 holes each, driving range, greens fees $70–$95; 831/899-7271.

Del Monte Golf Course: 6,007 yards, 18 holes, greens fee $108 (includes cart); 831/373-2700.

Pacific Grove Municipal: 5,553 yards, 18 holes, driving range, greens fee $32 Mon–Thurs, $38 Fri–Sun and holidays; 831/648-3175.

Poppy Hills Golf Course: 6,237 yards, 18 holes, greens fee $125 Mon–Thurs, $150 Fri–Sun; cart $30; 831/625-1513.

Rancho Cañada East & West: 6,113 yards, 18 holes, driving range, greens fee $80 West Course, $65 East Course; cart $36; 831/624-0111.

All That Jazz: the Monterey Jazz Festival. For a toe-tappin' time in Monterey, visit on the third weekend in September, when top talents like Wynton Marsalis strut their stuff at the Monterey Jazz Festival (831/373-3366; www.montereyjazzfestival.org), one of the country's best jazz jubilees and the oldest continuous jazz celebration in the world. Tickets and hotel rooms sell out fast, so plan early (die-hard jazz fans make reservations at least six months before show time). The web site posts the lineup of performers, provides online ticket sales, gives directions, and answers frequently asked questions.

Art in Monterey. The Monterey Museum of Art has two locations, one at the Civic Center on 559 Pacific Street, and one at La Mirada, a lovely old adobe mission-style historic home with galleries attached. Both locations have exhibits drawn from the museum's permanent collections, which feature California paintings, Asian art, international folk art, photography, and regional artists past and present. At the La Mirada location, tours of the historic upstairs rooms are given at 2 and 3pm Thursday through Sunday. (831/372-5477 or 831/372-3689; www.montereyart.org)

 Winery and Farm Tours. For a self-guided tour of wineries, stop in at the Monterey County Vintners Association (831/375-9400; www.montereywines.org), where you can get a wine-tasting and touring map of Monterey County's excellent vineyards and wineries, many of which have public tasting rooms and picnic grounds. If you prefer a guided tour, AgVenture Tours will take you for a day in the country, stopping at wineries so you can sip as much as you like while *they* drive. Their Carmel Valley Wine Tasting Tour visits three wineries from a list including Chateau Julian, Bernardus, Heller Estate/Durney Vineyard, and Talbott, and each tour involves a vineyard walk with a viticulturist, Carmel Valley points of interest, history, and golf resorts. There is also a Monterey Peninsula Sightseeing and Wine Tasting Tour, which includes Carmel, Big Sur, and 17-Mile Drive, as well as tastings in Carmel Valley, with the option of adding shopping, nature hikes, horseback riding, or the Monterey Bay Aquarium to the trip. Ask about other tours such as the Salinas Valley Agricultural Education Tour, where you see harvesting of crops. AgVenture Tours offers full-day tours of five to six hours, or minitours of three hours. (831/643-9463 or 888/643-9463; www.whps.com/agtours)

During the summer and fall, Monterey Bay Whale Watch takes passengers on 4- to 6-hour whale-watching excursions for humpback and blue whales departing from Fisherman's Wharf. In winter they offer 3-hour trips to watch gray whales. Call 831/375-4658 for reservations or reserve online at www.gowhales. com.

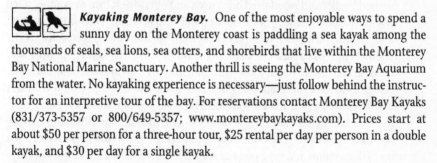 **Kayaking Monterey Bay.** One of the most enjoyable ways to spend a sunny day on the Monterey coast is paddling a sea kayak among the thousands of seals, sea lions, sea otters, and shorebirds that live within the Monterey Bay National Marine Sanctuary. Another thrill is seeing the Monterey Bay Aquarium from the water. No kayaking experience is necessary—just follow behind the instructor for an interpretive tour of the bay. For reservations contact Monterey Bay Kayaks (831/373-5357 or 800/649-5357; www.montereybaykayaks.com). Prices start at about $50 per person for a three-hour tour, $25 rental per day per person in a double kayak, and $30 per day for a single kayak.

 Monterey Bay Recreation Trail. The most scenic jog of your life waits along this trail, or just take it at walking speed. Near the entrance to the Maritime Museum you can rent bikes, reclining bikes, or two-person surreys for rolling along the Monterey Bay Recreation Trail. The paved pedestrian and bicycle path follows the coastline from Seaside through Monterey to Lover's Point in Pacific Grove. It passes Victorian homes, splashing surf, shops, eateries, and the Monterey

Bay Aquarium, with many places to pull over and enjoy the view. The section from Fisherman's Wharf to Cannery Row is lighted at night.

Sportfishing and Whale Watching. Gray whales come in very close to shore in Monterey Bay and are sometimes found bobbing in between boats at anchor. To see for yourself, or to do a little sportfishing, contact Monterey Sportfishing and Whalewatching (96 Old Fisherman's Wharf; 831/372-2203 or 800/200-2203). They have the biggest boats in the harbor, including Magnum Force, which takes 80 people for 2½-hour whale-watching tours twice a day at 10am and 1pm all year except in foul weather. The all-day sportfishing trips usually involve a maximum of 40 people. Call ahead, as prices and times may change.

Historic Garden Tour. Guided tours of Old Monterey's historic gardens, complete with cactus, sedums, California poppies, and old roses, are given every Tuesday, May through September, starting in the Cooper Molera House courtyard at Polk and Munras Streets. The tour is $5. In some of these gardens you can almost see the Californio señoritas brushing by on their way to a fandango. For information contact the Monterey State Historic Park (831/647-6204; www.mbay.net/~mshp/).

RESTAURANTS

CAFE FINA ★★

It's a surprise to find a fine restaurant in the carnival atmosphere of Fisherman's Wharf, but Cafe Fina certainly fits the bill. Owner Dominic Mercurio cooks with a wood broiler and wood-fired brick oven and offers fresh fish, mesquite-grilled chicken and beef, salads, house-made pasta with inventive herb sauces, salmon burgers, and pizzettes—little pizzas hot from the brick oven. Specialties are the seafood and pasta dishes, including clams with garlic butter, prawns and Pernod, and the flavorful Pasta Fina (linguine with baby shrimp, white wine, olives, clam juice, olive oil, tomatoes, and green onions). The food is delicious and carefully prepared, the atmosphere is casual and fun, and the view is a maritime dream. Be sure to pick up a business card on entering, which has a recipe for roasted garlic printed on the back. You can go inside and be seated or walk up to the window and get a pizza or deep-fried artichoke hearts to go. *47 Fisherman's Wharf, Monterey; 831/372-5200; $$; AE, DC, DIS, MC, V; no checks; lunch every day; full bar; no reservations; on Fisherman's Wharf.*

FRESH CREAM ★★★

At this upstairs aerie perched on a knoll, you can dine and have a bird's-eye view of Monterey Bay and Fisherman's Wharf. Specializing in French cuisine with

A GOOD DAY IN MONTEREY

8–9:30am:	*Breakfast at the Old Monterey Cafe.*
9:30–10:30am:	*Rent a bike or surrey and ride the 3½-mile Monterey Bay Recreation Trail.*
10:45–11:45am:	*Start at Pacific House, then walk the Path of History Walk in Old Monterey.*
11:45am–12:30pm:	*Visit the Monterey Maritime museum.*
12:30–1:30pm:	*Lunch at Cafe Fina on Fisherman's Wharf.*
1:45–4pm:	*Tour the Monterey Bay Aquarium.*
4:30–5:30pm:	*Let the kids unwind at Dennis the Menace Park.*
6:30–9:30pm:	*Have dinner at Fresh Cream overlooking the harbor lights.*

hints of California influence, Fresh Cream starts you off with a delightful complimentary caviar-and-onion tartlet, and thrills the eye and the palate all the way through dessert. Appetizers range from lobster ravioli with gold caviar to escargots in garlic butter with Pernod, or a smooth-as-silk goose liver pâté with capers and onions. Executive chef Gregory Lizza's luscious entrees include roasted duck with black currant sauce, the definitive rack of lamb dijonnaise, and a delicate poached salmon in saffron-thyme sauce. Vegetarians needn't feel left out; the tasty grilled seasonal vegetable plate is a cut above most veggie entrees. For dessert try the Grand Marnier soufflé or the amazing sac au chocolat, a dark chocolate bag filled with a mocha milk shake. Service tends to be a bit on the formal side; the wine list is extensive and expensive. This is the perfect place for a special night out. *99 Pacific St, Monterey; 831/375-9798; $$$; AE, DC, DIS, MC, V; checks OK; dinner every day; full bar; reservations recommended; dining@fresh cream.com; www.freshcream.com; at Suite 100C in the Heritage Harbor complex on Pacific St, across from Fisherman's Wharf.* ♿

MONTRIO ★★★

Curved lines, stools of woven branches and soft-sculpture clouds overhead punch up the decor of this converted 1910 firehouse, and the wait staff are cordial and insightful. The only even slightly edgy element is the food, which has the lusty, rough-yet-refined flavors characteristic of Rio Grill and Tarpy's, two other local favorites founded by Montrio co-owners Tony Tollner and Bill Cox. An oak-fired rotisserie grill in the open kitchen lets you watch the action. Try such dishes as grilled salmon over beans and black rice in a citrus-cumin broth, or duck with wild rice and a dried plum–juniper reduction. The wine list, which received *Wine Spectator* magazine's Award of Excellence, includes many fine vintages by the glass. Or you can opt to sample a wee dram of single-malt Scotch or small-batch bourbon—and if it's thrills you seek, try a Tombstone Martini, described on the menu as "soooo smooth it's scary." Desserts are worth the calories: white nectarine pecan crisp with vanilla bean ice cream is one. Surprisingly for such a stylish place, a kids' menu and crayons are available, which should keep junior diners as contented as their parents. *414 Calle Principal, Monterey; 831/648-8880; $$$; AE, DIS, MC, V; no checks; lunch Mon–Sat, dinner every day; full bar; reservations recommended; www.critics-choice.com/restaurants/montrio; on Calle Principal near Franklin St.* &

STOKES RESTAURANT AND BAR ★★★

Formerly Stokes Adobe, the name here was changed because too many people assumed the restaurant served basic Mexican food. Not likely in this sophisticated place. A recent inspired redesign has literally gilded the lily at the historic peach-colored adobe built in 1833 for the town doctor. Co-proprietors Dorothea and Kirk Probasco (Kirk formerly managed Carmel's Rio Grill as well as Pacific's Edge at the Highlands Inn) didn't miss a trick when they opened Stokes in 1996, snagging Brandon Miller as head chef and assembling a staff that is both well trained and friendly. The two-story adobe and board-and-batten house is surrounded by attractive gardens and reflects the Spanish character of Old Monterey. Inside, using hand-cut stencils, interior designer Daniel Peterson has applied intricate gold leaf panels and friezes of elaborate Renaissance design. A new entry has been created, and the interior walls now are distressed cafe au lait–colored plaster that looks like aged adobe (Peterson calls the style "Mediterranean villa gone to seed"). As you step in you pass a wood-burning fireplace. The large space has been divided into several airy dining rooms with terra-cotta floors, bleached-wood plank ceilings, and Mediterranean-inspired wooden chairs and tables. A charming narrow balcony offers additional romantic seating. The main dining room is airy, with walls of small-paned windows and seating covered in blue, teal, and tan fabrics. It's a soothing showcase for Miller's terrific food, which he describes as contemporary rustic. That means, for example, when he takes a pizza out of his new pizza oven, it won't always be perfectly round. You can come just for tapas such as fava bean crostini or crispy potatoes with aioli, or for a full meal. Popular items include grilled lavender pork chop with leek-lemon bread pudding and pear chutney, and a roasted half chicken on currant-candied pecan and crouton salad. Don't let the "rustic" label fool you; this is extremely refined cooking that respects the individual flavors of the high-quality ingredients. Desserts are wonderful here, especially the chocolate lava cake (as in volcano). *500 Hartnell St, Monterey; 831/373-1110; $$–$$$; AE, MC, V; checks OK; lunch Mon–Sat, dinner every day; full bar; reservations recommended; on Hartnell St at Madison St.* ♿

TARPY'S ROADHOUSE ★★★

Tarpy's may single-handedly give the word *roadhouse* a good name. Worth a hop in the car for a spin on Highway 68, this exuberant restaurant features a broad, sunny patio bursting with plants, shaded by market umbrellas out front and graced with handsome Southwestern decor inside, with rustic, bleached-wood furniture, golden stone walls, and whimsical art. Lunch emphasizes well-prepared sandwiches and salads, but dinner is when Tarpy's really shines. Appetizers might include grilled polenta with mushrooms and Madeira, fire-roasted artichokes with lemon-herb vinaigrette, and Pacific oysters with red wine–jalapeño mignonette. Entrees run the gamut from a bourbon-molasses pork chop or a Dijon-crusted lamb loin to sea scallops with saffron penne or a grilled vegetable plate with succotash. Desserts include lemon and fresh ginger crème brûlée, a triple-layer chocolate cake, and olallieberry pie. The wine list is modest and skewed toward the expensive side, but thoughtfully selected. *2999 Monterey-Salinas Hwy (Hwy 68), Monterey; 831/647-1444; $$$; AE, DIS, MC, V; no checks; lunch, dinner every day, brunch Sun; full bar; reservations recommended; www.tarpys.com; on Hwy 68 at Canyon Del Rey, near the Monterey Airport.* ♿

LODGINGS

CYPRESS GARDENS RESORT INN ★

Cypress Gardens Resort Inn is a pleasant upscale motel-style property about a mile from the beach. Its 46 rooms (all nonsmoking), decorated in light resort style, open onto extensive gardens and have refrigerators, microwaves, coffeemakers, new 25-inch TV/VCRs, and irons and ironing boards. All rooms have balconies or courtyard patios. The pool is the largest hotel pool in Monterey. The inn overlooks a nature preserve across the street and is within walking distance of the historic core downtown. Rates begin at well under $100 and go up to $250 for the two-level honeymoon suite. The inn offers off-season packages such as a $99 per night rate on weekdays in the winter that includes admission to the Monterey Bay Aquarium and a continental breakfast. *1150 Munras Ave, Monterey; 831/373-2761 or 877/922-1150; $$; AE, DIS, MC, V; no checks; www.magnason hotels.com; corner of Munras Ave and Cass St.*

The new Monterey Hostel is located in the historic Carpenters Union Hall (778 Hawthorne St; 831/649-0375) in new Monterey. The rate is $18 per person for dormitory-style bunkrooms.

HOTEL PACIFIC ★★★

The Hotel Pacific is a modern neo-hacienda hotel that blends in well with the authentic old Monterey adobes it stands amid. A sparkling fountain burbles beside the entrance; inside you'll find handwoven rugs, muted Southwestern colors, terra-cotta tiles, and beamed ceilings soaring above rounded walls. Connected by tiled courtyards with hand-carved fountains, arches, and flowered pathways, a scattering of low-rise buildings holds 105 small suites. All rooms have private patios or terraces overlooking the gardens, fireplaces, goose-down feather beds, three telephones, and two TVs (one in the bathroom). Ask for a room on the fourth level with a panoramic view of the bay, or a room facing the inner courtyard with its large fountain. A deluxe continental breakfast is provided in the morning, and guests may indulge in afternoon tea. Complimentary underground parking is available, too. *300 Pacific St, Monterey; 831/373-5700 or 800/554-5542; $$$; AE, DC, DIS, MC, V; checks OK; www.coastalhotel.com; on Pacific St between Scott St and Del Monte Blvd.* ⅄

THE JABBERWOCK ★★

You will indeed feel you have stepped through the looking glass and into another realm in this charming hilltop Craftsman-style inn. The name Jabberwock comes from a Lewis Carroll poem; it was the fearsome creature that gnashed its jaws and flashed its claws. This inn has none of that menace but plenty of whimsical elegance. Lines or words from the poem pop up everywhere, even on the walls, and the rooms bear names such as The Toves (which has a new whirlpool tub and fireplace) and Tulgey Wood (with a spacious detached bath). The delicious breakfast dishes (written on a board in backwards mirror-writing) are called "macachew slurry" and "snarkleberry flumptious." Set well back from the hubbub of nearby Cannery Row, this 1911 former convent has seven guest rooms, five with private baths. The spacious and grand Borogrove Room boasts wraparound picture windows, a very large antique bed, a romantic fireplace and sitting area, and grand views of the town and the inn's garden. The Mome Rath Room also has a bed big enough for any beast. The large, beautifully landscaped garden includes a pond, a waterfall, a nifty sundial, and, certainly no surprise, a rabbit who's very late. Decades ago the children of Monterey came here to be schooled in catechism by the convent's nuns, and sometimes one of those children, now an elegant senior, will drop by for a spot of sherry and share stories of what Monterey was like when he or she was a child. Another bonus to staying here: if you can recite the whole Jabberwock poem at breakfast, you're given a prize. Tablemates are permitted to help. *598 Laine St, Monterey; 831/372-4777 or*

888/428-7253; $$–$$$$; DIS, MC, V; checks OK; on Laine St at Hoffman Ave, 4 blocks above Cannery Row and the Monterey Bay Aquarium.

MERRITT HOUSE ★

The only place on the coast where you can stay in a historic 1830 adobe home is in the Old Monterey district at the Merritt House, a cream-colored two-story wood and adobe building with a Monterey balcony, set amid rose gardens on Pacific Street. The inn also has 22 newer rooms with balconies or terraces in two buildings around the gardens, but ask for suites number 24, 25, or 26 if you want to stay in the original home, where the rooms are large and furnished with antique reproduction furniture. The inn is named for former owner Josiah Merritt, who served as the first judge of Monterey County in 1851. The place is centrally located: you can leave your car parked and walk to several of Monterey's other historic buildings, which are on the Path of History tour, and it's a short stroll to the wharf and downtown shops. A continental breakfast is served at the formal dining table in a sunny morning room that opens onto the gardens. The winter "Quiet Season" rates can be quite reasonable. One word of warning: Pacific is a busy street, with traffic that continues late, and the rooms can be a bit noisy. *386 Pacific St, Monterey; 831/646-9686 or 800/541-5599; $$–$$$$; AE, DIS, MC, V; no checks; Pacific St between Franklin and Del Monte.*

MONTEREY PLAZA HOTEL AND SPA ★★★

Situated right at the edge of Monterey Bay, the Monterey Plaza Hotel brings big-city style and services to Cannery Row. In contrast to the California beach-house decor often found in waterfront hotels, this place strikes a note of classic, sleek traditionalism, with a spacious lobby that gleams with Brazilian teakwood walls, Italian marble, and red, Oriental-style carpeting. Beidermeier-style armoires and writing desks, cozy duvet bedspreads, and sumptuous marble baths carry the classic look into the hotel's 290 guest rooms and suites. And 24-hour in-room dining, a well-stocked honor bar, pay-per-view videos, and nightly turndown on request make guest rooms especially nice to cocoon in. Many of the rooms face the bay and feature sliding glass doors and private balconies that place you right above the lapping surf. A recent renovation of all rooms included new window treatments, bedding, and bath decor. The addition of the Plaza's 11,000-square-foot European-style spa has transformed it from simply a nice place to stay into something of a destination. Although the spa services are extra, use of the well-equipped fitness room is complimentary with any spa treatment. The hotel's Duck Club Restaurant enjoys an enviable location right on the water and serves American regional cuisine with an emphasis on wood-roasted specialties, including duck, beef, lamb, chicken, and fresh seafood. The adjacent Schooner's Bistro serves lighter fare, with a tasty range of starters, salads, sandwiches, and pastas. *400 Cannery Row, Monterey; 831/646-1700 or 800/334-3999; $$$$; AE, DIS, MC, V; checks OK; www.montereyplazahotel.com; at Drake St.*

OLD MONTEREY INN ★★★★

When was the last time you paid $300 for a room and felt you had underpaid? You may feel that way after a night at this elegantly appointed inn. Nestled among giant oak trees and gardens filled with rhododendrons, begonias, fuchsias, and ferns, this Tudor-style country inn built as a home in 1929 positively gleams with natural wood, skylights, and stained-glass windows. The 10 beautifully decorated guest rooms, each with a private bath, are filled with charming antiques and comfortable beds with plump down comforters and huge, fluffy pillows. Nine of the ten accommodations have fireplaces, and all rooms have TVs with VCRs and a telephone for outgoing calls only, to preserve guest privacy; hosts Ann and Gene Swett and their staff will be happy to take incoming calls and deliver the message to your room. For the utmost privacy, request the lacy Garden Cottage, which has a private patio, skylights, and a fireplace sitting room, but book it many months ahead because it is a favorite with honeymooners. The deluxe Ashford Suite is the largest, in a wing all its own, and was the master suite of the house. It has a sitting area with a fireplace, a separate dressing room, a king-size bed, an antique daybed, a very large "gentleman's tub," and a panoramic garden view. Another standout: the handsome Library guest room, with its book-lined walls, stone fireplace, and private sundeck. Breakfast, taken in the formal dining room or en suite, might include orange blossom French toast, crepes, artichoke strata, or waffles. The menu is posted the night before, and if you would prefer something else that better fits your diet or food regimen, just tell the staff that evening and they will prepare something special for you. Everything served is baked, not fried, and they do not serve meat. You'll also find a delightful afternoon tea and evening hors d'oeuvres. There are plenty of low-key ways to pamper yourself around here, such as lounging at the picnic tables in the rose garden or strolling around the acre-plus grounds. *500 Martin St, Monterey; 831/375-8284 or 800/350-2344; $$$$; MC, V; checks OK; omi@oldmonterey inn.com; www.oldmontereyinn.com; on Martin St near Pacific St.*

SPINDRIFT INN ★★★

With its soaring four-story atrium and rooftop garden, the Spindrift is an unexpected and elegant refuge amid the hurly-burly tourist world of Cannery Row. Downstairs in this former bordello, plush Oriental carpets muffle your footsteps, and a tall pair of attractive if politically questionable Italian blackamoor statues keep you company in the fireside sitting room. Upstairs, all 42 rooms have feather beds (many with canopies) with down comforters, fireplaces, hardwood floors, telephones, and tiled bathrooms with marble appointments. You'll also discover terry-cloth robes, cable TVs, and nightly turndown service. The corner rooms, with their cushioned window seats and breathtaking ocean views, are the best in the house. In the morning there will be a newspaper and a delicious breakfast of fruit, orange juice, croissants, and sweet rolls waiting outside your door on a silver tray. In the afternoon you are invited to partake of tea, pastries, wine, and cheese. *652 Cannery Row, Monterey; 831/646-8900 or 800/841-1879; $$$; AE, DC, DIS, MC, V; checks OK if mailed with reservation; www.spindriftinn.com; on Cannery Row at Hoffman St.* &

PACIFIC GROVE

In 1875, a Methodist summer retreat set up its tents near what is now Lover's Point. Before long board-and-batten cottages were built right over the tents, and in some of those former cottages current residents still find scraps of the original tent material in the eaves. As one might suppose, things were pretty buttoned up for a while, and Pacific Grove once even had an ordinance that residents' curtains must be open during the day so no hanky-panky could transpire. The town was incorporated in 1889, just about the time Robert Louis Stevenson visited and said, "I have never been in a place that seemed so dreamlike." This beautiful Victorian seacoast village is still a bit dreamlike and retains its decorous old-town character, though it's loosened its collar a bit since the early days, when dancing, alcohol, and even the Sunday newspaper were banned. Less tourist-oriented than Carmel, less commercial than Monterey, P. G. (as locals call it) exudes peace and tranquillity. Geographically, Pacific Grove begins at the Monterey Bay Aquarium and ends at the 17-Mile Drive gate.

The most charming sculpture on the Monterey coast stands in front of the Pacific Grove Post Office on Lighthouse Avenue. A brother and sister hold hands, both dressed as butterflies, ready to march in the town's annual Monarch Butterfly Parade.

ACTIVITIES

Coastal Trail. The best way to start your vacation in Pacific Grove is to stroll the 4 miles of trails that meander between Lover's Point Beach and Asilomar State Beach. In May the brilliant pink blooms of the coastal ice plant against the turquoise of the bay's water is enchanting. Start at grassy Lover's Point (named for lovers of Jesus Christ, not the more carnal kind), located off Ocean View Boulevard next to the Old Bath House Restaurant, and work your way west past the numerous white-sand beaches, tide pools, and rocky coves to Asilomar on the west side of Point Pinos. A second, shorter option is the mile-long Monterey Peninsula Recreation Trail,

MONARCH BUTTERFLIES

Are the only insects known to migrate annually • Travel up to 2,000 miles between ancestral wintering sites • Can fly 100 miles a day at altitudes up to 10,000 feet • Live only 6 to 9 months, so are guided on their annual migration purely by instinct • Congregate in groups of up to 50,000 in a single grove • Feed on milkweed, a poisonous plant that makes them inedible to birds.

which parallels Ocean View Boulevard from Lover's Point to the Monterey Bay Aquarium. Be sure to keep an eye out for sea otters sleeping atop the kelp beds—there are tons of them here.

Butterflies. Pacific Grove bills itself as "Butterfly Town, USA" in honor of the thousands of monarchs that migrate here from late October to mid-March. Two popular places to view the butterflies are the Monarch Grove Sanctuary (at Lighthouse Ave and Ridge Rd) and George Washington Park (at Sinex Ave and Alder St). To learn more about the monarchs, visit the informal and kid-friendly Pacific Grove Museum of Natural History, which has a video and display on the butterfly's life cycle, as well as exhibits of other insects, local birds, mammals, and reptiles. Admission is free. (At the intersection of Forest and Central Aves, Pacific Grove; 831/648-5716; www.pgmusems.org; open 10am–5pm Tues–Sun)

Lighthouse. At the tip of Point Piños (Spanish for "Point of the Pines") stands the small Cape Cod–style Point Pinos Lighthouse, the oldest continuously operating lighthouse on the West Coast: its 50,000-candlepower beacon has shone since February 1, 1855. This National Historic Landmark seems too short to be a proper lighthouse, but since it is high on a cliff, it serves sailors just fine. (On Asilomar Blvd at Lighthouse Ave, Pacific Grove; 831/648-3116; Thurs–Sun 1pm–4pm; free)

Victorian Beauties. P. G. is famous for its Victorian houses, inns, and churches, and hundreds of them have been declared historically significant by the Pacific Grove Heritage Society. Every October, some of the most beautiful and artfully restored are opened to the public on the Victorian Home Tour; call the Pacific Grove Chamber of Commerce (831/373-3304 or 800/656-6650) for details. If you can't make the tour, you can at least admire them from a distance along Lighthouse Avenue, Central Avenue, and Ocean View Boulevard.

Art Gallery. A perennial Best Art Gallery winner in the "Best of Monterey" survey by *Coast Weekly*, the nonprofit Pacific Grove Art Center has four galleries with rotating displays ranging from sculpture to photography to drawings and even children's artwork. Poetry readings, workshops, and the occasional concert are also on the menu if you time it right. (568 Lighthouse Ave at Forest Ave; 831/375-2208; Wed–Sat noon–5pm, Sun 1pm–4pm)

A Good Read. For good books and international gifts, amble over to Bookworks (667 Lighthouse Ave; 831/372-2242), where yellow crime tape festoons the mystery section and there's an easy chair for reading, along with an extensive array of magazines and newspapers.

Factory Outlets. This area's little cluster of outlets may seem small compared to huge new outlet malls in other places, but it was one of the first. Within the American Tin Cannery Premium Outlets factory outlet center are 40 high-quality clothing stores—Anne Klein, Bass, London Fog, Reebok, Big Dog—selling their wares for about half what you'd normally pay. Particularly worth a look are the amazing deals at the Woolrich outlet, where most items are 50 percent off. (125 Ocean View Blvd, around the corner from Monterey Bay Aquarium; 831/372-1442; Sun–Thurs 10am–6pm, Fri–Sat 10am–8pm)

RESTAURANTS

FANDANGO ★★★

Fandango, the name of a lively Spanish dance, is the perfect moniker for this kick-up-your-heels restaurant specializing in Mediterranean country cuisine. It's a big, sprawling, colorful place with textured adobe walls and a spirited crowd filling six separate dining rooms; the glass-domed terrace in back, with its stone fireplace and open mesquite grill, is especially pleasant. Start with a few tapas— perhaps spicy sausage, roasted red peppers, or a potato-and-onion frittata. If you're feeling adventurous, order the Velouté Bongo Bongo, an exotic creamy soup with oysters, spinach, and Cognac. For the main course, choose from the flavorful Paella Fandango (served at your table in a huge skillet), pasta puttanesca (tomatoes, basil, garlic, capers, and olives), bouillabaisse Marseillaise, osso buco, or the 26-ounce porterhouse steak, with tarragon and Cognac herbed butter. For dessert, try the profiteroles filled with chocolate ice cream and topped with hot fudge sauce. Olé! *223 17th St, Pacific Grove; 831/372-3456; $$$; AE, DC, DIS, MC, V; no checks; lunch, dinner every day, brunch Sun; full bar; reservations recommended; www.fandangorestaurant.com; on 17th St near Lighthouse Ave.* &

THE FISHWIFE AT ASILOMAR BEACH ★

The Fishwife (which also has a location in Seaside) has been voted Best Seafood on the Monterey Peninsula and Best Value by locals. Casual and easy, this is a perfect place to come after a long day at the beach. The feeling is a bit tropical, with cloth parrots and toucans suspended from the ceiling and brightly colored fish-shaped pillows tossed about the waiting area. The long roster of seafood dishes includes golden fried calamari, grilled snapper, mussels in garlic cilantro broth, grilled oysters, and prawns Belize, as well as a number of daily specials featuring fresh seasonal fish. The Boston clam chowder is justly famous. For heartier fare, there are steaks and a couple of pasta dishes such as fettuccine with alfredo or pesto sauce. Finish with mango cheesecake or their famous Key lime pie. The reasonable prices and separate kids' menu make this a good choice for folks with children in tow. *1996 Sunset Dr, Pacific Grove; 831/375-7107; $$; AE, DIS, MC, V; no checks; lunch, dinner every day; beer and wine; reservations recommended; www.critics-choice.com/restaurants/fishwife; on Sunset Dr in the Beachcomber Inn at Asilomar Beach.*

OLD BATH HOUSE RESTAURANT ★★★

Although many locals are quick to dismiss the Old Bath House as a pricey tourist restaurant (and it is indeed guilty on both counts), the food is meticulously prepared and the setting is undeniably romantic. This former bathhouse at Lover's Point has a fine view of the rocky coast and a wonderful wood interior with a low, carved ceiling. Chef Jeffrey Jake, formerly at Domaine Chandon in Yountville and Montrio in Monterey, has breathed new life into the continental menu. Expect starters such as grilled prawns and wild boar sausage, and artichoke and Gorgonzola cheese ravioli with a lemon-nutmeg cream sauce. Entrees may feature an oak-grilled lavender-thyme pork porterhouse; a Muscovy duck breast with a tart dried cherry–Merlot reduction and risotto with hazelnuts; or Beef Bindel, a filet mignon baked in a puff pastry with Black Forest ham and mushrooms. Tempting desserts include hot pecan ice-cream fritters and the aptly named Oceans of Chocolate (a bittersweet chocolate brownie with espresso cream cheese, vanilla or chocolate ice cream, and warm chocolate sauce). The service is impeccable and the wine list extensive. *620 Ocean View Blvd, Pacific Grove; 831/375-5195; $$$; AE, DC, DIS, MC, V; no checks; dinner every day; full bar; reservations recommended; www.oldbathhouserestaurant.com; on Ocean View Blvd at Lover's Point Park.*

PASTA MIA ★★

A small, century-old Victorian house provides a homey backdrop for Pasta Mia's hearty Italian fare. The soup and appetizers tend to be tried-and-true standards, such as minestrone, mozzarella fresca, and carpaccio, but the house-made pastas include some intriguing choices, such as a black-and-white linguine with scallops, caviar, cream, and chives, or half-moon pasta stuffed with pesto in a lemon-zest cream sauce dotted with chicken and sun-dried tomatoes. The corkscrew pasta with sausage and chicken in a pink sauce is satisfying and flavorful, as is the scampi in a light champagne cream sauce. Secondi piatti include veal marsala, breast of chicken with a garlic, wine, and rosemary sauce, and a daily fresh fish preparation. Portions are generous in this friendly, informal restaurant, though service can be slow at times. *481 Lighthouse Ave, Pacific Grove; 831/375-7709; $$; AE, MC, V; no checks; dinner every day; beer and wine; reservations recommended; on Lighthouse Ave near 13th St.* &

PEPPERS MEXICALI CAFE ★

This Pacific Grove hot spot (pun intended) with strings of red chile peppers dangling from the ceiling is known for its house-made tamales and chiles rellenos. The delicately flavored seafood tacos may be filled with mahimahi, swordfish, or salmon, whichever is available, and the spicy prawns Gonzalez, with tomatoes, chiles, cilantro, and lime juice, are also worth a try. The chips and salsa are dynamite, and a good selection of Mexican beers from Dos Equis to Tecate can cool your singed palate. Owner Scott Gonzalez is usually on hand to make sure everything runs smoothly, and the service is always friendly even though the place is usually packed. The wine list is awesome for this kind of place, with very good California varietals, including a Sauvignon Blanc from Frog's Leap and Bonny Doon's Ca'del Solo (Big House Red). Stay in a Mexican mood for dessert and have sopaipillas (a puffy fried sweet) or Mexican chocolate cake. *170 Forest Ave, Pacific Grove; 831/373-6892; $; AE, DIS, MC, V; local checks only; lunch Mon, Wed–Sat, dinner Wed–Mon; beer and wine; reservations recommended; on Forest Ave by Lighthouse Ave.*

RED HOUSE CAFE ★★

A trim, 103-year-old, red brick house in downtown Pacific Grove is the deceptively modest setting for some of the most adroit cooking on the Monterey Peninsula. It offers a handful of humble-sounding dishes at breakfast and lunch—items such as Irish oatmeal, Belgian waffles, pastries, a mixed green salad, roast beef on sourdough, a BLT, and eggs any way you like them as long as they're scrambled. Sit in one of the snug, country cottage–style dining rooms or enjoy the ocean breezes on the porch with its smattering of wicker chairs and tables for two. Often local salmon or other Monterey Bay seafood is on the menu, and the crab cakes are to die for, full of succulent crab and not much else. Locals love it here, and often have a favorite menu item they always order. Perfectly cooked, every dish demonstrates the kitchen's insistence on first-rate ingredients—heck, even the toast and jam tastes like a gourmet treat. On the sidewalk outside there is a large round embedded stone engraved with the word JOY. When you take your first bite you will see why. *662 Lighthouse Ave, Pacific Grove;*

831/643-1060; $; no credit cards; checks OK; breakfast, lunch Tues–Sun, dinner Thurs–Sat; beer and wine; no reservations; on Lighthouse Ave at 19th St.

TASTE CAFE & BISTRO ★★★

Although it's a bit hard to see on Forest Avenue, in a small mini-mall with only one entry, food lovers seek out Taste Cafe. You'll be hard-pressed to find higher-quality food for the same price anywhere else on the coast. Chef/owners Paolo Kautz and Sylvia Medina describe their preparations as a combination of rustic French, Italian, and California cuisines, and they work hard to glean the best and freshest produce, seafood, and meats from local suppliers. Lunch could be a grilled eggplant sandwich with smoked Gouda cheese and caramelized onion on toasted focaccia, or chicken apple sausages with au gratin potatoes. At dinner, start your meal with house-cured salmon carpaccio with a mustard-dill dressing, butternut squash agnolotti, or an organic red Oakleaf salad with crumbled blue cheese, balsamic dressing, sliced pears, and glazed pecans. Move on to entrees such as tortellini florentine, marinated rabbit with braised red cabbage, and lean pork medallions with sautéed napa cabbage, onions, celery, and apples. Be sure to save room for one of Sylvia's wonderful desserts: warm brioche pudding with apricot coulis and crème fraîche or a hazelnut-chocolate torte. The interior is simple, airy, and high-ceilinged. The word is out on this terrific restaurant, so be sure to call well ahead for reservations, especially for weekend dinners. *1199 Forest Ave, Pacific Grove; 831/655-0324; $$; AE, MC, V; checks OK; dinner Tues–Sun; full bar; reservations recommended Thurs–Sun; in a mini-mall on Forest Ave at Prescott Ave, enter only off Forest.* &

LODGINGS

THE ASILOMAR CONFERENCE CENTER ★

Many of the original buildings at Asilomar, located at the tip of the Monterey Peninsula on a wooded stretch of beach, were designed by famed Bay Area architect Julia Morgan. Donated to the YWCA by Phoebe Apperson Hearst and now owned by the State Division of Parks and Recreation, Asilomar is in a beautiful setting ranging from forests to native sand dunes. Its 105 acres of parklike grounds include a large, heated swimming pool, wooded trails, and a fine beach where you can watch otters, seals, and, depending on the season, whales. There are 314 units in the complex; the older rooms, designed by Morgan, have hardwood floors and are much smaller and more rustic than the newer suites with their wall-to-wall carpeting, fireplaces, and kitchenettes. The apartment-style Guest Inn Cottage and Forest Lodge Suite can accommodate a large group or family. Breakfast is included, served in a cafeteria-style restaurant on the premises, but you're better off going into town to eat. Independent guests may feel a bit out of place, as most of the people who stay here are participants in a conference or group meeting. The upside is that Asilomar usually has rooms during the holidays when other lodgings are full, as there are fewer group bookings then. *800 Asilomar Blvd, Pacific Grove; 831/372-8016; $$; AE, MC, V; checks OK; www. visitasilomar.com; on Asilomar Blvd at Sinex Ave.* &

GATEHOUSE INN ★★

This big yellow Victorian looks a bit like the haunted house at Disneyland, but much cheerier. When State Senator Benjamin Langford built the ocean-view mansion in 1884, Pacific Grove was less a town than a pious Methodist meeting ground, separated from wicked, worldly Monterey by a white picket fence. Langford's domain is now an enticingly eccentric B&B. Decorated in an interesting mix of Victoriana and art deco, the inn's nine guest rooms have private baths and queen-size beds, with the exception of the Cannery Row Room, which has a king-size bed. The Langford Suite ranks as the inn's most luxurious, with an ocean-view sitting room, a potbellied stove, and a claw-footed bathtub that's just a step away from the bed and commands a stunning view of the coast (talk about soaking it all in!). In the morning, the sun just streams in. Looking for something more exotic? You might try the Turkish Room. Three other rooms are entered off the courtyard, including the Steinbeck Room and the Italian Room, which has a pressed tin ceiling and a Venetian chandelier. You'll find delicious hors d'oeuvres, tea, and wine in the lobby every evening and a full breakfast buffet in the morning, and you can even help yourself to cookies and beverages from the kitchen any time of day or night. As in many inns here in high season, a two-night stay is required on weekends. *225 Central Ave, Pacific Grove; 831/649-8436 or 800/753-1881; $$–$$$; AE, DIS, MC, V; checks OK; on Central Ave at 2nd St.* &

GRAND VIEW INN ★★★

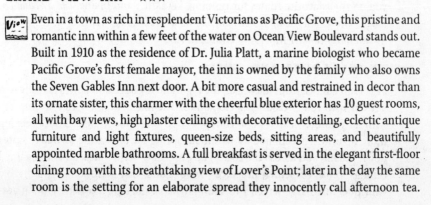 Even in a town as rich in resplendent Victorians as Pacific Grove, this pristine and romantic inn within a few feet of the water on Ocean View Boulevard stands out. Built in 1910 as the residence of Dr. Julia Platt, a marine biologist who became Pacific Grove's first female mayor, the inn is owned by the family who also owns the Seven Gables Inn next door. A bit more casual and restrained in decor than its ornate sister, this charmer with the cheerful blue exterior has 10 guest rooms, all with bay views, high plaster ceilings with decorative detailing, eclectic antique furniture and light fixtures, queen-size beds, sitting areas, and beautifully appointed marble bathrooms. A full breakfast is served in the elegant first-floor dining room with its breathtaking view of Lover's Point; later in the day the same room is the setting for an elaborate spread they innocently call afternoon tea.

If paying $8 to drive the 17-Mile Drive seems outrageous to you, drive the 5-mile coastline of Pacific Grove along Sunset Drive and Ocean View Boulevard three-and-a-half times instead. The scenery is similar and just as beautiful.

These two sister inns have their own chef, who cooks up savories as well as sweets for the afternoon tea, so you may not even have to go to dinner afterward. Complimentary off-street parking is available, too. *557 Ocean View Blvd, Pacific Grove; 831/372-4341; $$–$$$$; MC, V; checks OK; www.pginns.com; on Ocean View Blvd at Grand Ave.* &

THE INN AT 213 SEVENTEEN MILE DRIVE ★★★

This 1920s Craftsman home is a perfect reincarnation of elegant living of that era. Innkeepers Tony and Glynis Greening are avid gardeners and it shows in the perfect setting they have created. They aren't too bad at decorating either—the decor inside the inn is of a very high caliber. The fine woodwork and built-in bookcases and other trim in the living and dining rooms are evocative of the Greene and Greene architectural style. The 14 rooms are perfectly appointed, each decorated quite differently from the others. In the main house the Blue Heron room is popular, with its king-size brass bed, balcony overlooking the bay, Oriental rugs, and a sitting room complete with daybed. Several of the rooms are very large and feel almost like apartments. Asiaphiles should book the Avocet, an elegant Oriental-style room decked out in red, cream, and black. The Pelican, in a separate cottage in the rose garden, is the only room with a fireplace; its king bed is covered in soft florals. Redwood Chalet rooms, also separate, sit under the redwoods. The inn offers a complete breakfast in the morning and wine and hors d'oeuvres in the afternoon. It's only a 200-yard stroll to the Butterfly Sanctuary, and often you will look up to find monarchs fluttering in the trees. A three-block walk takes you to the water, or a half-mile hike delivers you to Lover's Point, where you can take the recreation path by the bay for a long, scenic walk. Tony and Glynis are both long-distance athletes and will be happy to advise you on their favorite routes for running, kayaking, and biking. *213 17-Mile Dr, Pacific Grove; 831/624-9514 or 800/526-5666; $$$–$$$$; AE, MC, V; checks OK; www.innat17.com; 17-Mile Dr at Lighthouse Ave.*

LIGHTHOUSE LODGE AND SUITES ★★

Less than a block from the ocean, the Lighthouse Lodge and Suites is really two entities with rather distinct personalities. The lodge, a Best Western property with an outdoor heated pool, consists of 68 motel-like rooms. Those seeking more luxurious accommodations should spring for one of the 31 newer suites down the hill and across the road. The Cape Cod–style suites, all with beamed ceilings, plush carpeting, fireplaces, wing chairs, vast bathrooms with marble whirlpool tubs, large-screen TVs, mini-kitchens, and king-size beds, glow in peacock hues of purple, green, and fuchsia. The overall effect is a bit nouveau riche, but riche all the same. After a made-to-order breakfast in the fireside lounge, take a morning stroll around the grounds, cleverly landscaped with fountains and native plants. *1150 and 1249 Lighthouse Ave, Pacific Grove; 831/655-2111 or 800/858-1249; $$ (lodge), $$$ (suites); AE, DC, DIS, MC, V; no checks; www.lhls. com; on Lighthouse Ave at Asilomar Blvd.* &

THE MARTINE INN ★★★

Perched like a vast pink wedding cake on a cliff above Monterey Bay, this villa with a Mediterranean exterior and a Victorian interior is one of Pacific Grove's terribly elegant bed-and-breakfasts. Built in 1899 for James and Laura Parke (of Parke-Davis Pharmaceuticals fame), the inn has 25 spacious guest rooms, all with private baths and high-quality antiques, including lamps with interesting shades. Owner Dan Martine has accumulated the best collection of ornately carved armoires on the planet, including one 1840s bedroom set of bedstead, armoire, and dresser, each crowned with a three-quarter relief carving of opera sensation Jenny Lind's head, and another set featured at the World's Fair. Three rooms in the auxiliary building have recently been renovated. Most rooms have fireplaces; all have views of the water or the garden courtyard with its delightful dragon fountain. If you feel like splurging, the Parke Room at the very top of the house is outstanding. Originally the master bedroom, it has three walls of windows, with views of the waves crashing against the rocks, an 1860s Chippendale Revival bedroom set complete with four-poster canopy bed, a sitting area, a clawfooted tub, and a massive, white brick corner fireplace. No matter which room you choose, you'll find a silver basket of fruit and a rose waiting for you upon arrival, and a newspaper at your door in the morning. Several intimate sitting rooms offset three large common areas: the library, the main dining room (with a dazzling view of the bay), and the breakfast parlor. The personable Mr. Martine is your host and will be happy to show you his collection of five vintage roadsters, including a 1925 MG, which he races. The Martine serves an elaborate and well-prepared breakfast at a table set with old Sheffield silver, crystal, and lace, and offers wine and hors d'oeuvres in the late afternoon in the formal parlor with its baby grand piano. *255 Ocean View Blvd, Pacific Grove; 831/373-3388 or 800/852-5588; $$$–$$$$; AE, DIS, MC, V; checks OK; www.martineinn.com; on Ocean View Blvd, 4 blocks from Cannery Row.* &

PACIFIC GARDENS INN ★

Not far from Asilomar Beach, shaded by pines, oaks, and Monterey cypress, sits the Pacific Gardens Inn. It looks a bit like an upscale midwestern motel, but the furniture is well-chosen, with wing chairs and comfortable couches, and the decor is simple and contemporary but not cold. The rooms and suites are large and the value for the price is terrific; the one- and two-bedroom suites have the usual amenities plus a fully equipped kitchen and large living room. Complimentary continental breakfast is served daily and the hosts put out cheese and wine in the afternoon. All but three of the rooms have wood-burning fireplaces, all have popcorn poppers and coffeemakers, and laundry facilities are also available to guests. This inn is not located in town, but you're just 10 minutes from some famous golf courses—Pebble Beach, Spyglass Hill, and Poppy Hills. *701 Asilomar Blvd, Pacific Grove; 831/646-9414 or 800/262-1566; $–$$; AE, MC, V; checks OK; www.pacificgardens.com; just off Hwy 68 at Asilomar Blvd, near the entrance to the Asilomar Conference Center.* &

PEBBLE BEACH

How much is a room and a round of golf at Pebble Beach these days? Put it this way: if you have to ask, you can't afford it. If the 6,000-or-so residents of this exclusive gated community had their way, Pebble Beach would probably be off-limits to mere commoners. Perhaps more of an indignity, though, is the $8-per-car levy required to trespass on their gilded avenues and wallow in envy at how the ruling class recreates. If you have no strong desire to tour corporate-owned hideaways and redundant—albeit gorgeous—seascapes along 17-Mile Drive, save your lunch money: you're not missing anything that can't be seen elsewhere along the Monterey coast. Just drive along the coast on Ocean View Boulevard in Pacific Grove and you'll see much the same views.

ACTIVITIES

View **17-Mile Drive.** If you want to do this drive anyway, you can choose from five entrances, manned by spiffy security guards, which lead into this fabled enclave that serves as home and playground of the absurdly wealthy. Though it can be whizzed through in about 30 minutes, two to three hours is the average touring time. The toll includes a map and guide, but you won't need it: just follow the dotted red line painted on the road. Among the 21 "points of interest" you'll see everything from a spectacular Byzantine castle with a private beach (the Crocker Mansion near the Carmel gate) to several tastefully bland California nouvelle country-club establishments in perfectly maintained forest settings. Other highlights include the often-photographed gnarled Lone Cypress clinging to its rocky precipice above the sea; miles of hiking and equestrian trails winding through groves of native pines and wildflowers, with glorious views of Monterey Bay; and Bird Rock, a small off-

Though bicyclists can enter any gate into Pebble Beach on weekdays for free, on weekends and holidays they may enter only through the Pacific Grove gate.

shore isle covered with hundreds of seals and sea lions (bring binoculars). For more information, contact Pebble Beach Security at 831/624-6669.

Trail Rides on the Beach. All levels of riders are welcome at Pebble Beach Trail Rides (831/624-2756; www.ridepebblebeach.com), operated by the Pebble Beach Equestrian Center at Portola Road and Alva Lane in Pebble Beach. They offer four beach trail rides daily or you can arrange for a private ride. Rides wander through the Del Monte Forest and onto the beach. Along the way you ride past golfers in the distance, swinging away on the Cypress Hill and Spyglass Hill courses.

LODGINGS

THE INN AT SPANISH BAY ★★★★

Set on the privately owned 17-Mile Drive, this sprawling modern inn defines deluxe. Its 270 luxuriously appointed rooms and suites perched on a cypress-dotted bluff have gas fireplaces, quilted down comforters, and elegant sitting areas. Most have private patios or balconies with gorgeous views of the rocky coast or the Del Monte Forest. Three of the most deluxe suites even come with grand pianos. The bathrooms, equipped with all the modern conveniences you could want, are appropriately regal. Hotel guests have access to the world-famous Pebble Beach, Spanish Bay, and Spyglass Hill golf courses, as well as eight championship tennis courts, a fitness club, an outdoor swimming pool, and miles of hiking and equestrian trails. The resort recently created a new Italian restaurant, Peppoli, which serves rich Tuscan fare, prepared by chef Stephen Blackwell. *1700 17-Mile Dr, Pebble Beach; 831/647-7500 or 800/654-9300; $$$–$$$$; AE, DC, MC, V; checks OK; www.pebblebeach.com; on 17-Mile Dr, near Pacific Grove entrance in Pebble Beach.* &

THE LODGE AT PEBBLE BEACH ★★★

Despite greens fees of $375 (with a cart), Pebble Beach remains the mecca of American golf courses, and avid golfers feel they have to play it at least once before retiring to that Big Clubhouse in the Sky. The guest rooms are tastefully decorated, swathed in soothing earth tones and outfitted with a sophisticated, modern decor. There are 161 suites and rooms, most with private balconies or patios, brick fireplaces, sitting areas, and gorgeous views. All the usual upscale amenities are provided, from phones by the commode and honor-bar refrigerators to robes and cable TVs. The whole effect is very East Coast country club. Four restaurants cater to visitors, most notably Club XIX, where chef Philip Baker features his elegant mix of French and Californian cuisine, and the Stillwater Bar and Grill, with a menu that offers seafood, steak, and even hamburgers. Jackets for men are required at Club XIX. *17-Mile Dr, Pebble Beach; 831/624-3811 or 800/654-9300; $$$; AE, DC, DIS, MC, V; checks OK; www.pebblebeach.com; 17-Mile Dr, near the Carmel gate in Pebble Beach.* &

CARMEL-BY-THE-SEA

In the not-so-distant past, Carmel was regarded as a reclusive little seaside town with the sort of relaxed Mediterranean atmosphere conducive to such pursuits as photography, painting, and writing. Robert Louis Stevenson, Upton Sinclair, and Ansel Adams all found Carmel so peaceful and intellectually inspiring as to settle down here. They wanted to be left alone and fought street improvements and numbered house addresses to ensure their seclusion. Not anymore. The charmingly ragtag bohemian village of yesteryear has long since given way to a major tourist hot spot brimming with chichi inns, art galleries, and house-and-garden shops offering $300 ceramic geese and other essentials. Traffic—both vehicular and pedestrian—can be maddeningly congested during the summer and on weekends, and prices in the shops, hotels, and restaurants tend to be high. The funny thing is, no matter how crowded or expensive Carmel gets, nobody seems to mind. Enamored of the village's eclectic dwellings, outrageous boutiques, quaint cafes, and silky white beaches, tourists arrive in droves during the summer to lighten their wallets and darken their complexions. In fact, most lodgings are booked solid from May to October, so make your reservations far in advance and leave plenty of room on the credit cards—you'll need it. And bring your dog if you have one; many inns welcome them with doggy biscuits at the desk and pet beds in the rooms, and in many shops it's perfectly OK to bring Fido in to browse.

Until quite recently Carmel had an ordinance against women wearing high heels (irregular pavement made walking difficult). There are no rules against dogs, however, and Carmel Beach is one of the few beaches on the coast where dogs are welcome off-leash.

ACTIVITIES

Storybook Cottages. One of Carmel's great love stories concerns Hugh Comstock and his wife, Mary, who designed what she called Hotsy Totsy dolls in the 1930s. She asked hubby Hugh if he could design and build a charming cottage that such a doll might live in, for her to use as a shop to feature her creations. The result changed Carmel forever. The Tudor/Cotswolds/fairy-tale style of the little cottage he designed stole a lot of hearts, and he was asked to build many more. His original is now the Tuck Box restaurant, and you will see its progeny all over town. The Chamber of Commerce, located on San Carlos between Fifth and Sixth Avenues, above the Hog's Breath Inn, has maps with the cottages clearly marked so you can seek them out on your own.

GETTING AROUND CARMEL

Along with a ban on streetlights, franchises, and billboards, Carmel-by-the-Sea has also outlawed that scourge of modern society, the street address. That's right, no business or home within city limits has a numerical street address. Instead, people have homes with names like Periwinkle and Mouse House, and residents must go to the post office to pick up their mail. Fortunately, Carmel-by-the-Sea is small enough that this doesn't create much of a problem navigating your way around town, though a street map comes in real handy. There are free maps at the Carmel Visitors Center (on San Carlos St between 5th and 6th Aves above the Hog's Breath Inn; 831/624-2522 or 800/550-4333; www.carmelcalifornia.org).

Shopper's Heaven. Dress in your best "sophisticated casual" garb and stroll down Ocean Avenue with your credit cards at the ready. Carmel is for power shoppers—those who don't blanch at astronomical price tags. There *are* shops heralded as outlets, such as the Coach store on Ocean, where you can spend $180 on a handbag instead of $230, but it's not Wal-Mart. Even if you can't afford a lizard-skin gym bag or a Waterford crystal birdbath, it's still fun—and free—to window-shop among Carmel's oh-so-chic boutiques. Wander the side streets for some of the best shops. Don't miss Phideaux, on Ocean, which has everything for the well-dressed and coddled dog. Other intriguing stores include Ladyfingers for designer jewelry created by famous artists such as Michael Good and Michael Sugarman (on Dolores St between Ocean and 7th Aves); Augustina Leathers for fashion-forward leather jackets, vests, and boots (on San Carlos northwest of 6th Ave); Handworks for beautifully made modern furniture and crafts (two locations, both on Dolores St, one between 7th and 8th Aves, one between 4th and 5th Aves); the Dansk II outlet for housewares (on Ocean Ave and San Carlos St); and the Secret Garden for pretty garden accessories (on Dolores St between 5th and 6th Aves). You haven't shopped Carmel until you have browsed the two upscale suburban malls: the flower-filled rustic Barnyard (on Hwy 1 at Carmel Valley Rd) and the Crossroads (on Hwy 1 at Rio Rd) nearby.

Galleries. A good collection of quality art galleries can be found between Lincoln and San Carlos Streets and Fifth and Sixth Avenues. Particularly noteworthy is the Weston Gallery (6th Ave at Dolores St; 831/624-4453), which showcases 19th- and 20th-century photographers' works, including a permanent display featuring such famous Carmelites as Edward Weston, Ansel Adams, and Imogen Cunningham. If it's fine historical California landscape paintings you love, try James J. Rieser Fine Art (Dolores St between 5th and 6th Aves; 831/620-0530).

Carmel's Beaches. When you hit town, check the local paper, the *Carmel Pine Cone*, for the time the sun will set that day. A half hour before, stroll down Ocean Avenue to Carmel Beach City Park, where families and lovers young and old gather to watch the spectacular sunsets. Dogs are welcome on this beach. It's also a good beach for sunning; although the water is unsafe for swimming, the soft white sand and towering cypresses are worth the price of sunbathing among the hordes. Better yet, head a mile south on Scenic Drive (the street running alongside the beach) to spectacular Carmel River State Beach, where the locals go to hide from tourists. The Carmel River enters the Pacific here, and the nearby bird sanctuary is often frequented by pelicans, hawks, sandpipers, and the occasional goose. Middle Beach and Monastery Beach lie beyond.

Carmel Walks. Without doubt, the best way to see Carmel is on foot. Carmel Walks (831/642-2700; www.carmelwalks.com) offers a two-hour guided walk of the town's most interesting paths and courtyards, including Hugh Comstock's storybook cottages and the homes of famous former denizens such as feminist Mary Austin, photographer Edward Weston, and poet Robinson Jeffers. Tours cost $20 and are offered Tuesday through Friday at 10am, Saturdays at 10am and 2pm; meet in the courtyard of the Pine Inn (Lincoln St at Ocean Ave).

Books and Bagels. The only thing better than a good bookstore is a good bookstore with a good cafe. Within the sea of Carmel's exorbitant boutiques and restaurants is the refreshingly unpretentious (and inexpensive) Thunderbird Bookshop (831/624-1803) and Cafe (831/624-9414), located within the Barnyard shopping complex at Highway 1 and Carmel Valley Road. Peruse the largest book selection on the Central Coast, then sit your fanny at the adjacent cafe armed with a decaf latte and your new read. Now that's vacationing. Open every day 10am to 8pm.

Carmel Mission. This is how a mission ought to look. At the south end of Carmel on the corner of Rio Road and Lasuen Drive is the restored Mission San Carlos Borromeo del Río Carmelo, better known as the Carmel Mission. Established in 1770, this was the headquarters of Father Junípero Serra's famous chain of California missions, as well as being his favorite (Serra is buried in front of the altar in the sanctuary). The vine-covered baroque church with its 11-bell Moorish tower is one of California's architectural treasures. The mission houses 3 extensive museums, and its surrounding 14 acres are planted with native flowers and trees. The cemetery has more than 3,000 graves of Native Americans who worked and lived in the mission; in place of a gravestone, many plots are marked by a solitary abalone shell. (3080 Rio Rd at Lasuen Dr, several blocks west of Hwy 1; 831/624-3600)

Mission Trails Park. If the Carmel crowds are getting to you, head to the intersection of Mountain View Avenue and Forest Road (off Ocean Avenue) and bask in the glorious silence of this park. Even on the busiest weekends, the north end of the park is usually deserted, allowing those in the know a few hours' respite among the 35 shaded acres of tree-lined trails with footbridges and native plants. Dogs are permitted, and plastic doo-doo bags are provided to keep things tidy.

Touring Tor House and Hawk Tower. Ready for a real-life romantic story? Tour Tor House, the former home of poet Robinson Jeffers. Constructed over several years beginning in 1914, the rustic granite building looks as if it was transplanted from the British Isles. More intriguing, however, is the nearby four-story Hawk Tower, which Jeffers built as a retreat for his beloved wife, Una, with thousands of huge granite rocks he hauled up from the beach below his house. When friends such as Edna St. Vincent Millay and George Gershwin came, they were offered a glass of Una's Celtic wine as they sat and talked by the fireplace. Guided tours of the house and tower are available for $7 on Friday and Saturday at 10am and 3pm by reservation only; no children under 12. (26304 Ocean View Ave at Stewart Wy; 831/624-1813)

Theater. Carmel has an active theater scene, perhaps best represented by the Pacific Repertory Theatre company, which puts on an outdoor musical and Shakespeare festival each summer and performs other classics such as *The Madness of George III* and *Death of a Salesman* in its indoor theater, located in a former school auditorium, year-round. A recent renovation has made both seats and sight lines more comfortable. Tickets are reasonably priced; call 831/622-0700 or 831/622-0100 for details.

For the Serious Music Lover. The annual monthlong Carmel Bach Festival offers numerous concerts, recitals, lectures, and discussion groups—some are even free. In addition to Bach masterpieces, you'll hear scores by Vivaldi, Scarlatti, Beethoven, and Chopin. The most sought-after ticket of the event is the formal concert in the mission (book far ahead for that one). The classical music celebration begins in mid-July; series tickets are sold starting in January, and single-event tickets (ranging from $10 to $50) go on sale in April. (831/624-2046 for tickets, 831/624-1521 for festival facts)

RESTAURANTS

ANTON & MICHEL ★★

This longtime Carmel favorite overlooks the Court of the Fountains with its Louis XV lions and verdigris garden pavilions. Anton & Michel's elegant dining room has pink walls, white wainscoting, and tall, slender pillars adorned with curlicue cornices. Despite the interesting decor, the continental cuisine isn't very daring, but chef Max Muramatsu trained at Maxim's in Paris and Tokyo and his food is delicious and extremely well prepared. Standouts include the rack of lamb with an herb-Dijon mustard au jus, grilled veal with a spinach-Madeira sauce, and medallions of ahi tuna with a black-pepper-and-sesame-seed crust and a wasabi-cilantro sauce. Anton & Michel also offers traditional French desserts such as crepes suzette, cherries jubilee, and chocolate mousse cake with sauce anglaise. Service is courtly, and the extensive wine list has garnered many *Wine Spectator* magazine awards. *Mission St between Ocean and 7th Aves, Carmel; 831/624-2406; $$$; AE, DC, DIS, MC, V; no checks; lunch, dinner every day; full bar; reservations recommended; www.carmelsbest.com.* &

CASANOVA RESTAURANT ★★

The former home of Charlie Chaplin's cook, this sunny cottage with a Mediterranean feel attracts happy throngs of locals and tourists alike. Casanova specializes in Italian and French country–style dishes; the pasta creations, such as linguine with seafood served in a big copper pot, are particularly fetching. At dinner, there is a required three-course prix fixe menu, so don't go here if you just want to graze on appetizers. Lunch on the big patio out back is informal and fun, with heaters keeping patrons warm on chilly afternoons. Inside, the cottage is a jumble of nooks and crannies decked out in rustic European decor. Casanova prides itself on its extensive and reasonably priced wine list, including the well-received Georis Merlot and Cabernet, produced by one of the restaurant's owners. Cap off your meal with one of Casanova's superb desserts; the many choices include a Basque-style pear tart and a chocolate custard pie with whipped cream, nuts, and shaved dark and white Belgian chocolates. *On 5th Ave between San Carlos and Mission Sts, Carmel; 831/625-0501; $$; MC, V; no checks; lunch, dinner every day, brunch Sun; full bar; reservations recommended; www.casanovarestaurant.com.* &

FLYING FISH GRILL ★★

Hidden on the ground level of the Carmel Plaza shopping center, this ebullient newcomer is worth seeking out for its fun, stylish atmosphere and its delicious Pacific Rim seafood. The interior is a maze of booths and tables flanked by an expanse of warm, polished wood and crisp blue-and-white banners. Chef/owner Kenny Fukumoto offers such creative dishes as Yin-Yan Salmon (roast salmon on angel hair pasta sprinkled with sesame seeds and served with a soy-lime cream sauce); catfish fillets with fermented Chinese black beans, ginger, and scallions steamed in paper pouches; pan-fried Chilean sea bass with almonds, whipped potatoes, and a Chinese cabbage and rock shrimp stir-fry; and his specialty, rare peppered ahi tuna on angel hair pasta. New York steak and a couple of flavorful Japanese clay pot dishes (seafood or beef) that you cook at your own table round out the menu. There's also a tempting lineup of desserts, including Chocolate Decadence, a warm banana sundae, and an assortment of delicate sorbets. *On Mission St between Ocean and 7th Aves, Carmel; 831/625-1962; $$; AE, DIS, MC, V; no checks; dinner Wed–Mon; beer and wine; reservations recommended; in the Carmel Plaza.*

GRASING'S ★★★

Noted chefs Kurt Grasing and Narsai David teamed up to open this eponymous restaurant (formerly the Sixth Avenue Grill), which serves a more casual version of the contemporary California-Mediterranean cuisine Grasing previously turned out at tony eateries like San Mateo's 231 Ellsworth. At lunch, you'll find superb pastas, salads, sandwiches, and entrees such as bronzed salmon with grilled portobellos, roasted potatoes, and garlic. Dinner starters might include potato, wild rice, and zucchini pancakes with house-cured salmon and crème fraîche or a savory three-onion tart with a fennel sauce and balsamic syrup; main courses range from wild-mushroom stew with creamy polenta to roast duck with an orange-port glaze. The dining room is a cheerful stage for Grasing's inspired cooking, with Milano-modern furnishings, textured ocher walls, cathedral ceilings, and witty sculptures and art. The wine list is ample and thoughtfully selected, desserts are diet-busting delights, and there's a small patio for dining alfresco. *6th Ave, Carmel; 831/624-6562; $$; AE, DC, MC, V; local checks only; lunch, dinner every day; full bar; reservations recommended; www.grasings.com; at Mission St.* &

THE GRILL ON OCEAN AVENUE ★

This warm and unpretentious restaurant has a hostess manager who makes you feel as if you are coming home, and attentive but unstuffy service. Sit by the window to watch the elegant strollers go by on Ocean Avenue, or choose a table in the back for more privacy. The menu is a fusion of fresh California cuisine and Asian tastes. Lunch offers duck quesadilla, wood-grilled portobello mushroom and polenta, or prawns tempura salad. The oak-wood-fired grill produces dinner items such as marinated chicken breast with plum vinaigrette marinade and hoisin sauce; Pacific salmon; and marinated pork loin. Also on the main course dinner menu are Monterey Bay sand dabs (a delicate white fish) with herb-citrus sauce. The restaurant is in a charming Tudor-front building on Ocean. It is very quiet, and so well-insulated that you cannot hear the usual restaurant sounds of serving, or even a conversation at the next table. *Ocean Ave between Dolores St and*

Lincoln Ave, Carmel; 831/624-2569; $$; AE, DC, MC, V; no checks; lunch, dinner every day; full bar; reservations recommended; www.carmelsbest.com. &

HOG'S BREATH INN

The Hog's Breath Inn is located at the bottom of a set of steps leading to a big outdoor courtyard. When you hear music so loud you can hardly think, you'll know you've found it. Although it is no longer owned by former mayor and movie star Clint Eastwood (he still owns the building), you'll always find a horde of tourists and locals cruising, carousing, and plowing their way through the pub grub here. The dishes are still named after Clint's films, like the Dirty Harry burger on a fresh-baked bun, and the aptly named For a Few Dollars More 16-ounce New York steak. (A word to the wise: Prices vary wildly here—most dinner entrees will run you around $15 to $25, but the $9.50 burger or the $9.95 roast chicken sandwich might make your day.) Thanks to half a dozen heat lamps and fireplaces, you can eat outside on the brick patio, with its immense scenic mural of Carmel Valley, in just about any weather. Just don't expect prompt service. *San Carlos St between 5th and 6th Aves, Carmel; 831/625-1044; $$; AE, DC, MC, V; no checks; lunch Mon–Sat, dinner every day, brunch Sun; full bar; no reservations.*

KATY'S PLACE ★

A few steps from the city library is Katy's Place, the insider's favorite spot in Carmel to go for breakfast. The country-kitchen-style restaurant specializes in comfort food: big helpings and endless variations of pancakes, waffles, and eggs, including a dynamite eggs Benedict. Eat in the pretty dining room or on the patio under the redwood trees. This is a wonderful place to bring the kids. *Mission St between 5th and 6th Aves, Carmel; 831/624-0199; $; no credit cards; local checks only; breakfast, lunch every day; beer and wine; no reservations.* &

LA BOHÈME ★★

If you tend to have trouble choosing what to have for dinner, head for La Bohème. You won't have to make a choice at all in this small, romantic restaurant where the walls are painted a pale blue and dotted with cream puff clouds. La Bohème serves only one, prix-fixe menu for under $30 per person, and the selection changes nightly. How do you know if it's something you'll like? Calendars that list the entrees each day for an entire month are put just outside the door to the street, and patrons in the know make it a point to pick up this schedule as soon as they hit town. The three courses include a salad, a bowl of soup, and a main course—perhaps lamb with mint, garlic, and wine; beef bourguignon, or filet mignon with Madeira wine sauce. The soups, such as salmon bisque, and the salads, with Carmel Valley organic greens, are universally wonderful. Two of the most sought-after tables are tucked inside a topsy-turvy little toy house—part of the whimsical street scene mural. While this restaurant is not always consistent, when everything works, La Bohème's cuisine ranks among the best in Carmel, at bargain prices to boot. *Dolores St at 7th Ave, Carmel; 831/624-7500; $$; MC, V; no checks; dinner every day; beer and wine; no reservations; www.laboheme. com.*

LA DOLCE VITA ★★

Those in the mood for authentic Italian food in a casual atmosphere will enjoy this restaurant, a local favorite. The terrace, which overlooks the street, is popular both for sunny lunches and moonlit dinners (heaters take the chill off when necessary). Decorated in an Italian-flag color scheme—green chairs, Astroturf, and plastic red-and-white tablecloths—it's a wonderfully unassuming place to sit back, sip a glass of wine, and revel in *la dolce di far niente*: the joy of doing nothing. The main dining room is a bit more gussied up; it resembles a cozy trattoria with slate floors, light wood furniture, and peach-toned walls bedecked with garlic braids. Specialties include the transporting ravioli alla Rachele (homemade spinach ravioli stuffed with crab and cheese in a champagne cream sauce, topped with scallops and sun-dried tomatoes) and gnocchi della nonna (fresh potato dumplings with choice of a tomato or Gorgonzola-sage-cream sauce—ask for a little of both). A range of individual-size pizzas is also available, along with secondi piatti ranging from traditional osso buco to calamari steak drizzled with sun-dried tomato pesto, lemon juice, and crisp Orvieto wine. The wait staff can be a bit cheeky at times, but hey, with food this bellissima, you're not likely to get your feathers ruffled. *San Carlos St between 7th and 8th Aves, Carmel; 831/624-3667; $$; MC, V; local checks only; lunch, dinner every day; beer and wine; reservations recommended.* &

LINCOLN COURT RESTAURANT ★★

This elegant restaurant is in the location of the former Sans Souci restaurant, in a courtyard complex off Lincoln Street. Chef/owners Wendy Brodie and Bob Bussinger and chef de cuisine Michael Bussinger feature "old-style fine dining with a fresh twist." The decor is quite luxe, with bronze raw silk draperies swooping everywhere and an ironic combination of old and new accessories. On each table are a sleek chrome salt and pepper set, for example, right next to an old former oil lamp. Walls are buff-colored, setting off black chairs with bronze detail. Michael's appetizers include a foie gras terrine with marinated figs, plums, fines herbes, and dried plum reduction with a raisin bread croustade; and a chilled Castroville artichoke served with preserved lemon remoulade and yam and artichoke chips. The brightest salad is literally red; Brodie's "salad rouge" includes radicchio, pears poached in red wine, grapes, rose petals, honey balsamic vinaigrette, Maytag blue cheese, and candied pecans. The usual filet mignon is far from usual here; they complement it with sage butter and a Madeira-roasted portobello cap stuffed with caramelized onions, fava beans, and rapini. The half Sonoma duck includes duck done three ways—pan-seared breast, leg and thigh confit, or roulade of duck breast, in an espagnole and port wine reduction, served with black lotus rice pilaf and rainbow chard. Save room for the serious desserts, such as the orange-pecan crème brûlée. Plan to spend the whole evening; dinner here is an event. *Lincoln St between 5th and 6th Aves, Carmel; 831/624-6220; $$–$$$; AE, DC, MC, V; local checks only; dinner Tues–Sun; full bar; reservations recommended; www.lincolncourtrestaurant.com.*

PACIFIC'S EDGE ★★★

 Perched on an eyebrow cliff over Highway 1 in the Highlands area is Pacific's Edge, the Highlands Inn Park Hyatt Hotel's flagship restaurant, one of the best (and most expensive) dining establishments in the area. If you are going to break the bank for one special evening, this is the place, as it serves inspired California cuisine in a gorgeous setting blessed with panoramic views (reserve well in advance for a table at sunset). Starters might include farm-fresh artichokes with basil mayonnaise, potato-wrapped ahi tuna, or grilled quail with creamy rosemary polenta. Entrees range from grilled Monterey Bay salmon in an onion-rosemary sauce to roasted rack of lamb with white truffle potatoes. Chef Rick Edge also provides a tasting menu every night, with a choice of three, four, or five courses. Wines are additional. One great reason to eat here is the view right down the rocks to the water, and at night it is magical. *120 Highlands Dr, Carmel; 831/622-5445 or 800/682-4811; $$$; AE, DC, DIS, MC, V; checks OK; dinner every day, brunch Sun; full bar; reservations recommended; gm@highlands-inn.com; www.highlands-inn.com; on Hwy 1, 4 miles south of Carmel.* &

RIO GRILL ★★

"All great civilizations have been based on loitering," says the painted wall over the bar at the Rio Grill. This noisy Southwestern-style grill is packed with a lively, young—and yes, loitering—crowd from opening to closing. The salads, such as organic mixed greens with aged goat cheese, seasoned walnuts, and curry vinaigrette, are wonderfully fresh, and appetizers, like the ever-popular onion rings and fried Monterey Bay squid with orange-sesame dipping sauce, draw raves. The tasty barbecued baby back ribs and the herb-crusted chicken with crispy broccoli-corn risotto cakes are good bets for the main course, as is the pumpkin-seed-crusted salmon with chipotle-lime vinaigrette and roasted red pepper–potato cakes. Don't miss the french fries with rosemary aioli. Desserts include a killer olallieberry pie and caramel-apple bread pudding. While the atmosphere may be chaotic, the service isn't, and the grill boasts a large wine list, with many selections available by the glass. *101 Crossroads Blvd, Carmel; 831/625-5436; $$; AE, DIS, MC, V; no checks; lunch, dinner every day, brunch Sun; full bar; reservations recommended; www.critics-choice.com/restaurants/riogrill; in the Crossroads Shopping Center at Hwy 1 and Rio Rd.* ⅋

ROBERT'S BISTRO ★★★

Wooden beams adorned with hanging dried flowers, golden-hued stucco walls, Provençal furnishings, and not one but two roaring stone hearths beckon visitors to relax at this temple to earthy cuisine. It's in an odd location (tucked into a busy shopping center), but the older, moneyed clientele isn't here for the French farmhouse atmosphere—they've come to sample Robert Kincaid's culinary magic. His updated bistro fare includes such appetizers as an exceptionally creamy (and delicious) onion tart; a quenelle of chicken in an artichoke bottom with julienne of apples, pecans, and blue cheese; and lobster ravioli. Main courses include roast rack of lamb with a mustard crust, and roulade of poached duck breast with morel and shiitake mushroom ragout on polenta cream, with black currant sauce. The *San Francisco Chronicle* deemed the roast duckling the best on the Monterey Peninsula. Desserts include delicious treats such as the signature chocolate bag with chocolate shake as well as pithivier, a wonderfully light and tasty marriage of flaky puff pastry and almond cream. The service is both warm and impeccable, a rare combination, but the wine list disappoints: it's not as extensive as one would expect at a restaurant of this caliber and it's tipped toward pricier vintages. *217 Crossroads Blvd, Carmel; 831/624-9626; $$$; AE, DIS, MC, V; local checks only; dinner every day; beer and wine; reservations recommended; in the Crossroads Shopping Center at Hwy 1 and Rio Rd.* ⅋

LODGINGS

CARMEL RIVER INN ★

Families favor these 24 painted wooden cottages and 19 seafoam green motel units that offer utilitarian but homey accommodations at reasonable prices. Though the inn's close to the highway, noise isn't a problem because it is set back along the Carmel River and surrounded by a natural buffer of trees. The rustic Sierra-style units will be refurbished in 2002. The cabins remain the best places to stay; a few have full kitchens or kitchenettes and log-style furniture, and some have fireplaces and two bedrooms. Guests have use of a heated outdoor pool year-round. *Hwy 1 at Oliver Rd, Carmel; 831/624-1575 or 800/882-8142; $$; AE, DC, DIS, MC, V; no checks; www.carmelriverinn.com.* ⅋

For no-cost help in finding a room in Carmel in your price range, call A Place to Stay, a.k.a. RoomFinders for the Monterey Peninsula, 800/364-1867 or 831/624-1711. Hours are Monday to Friday, 9am–5pm.

CYPRESS INN ★★

One of the more elegant hotels in Carmel, this Spanish Colonial–style inn in the center of town has fairly recently undergone a general renovation of all rooms that brought the inn up to date while preserving its Old Carmel charm. The 34 guest rooms received new paint, wrought-iron beds, carpets, and TVs, and the bathrooms have been outfitted in new ceramic or marble tile. Movie star and animal-rights activist Doris Day owns the inn, and pets, naturally, are more than welcome; the immaculate hotel even provides dog beds for its four-footed guests. Try to book a tower suite, with the bedroom reached by a winding stair, plus whirlpool tub, arched windows, and bookshelves complete with books. All rooms contain some thoughtful touches: fresh fruit, bottles of spring water, chocolates left on the pillow at night, and a decanter of sherry. Some have sitting rooms, wet bars, private verandas, and ocean views. Light sleepers should ask for a room on the second floor. Downstairs there's a spacious Spanish-style open-beam living room with a comforting fire and a friendly bar that dishes out coffee and a continental breakfast in the morning, as well as libations of a more spirited kind at night. Posters of Doris Day movies add a touch of glamour and fun to the decor. *Lincoln St at 7th Ave, Carmel; 831/624-3871 or 800/443-7443; $$$; AE, MC, V; no checks.*

THE HAPPY LANDING ★★

You wouldn't be surprised to see the cheery plaster gnomes here come to life and start scampering around this adorable B&B's garden courtyard, a storybook setting complete with gazebo, fountain, and flower gardens. The aptly named pink-and-green Comstock-designed former home plus little cottage rooms around the courtyard were built in 1925 as a summer retreat for two lucky sisters from San Jose. It has been divided into seven cozy guest rooms. All rooms have private baths and televisions (but no phones), all but one are grouped around the courtyard, and three have fireplaces (have-nots can console themselves with the large adobe-and-stone hearth in the reception room). The best rooms are the two spacious suites, which are equipped with wet bars, but all the rooms boast at least a few charming details befitting a Comstock creation: wood-beamed cathedral ceilings, stained-glass windows, hand-painted sinks, curved archways, and cunning little windows and doors in surprising places. Lovers of pristine modernity may not be comfortable here—some of the furniture is comfortable more than fashionable. Others will be utterly charmed. A full breakfast is delivered to guests in the morning (just raise your blinds as a discreet signal you're ready to receive it), and tea and sherry are served in the grand, antique-laden sitting room every afternoon. *Monte Verde St between 5th and 6th Aves, Carmel; 831/624-7917; $$–$$$; MC, V; checks OK.*

HIGHLANDS INN ★★★

 Set high above the rocky coastline south of Carmel with fine views of Yankee Point, the Highlands Inn, now a Park Hyatt hotel, is a sprawling modern complex of glowing redwood and soaring glass. In the main lodge, a skylit promenade leads to a series of glass-walled salons built for watching sunsets. In the fireside lobby you'll find deep leather settees, a granite fireplace, a grand piano, and elaborate floral displays. Outside, flower-lined walkways connect the cottagelike collection of rooms and suites. Every suite and town-house unit comes with a full parlor, kitchen, and bath with a massive spa tub. The 142 guest rooms are furnished with jewel-toned accents and fabrics and carpeting with earth tones. Most rooms have fireplaces, private decks, and fabulous views of the ocean, landscaped grounds, and evergreen-draped hills. Another perk is the inn's elegant three-star restaurant, Pacific's Edge (see review under Restaurants, above), and the less formal California Market, which boasts wonderful coastline views and serves casual, well-prepared California fare. *102 Highland Dr, off Hwy 1, south of Carmel; 831/620-1234 or 800/682-4811; $$$–$$$$; AE, DC, DIS, MC, V; checks OK; gm@highlands-inn.com; www.highlands-inn.com; on Hwy 1, 4 miles south of Carmel.* ♿

LA PLAYA HOTEL ★★

Originally built in 1904 as a wedding gift for a member of the Ghirardelli chocolate family, this Mediterranean villa–style luxury hotel spills down a terraced, bougainvillea-and-jasmine-strewn hillside toward the sea. The recently updated but classic and subdued lobby sets the tone, with Greek caryatid priestess figures holding up the fireplace mantel. Paths lit by gas streetlamps wind among lush gardens with cast-iron gazebos and past a heated swimming pool festooned with mermaids, La Playa's mythical mascots. The 75 guest rooms and suites are comfortable, with hand-carved furniture, color TVs, and nightly turndown service. Many overlook the gorgeous courtyard. To do La Playa right, invest in one of the five cottages, some of which are nestled in the gardens. These have varying numbers of rooms, and four of them offer full kitchens, fireplaces, and private patios. The hotel's restaurant, the Terrace Grill, has a fine view of the gardens and serves such tasty seasonal fare as artichoke ravioli, grilled shrimp risotto, and chicken breast stuffed with dried cherries, cranberries, and walnuts. *Camino Real at 8th Ave, Carmel; 831/624-6476 or 800/582-8900; $$–$$$$; AE, DC, MC, V; checks OK; www.laplayahotel.com.* ♿

LINCOLN GREEN INN ★★

If you're looking for a place to pop the question and promise a rose garden in a cottage built for two, you could do worse than make your pitch in one of Lincoln Green Inn's four cottages. Located at Carmel Point just across the road from picturesque River Beach, the white, green-shuttered cottages, with names like Robin Hood, Maid Marian, Friar Tuck, and Little John, occupy a bucolic English garden setting. Each cottage features a living room with cathedral ceiling and stone fireplace; three have full-size kitchens. The Lincoln Green Inn is about as close as you can get to your own Carmel summer house without spending a fortune; it's a nice place for families or groups, with each couple having its own cottage, affording closeness and privacy in equal measure. The cottage interiors have just been totally remodeled, with new furniture, carpets, and wall coverings. Antiques and sailing ship images accent a clean, elegant East Coast–Hamptons style decor. The absolutely darling cottages in their flowered hillside setting will charm most romantics. There is no proprietor on site; just step into the tiny wooden phone booth to call the management. *Carmelo St at 15th Ave, Carmel; 831/624-1880 or 800/262-1262; $$–$$$$; AE, DIS, MC, V; checks OK.*

MISSION RANCH ★★★

Actor and former Carmel mayor Clint Eastwood owns this inn located on a former dairy farm. Nestled in back of the Carmel Mission, the Ranch overlooks a carpet of pastureland that gives way to a dramatic view of Carmel River Beach, with the craggy splendor of Point Lobos stretching just beyond. When Eastwood bought the property in the late 1980s, he poured a ton of money and a lot of love into restoring the Victorian farmhouse, cottages, bunkhouse, and other buildings, determined to be true to the original spirit of the place. The result is simply wonderful. The peaceful, Western-style spread offers everything a guest needs to feel comfortable and not a single silly frill. Most of the 31 rooms are housed in Western ranchlike buildings with slight porch overhangs like those we used to see on *Bonanza*. They are sparsely but tastefully appointed, with props from Eastwood's films, such as the clock from *Unforgiven*, nonchalantly scattered among the furnishings. Handmade quilts grace the custom-made country-style wooden beds that are so large you literally have to climb into them, and each guest room has its own phone, TV, and bathroom. Rates include a continental breakfast served in the tennis clubhouse. The informal and Western-themed Restaurant at Mission Ranch, which operates under separate management, serves hearty American-style fare. The place's only flaw is that the piano bar can get a little rowdy, and guests in the structures closest to the restaurant may find themselves reaching for earplugs in the middle of the night. Otherwise, Stetsons off to Clint.

26270 Dolores St, Carmel; 831/624-6436 or 800/538-8221; $$–$$$; AE, MC, V; checks OK; Dolores St at 15th Ave. &

THE PINE INN ☆

The Pine Inn is the oldest lodging in Carmel, opened in 1889. Located right on Ocean, within steps of shopping and just a short stroll to the beach, it is also one of the best lodging values in Carmel, with standard rooms starting at $125. The lobby is drop-dead luxurious, with red brocade antique furniture, gilt mirrors, a huge formal fireplace, and Oriental rugs. It's respectable enough for your wealthiest aunt but also romantic enough for a discreet escape for two. This is a full-service hotel complete with bellmen and a restaurant, Il Fornaio. Room decor is romantic; feather beds have a padded upholstered headboard with a cornice canopy, and there are armoires, Sheraton highboys, brass lamps, and formal chairs. Some rooms are a bit small, and if you are in the back of the hotel, you may hear noise from outside. Balance this with free parking (limited), a complimentary newspaper, the plush glamour of the lobby, and a continental breakfast each morning, however, and it's still a great find in this pricey town. *Ocean Ave between Monte Verde St and Lincoln St, Carmel; 831/624-3851; $$–$$$; AE, DC, DIS, JCB, MC,V; checks OK; www.pine-inn.com.*

THE STONEHOUSE INN ☆☆

This ivy-covered stone structure is one of those inns people return to again and again—and many have been doing just that since it opened as a hostelry in 1948. Prior to that, the 1906 building was the home of Nana Foster, and the six prettily decorated guest rooms are named after local writers and artists who were her frequent guests. The Jack London Room has gabled ceilings, a queen-size brass bed, and a ruffled daybed with a sea view. The Sinclair Lewis Room has a king-size bed, a writing desk, and a fine view of the ocean (though who knows what Lewis, that loather of the bourgeois, would think of the giant teddy bears). Only the downstairs Ansel Adams and Robinson Jeffers Rooms have private bathrooms— a definite detraction for some folks. Downstairs, you may lounge in the wing chairs before the fireplace and help yourself to wine in the early evening, and there is a full breakfast each morning. *On 8th Ave, between Monte Verde and Casanova Sts, Carmel; 831/624-4569 or 800/748-6618; $$; AE, MC, V; no checks.*

CARMEL VALLEY

Carmel Valley is a relaxed, ranchlike enclave where horses and wine are the main draw for those who need wide open spaces. There's no coastal fog here, so prepare for sunny skies for your outing. Some of California's most luxurious golf resorts lie in this valley, and it's also studded with interesting specialty nurseries and wine-tasting rooms. Some believe this valley's growing conditions are similar to those of the Bordeaux wine area of France. From Carmel, take Highway 1 to Carmel Valley Road.

ACTIVITIES

Earthbound Farm. Roughly 3½ miles after entering the valley you will come to Earthbound Farm, an organic farm that operates a large produce stand along with interesting programs on growing and cooking organic foods. Pick up the copies of farm recipes such as one for arugula salad. Any day of the week you can buy products such as figs, strawberries, honey, and tomatoes, and on Saturdays there are chef walks though the gardens, bug walks, or flower-arranging walks and workshops. Garlic braiding, compost workshops, and harvest walks are also on the schedule. (7250 Carmel Valley Rd; 831/625-6219)

Wine Tasting. About 5½ miles into the valley you'll see a French-style château. It's the Chateau Julien Wine Estates, open for tastings and picnics. Each of its wines are produced from 100 percent Monterey County grapes. Taste estate wines such as the 1999 Chardonnay, the 1998 Cabernet Sauvignon, and the 1998 Merlot. In the cool, high-ceilinged tasting room, be sure to pick up copies of recipes such as "pears in port with juniper and ginger" (8940 Carmel Valley Rd; 831/624-2600; Mon–Fri 8am–5pm and Sat–Sun 11am–5pm). Two other tasting rooms to try are Heller Estate Durney Vineyards, in a bright peach adobe house, which has a great 1997 estate-bottled Cuvee Gold, a summer wine good with spicy cuisine (69 W Carmel Valley Rd; 831/659-6220; Mon–Fri 11am–5pm, Sat–Sun 10am–5pm); and Georis, an upper Carmel Valley winery proud of its Merlots and Cabernet Sauvignons. Getting to this tasting room is like a treasure hunt—go through the Corkscrew restaurant on Carmel Valley Road just past the Heller/Durney tasting room, to an old adobe with gardens, courtyards, and Spanish antiques. It's worth the trouble to find (4 Pilot Rd; 831/659-1050; every day 11am–5pm, open till 6pm June–Oct).

Garland Ranch Regional Park. Roughly 9 miles into the valley, pull into the parking lot for the Garland Ranch, a park with many acres of open space. Follow the trail sign down the steps into the woods, across a wooden bridge over the murmuring Carmel River, strewn with mossy stones, and on into an open valley with the Santa Lucia Mountains rising ahead. Many people walk their dogs here or hike the scenic trails, or do bird-watching—pick up a Checklist of Birds brochure at the usually unstaffed visitor center to mark those you've seen. The center also has maps showing where to hike: try the 1¼-mile Lupine Loop or the 1½-mile Rancho Loop. The park has an area set aside for mountain biking, too, plus picnic tables in the lower area just beyond the Carmel River.

LODGINGS

BERNARDUS LODGE ★★★★

You'll sigh with satisfaction the moment you enter Bernardus Lodge, Carmel Valley's newest boutique resort, where check-in is seamless from the time you drive up, and you're offered a glass of chilled white wine on entering the lobby. The simple, elegant colonial-flavor lodge is the vision of Bernardus Vineyard and Winery owner Ben Pon, who spared no expense getting everything just right. Situated on a terraced hillside dotted with ancient oaks and pines and affording grand vistas of the surrounding Santa Lucia Mountains, the lodge offers terracotta- and lemon-colored buildings that hold 57 guest rooms and suites, two restaurants, two tennis courts, boccie and croquet courts, a swimming pool, and a full-service spa and salon. Understated elegance is a key theme here; Pon has mercifully deleted the nouveau from the riche. Generously sized guest rooms feature stone fireplaces, antique wardrobe armoires, a sitting area with sofa and chairs, vaulted ceilings, French doors, private patios, and king-size featherbeds with down comforters and soft-as-silk Frette linens. Portable phones allow you to take calls even when you're by the pool or on the courts. The lodge spa is a restorative haven; be sure to reserve spa treatments when you make your room reservation—weekend appointments fill up far in advance. Under the direction of award-winning chef Cal Stamenov, formerly of Highlands Inn and, before that, Domaine Chandon in Yountville, Marinus restaurant offers French-inspired wine-country cuisine. Wickets Bistro, a less formal environment, also draws upon Bernardus's extensive wine list and penchant for local, fresh ingredients. Although jacket and tie are optional in both establishments, a slightly snooty wait staff may make you wish you'd worn your Sunday best. *415 Carmel Valley Rd, Carmel Valley; 831/658-3400 or 888/648-9463; $$$$; AE, CB, DC, DIS, MC, V; no checks; www.bernardus.com; at Los Laureles Grade.* &

CARMEL VALLEY RANCH ★★★

Nestled on a 1,700-acre spread, this haven for golf and tennis enthusiasts (and corporate retreaters) is about as plush a ranch as you're ever likely to encounter. Outfitted in earth tones, burgundies, and greens, the 144 guest suites are arranged in low-lying, condo-like clusters on the rolling hills; each comes equipped with cathedral ceilings, a wood-burning fireplace, a well-stocked refreshment center, two TVs, a trio of phones, a private deck, and a richly appointed bathroom. The furnishing fabrics are a bit weathered looking and could use some updating. Some of the pricier suites come with a dining area, a kitchenette, and a private outdoor whirlpool tub (discreetly enclosed, of course). You might need that whirlpool after partaking of the ranch's activities: golf at the

Pete Dye 18-hole course, tennis on one of a dozen clay and hard-surface courts, guided nature hikes, biking, horseback riding, workouts with a personal trainer at the fitness club, or a dip in one of two swimming pools. When you're ready to relax, you can also indulge in a facial or a manicure, a soak in one of the fitness center's six whirlpool spas, or perhaps a couple's massage followed by champagne and chocolate-covered strawberries. The ranch has three restaurants, including the elegant Oaks, which serves refined American regional cooking in a formal room graced by Old California antiques, a towering stone fireplace, and a phalanx of windows affording a panoramic view of the oak-covered hills. *1 Old Ranch Rd, Carmel Valley; 831/625-9500 or 800/422-7635; $$$$; AE, MC, V; checks OK; www.wyndham.com; off Carmel Valley Rd.* &

QUAIL LODGE ★★★

The venerable Peninsula Hotel Group has bought Quail Lodge, and alert guests will notice the Asian-inspired touches that show up everywhere. This posh resort catering to golfers and tennis players has 100 guest rooms set along winding paths flanking a meticulously kept 18-hole course and a series of pretty little ponds. Comfort, not ostentatious luxury, is the byword here, and Quail Lodge does comfort very well indeed. Decorated in nature-inspired shades of green, yellow, and red, even the least expensive rooms are spacious and have private balconies or patios. Higher-priced units feature fireplaces, whirlpool tubs, and separate living rooms. Nice touches abound: all rooms have a coffeemaker, robes, room service, a minibar, a refrigerator, cable TV, and a bathroom equipped with every amenity. Ask for one of the rooms in the 100s building, which have just been completely made over and enlarged 25 percent. Each now has two fireplaces, two TVs, a minibar, Asian cabinets, and lush draperies dividing the living room and bedroom. Many have improved views of the lake. The resort has two pools and a large hot tub for your dipping pleasure. The Covey Restaurant offers Wine Country cuisine, such as venison osso buco, sweetbread salad, crab-crusted halibut, and other fare that reflects an emphasis on fresh local products. Hearty, well-prepared, reasonably priced breakfasts and lunches are served at the clubhouse, a pleasant quarter-mile stroll away. Guests are entitled to reduced greens fees at the private club and use of the tennis courts. *8205 Valley Greens Dr, Carmel Valley; 831/624-2888 or 888/828-8787; $$$$; AE, DC, MC, V; checks OK; info@quail-lodgeresort.com; www.quail-lodge-resort.com; 3½ miles east of Hwy 1, just off Carmel Valley Rd.* &

STONEPINE ★★★★

This exquisite Mediterranean villa (the former country home of the Crocker banking family) rises in terraced splendor against the Carmel Valley's oak-covered hills. Surrounded by cypress, imported stone pines, and wisteria trailing from hand-carved Italian stone pillars, the inn has 16 guest rooms divided among Château Noel (named after owner Noel Hentschel), the Paddock House, and the idyllic (and astronomically expensive) Briar Rose Cottage, a two-bedroom affair with a private rose garden, living room, dining room, kitchen, and bar. The suites in the main house are studies in formal splendor; all have French antique furnishings, spa tubs, down comforters, and fluffy robes, and five of them feature fireplaces. The cost of your room includes a big breakfast; for an additional charge you may partake of a wine reception followed by an elegant five-course estate dinner in the dining room. During the day, float in the jewel-like swimming pool, play tennis, explore the ranch's 330 acres, or horse around at the Stonepine Equestrian Center. Beware: The equestrian staff takes horseback riding mighty seriously, and more than one city slicker has suffered a bruised ego as well as a sore derriere after a turn on the trails. *150 E Carmel Valley Rd, Carmel Valley; 831/659-2245; $$$$; AE, MC, V; checks OK; www.stonepinecalifornia.com; 13 miles east of Hwy 1.* &

BIG SUR COAST

Spanish settlers called this 90-mile stretch of rugged, impassable coastline *El País Grande del Sur*, or "the big country to the south" (that is, south of their colony at Monterey). A narrow, twisting segment of Highway 1 (built with convict labor in the 1930s) snakes through this coastal area between Carmel and San Simeon, and the mist-shrouded forests, sloping grassy meadows, plunging cliffs, and cobalt sea make the drive one of the most beautiful in the country, if not the world. In fact, the region is so captivating that some folks favor giving it national park status; others recoil in horror at the thought of involving the federal government in the preservation of this untamed land.

Big Sur is surprisingly important in this country's recent political and social history. Literary free thinkers such as Jack Kerouac came early, drawn by a self-exiled Henry Miller. In the early 1960s the human potential movement was born in experimental gatherings at Esalen. The importing of Asian meditation and Eastern religion started here, thanks to such Eastern-influenced thinkers as Alan Watts. The philosophy still holds today. People who choose to live in Big Sur have done so consciously, and seem happy with their choice. Service is given with a smile and a generous heart that matches the beauty of the landscape. Travelers are drawn here not only for how it looks but how it feels.

Despite Big Sur's popularity—summer weekends mean slow traffic on the two-lane highway—the area has remained sparsely

The acknowledged honorary poet of the Big Sur area was poet Robinson Jeffers, who called this rugged part of the coast "this jagged country which nothing but a fallen meteor will ever plow."

ESALEN—A RETREAT FOR MIND, BODY, AND SPIRIT

To Esalen we can give thanks—or blame—for bringing terms like self-actualization, peak experience, encounter group, and Gestalt therapy into the popular lexicon, and for that essential contribution to instant enlightenment, the hot tub. Originally located at the ocean's edge, the baths were a source of controversy during Esalen's first two decades, generating rumors of drug use and public sex. Founders Michael Murphy and Richard Price tried to keep the lid on, so to speak, by declaring the baths chastely separate-sex, but the demand for coed nudity eventually overrode them. In 1998, El Niño storms caused extensive damage to the baths and the towering slope that rises above them. The baths were moved to the top of the bluff, where they'll remain until the hillside and the baths are repaired. They're still coed and clothing-optional and continue to be popular with Esalen guests, but the wild antics are long gone. Hey, it's not the '60s anymore.

Almost 40 years have passed since the heady days when Alan Watts and Joseph Campbell debated the mysteries of the universe, Joan Baez gave impromptu concerts, and George and Ringo flew in with the Maharishi in tow, but Esalen continues to be a countercultural enclave for spiritual seekers. A smorgasbord of workshops dealing with trauma, art and creativity, massage, yoga-martial arts, and relationships offer enough options to keep anyone's body, mind, and spirit in proper working order. Workshops are either two-day (Fri–Sun) or five-day (Sun–Fri) and cost $485 and $885 respectively. Shared lodgings and all meals are included. For more information, call 831/667-3000 or visit www.esalen.org.

—Christi Phillips

populated. Most visitors are day-trippers vacationing in the Monterey area who come to see what all the fuss is about. Others whiz through in rented convertibles on their way south. But those in the know journey here for a few days of camping, cabin-renting, backpacking, or luxuriating in the elegant (and exorbitantly priced) resorts. Even if you're only visiting for the day, start early, fill your tank, take a camera and binoculars, bring a jacket, wear comfortable shoes, drive slowly, and take at least one hike.

Keeping your Big Sur visit low-stress is challenging since driving Big Sur can be a bit confusing. Some of the park names sound so similar (too many Pfeiffers!), and it's hard to watch the road, take in the scenery, and still be ready to stop in time when you come to a park or gallery of interest. It will help if you can come either off-season or midweek when traffic along Highway 1 is fairly light. Another tip: Come in the spring, April through early June, when the golden California poppies, yellow mustard, and purple lupines brighten the windswept landscape.

ACTIVITIES

 Point Lobos. Whether you're in Big Sur for a day or for a week, spend some time in the gorgeous 1,276-acre Point Lobos State Reserve (on Hwy 1, 3 miles south of Carmel; 831/624-4909). More than a dozen trails lead to ocean coves, where you might spy sea otters, harbor seals, California sea lions, large colonies of seabirds, and, between December and May, migrating California gray whales. Take the cliff-top trail under wind-twisted Monterey pines. Docents are available on weekends to explain the natural features of the reserve. Wherever you trek through Big Sur, however, beware of poison oak (Remember: Leaves of three, let it be).

 Bixby Bridge. That magnificent arched span crossing over Bixby Creek Canyon is the Bixby Bridge, aka the Rainbow Bridge, completed in 1932. At 268 feet high and 739 feet long, with a 320-foot arch, it's one of the world's highest single-span concrete bridges and a favorite stop for camera-wielding tourists. Photo tip: For the best shooting angle, drive a few hundred yards up the dirt road at the north end of the bridge (Old Coast Rd).

The Point Sur Lighthouse. Towering 361 feet above the surf atop Point Sur, on a giant volcanic-rock island easily visible from Highway 1 south of the Bixby Bridge, you'll see the Point Sur Lighthouse, now the Point Sur Lightstation State Historic Park. The lighthouse was built in 1889 and is the only complete turn-of-the-century light station open to the public in California. Inexpensive (though physically taxing) three-hour guided lighthouse walking tours are offered on weekends year-round and on Wednesdays and Thursdays in summer. Don't forget your jacket and $5 for admission. Several times a year they also offer moonlight tours, where you hear about the ghosts of light-keepers past. Call for schedule information. (Off Hwy 1, 19 miles south of Carmel in Big Sur; 831/625-4419)

 Andrew Molera State Park Hiking and Beachcombing. A popular retreat for hikers and bicyclists is the 4,800-acre Andrew Molera State Park, the largest state park on the Big Sur coast. More than 15 miles of trails zigzag through grasslands, and redwood forests and along the Big Sur River. An easy mile-long walk from Creamery Meadow to Molera Beach leads through a meadow laced with wildflowers to a 2-mile-long beach harboring the area's best tide pools. This beach has the most driftwood of any beach in Big Sur, so much in fact that you are legally permitted to gather up to 50 pounds! You must stick to gathering wood that is "down and dead" and found only on the

A stop for refreshments or a sunset dinner in the gazebo at the breathtaking Rocky Point Restaurant hanging high over the coast, north of Big Sur and south of Point Lobos, is a don't-miss on a Big Sur visit; 831/624-2933; www.rocky point.com.

beach, though, not in the woods. The moderate to difficult hike on Molera 8-Mile Loop combines the Ridge Trail, the Panorama Trail, and the Bluffs Trail and passes through redwood groves at the far south end of the park. On the western side of the loop there is a trail marked "To Beach," which leads down to the water. (On Hwy 1, 21 miles south of Carmel; 831/667-2315)

Horseback-Ride the Big Sur Coast. Molera Horseback Tours offers scenic coastal horseback tours, from the Beach Bonanza to the Sunset Serenade, every day in Andrew Molera State Park, from April 1 to January 1, if the weather cooperates. The ride winds through bay laurel and redwoods, then up on the ridge over the water. All rides also go on the beach. No riding experience is necessary. There are several kinds of rides, departure times, and prices available. It's OK to call at the last minute; they may be able to accommodate you. (831/625-5486 or 800/942-5486; www. molerahorsebacktours.com)

Old Coast Road. Across from the entrance to Andrew Molera State Park is the southern access point to Old Coast Road, a maintained but bumpy dirt road (without guardrails) that passes through 10 miles of dense redwood groves and climbs sky-high onto chaparral-covered ridges—with spectacular views of pastures, canyons, and the coast—before exiting back onto Highway 1 at Bixby Bridge. It takes about an hour to drive this lonely 10 miles, so check your tires, gas, and suspension before you attempt it. A four-wheel-drive vehicle isn't required for the hour-long mini-adventure, but this isn't for the fainthearted, either. The prize at the end of the road is a dramatic and beautifully framed view of Bixby Bridge, with islands offshore visible under it, traffic passing on it, and clouds scudding over it. The road is usually closed during the rainy winter season.

Hiking and Camping at Pfeiffer–Big Sur State Park. One thing Big Sur isn't short of is hiking trails. Pfeiffer–Big Sur State Park has dozens of trails—many with panoramic views of the sea—that crisscross the park's 810 acres of madrone and oak woodlands and misty redwood canyons. The most popular easy hike is the Pfeiffer Falls trail, a 1¼-mile hike along Pfeiffer–Big Sur Creek through one of the park's finest redwood groves. The trail ends at a 60-foot-high waterfall. The Big Sur River meanders through the park, too, attracting anglers and swimmers hardy enough to brave the chilly waters. For overnighters, Pfeiffer–Big Sur offers 218 ultracivilized camping facilities that include showers, a laundry, a store, an amphitheater for ranger-led campfire talks, and (bless 'em) flush toilets. (Between Andrew Molera State Park and Pfeiffer Beach; park reservations: 800/444-7275; information: 831/667-2315)

To the Beach on Wheels. Though entrance to Pfeiffer–Big Sur State Park costs a hefty $5, the park's best attraction is free. Exactly 1½ miles south of the park's entrance on Highway 1 is the unmarked turnoff to Sycamore Canyon Road, a narrow 2⅓-mile paved road (motor homes can forget this one) that leads to beautiful but blustery Pfeiffer Beach, the only beach in Big Sur accessible by car. Even if the sun's a no-show, it's still worth a trip to marvel at the white-and-mauve sands, enormous sea caves, and pounding surf.

Miller Time, as in Henry. Three miles south of Nepenthe Restaurant on Highway 1 is the Coast Gallery (831/667-2301), a showplace for local artists and craftspeople featuring fine sculpture, pottery, jewelry, and paintings. The large upstairs gallery is dedicated to watercolors by author Henry Miller, who lived nearby for more than 15 yeasrs, and who had painted for 50 years by the time he died. Most of the prints were originally done as stone plate lithographs or serigraphs. The gallery's casual Coast Cafe (see above) has a great view of the ocean through 6-foot round windows, or you can sit outside on the terrace. Choose from soup, sandwiches, baked goods, wine, and espresso drinks—the quiche is especially good. The author's fans will also want to seek out the Henry Miller Library (831/667-2574; www.henrymiller.org), located in the former home of friend Emil White. In addition to a great collection of Miller's books and art, the library serves as one of Big Sur's cultural centers and features the art, poetry, prose, photography, and music of locals as well as famous friends of Henry's such as Jack Kerouac, Alan Watts, and poet Robinson Jeffers. It's open Wednesday through Sunday and is located just beyond Nepenthe Restaurant on the east side of Highway 1.

> *"It was here in Big Sur that I first learned to say Amen!" —Henry Miller in* Big Sur and the Oranges of Hieronymus Bosch

Hidden Secrets Hike. If you only have the time or energy for one short hike while touring Big Sur, head for the secret cove at Partington Canyon. Don't bother looking for it on the map; it's not there. Instead, look for a long, horseshoe-shaped turn around a small canyon leading to the ocean, exactly 2 miles north of Julia Pfeiffer Burns State Park turnoff and 6 miles south of Nepenthe (you'll see several dirt pull-offs where you can park). Walk down the canyon on the fire road toward the ocean, turn right at the "Underwater Forest" display board, then left across the sturdy wooden footbridge, and through an 8-foot-high, 100-foot-long, hand-carved, timber-reinforced tunnel that leads to a dazzling hidden cove, where a convenient bench lets you sit and look out at the water swept by kelp, where sea otters sometimes play. The story goes that John Partington built the tunnel for his tan-oak cutting and shipping operation, where sleds filled with tan-oak bark were pulled down the mountain and loaded onto ships anchored in the placid cove. Take water with you for this hike, as the steep climb back up to the road is in full sun.

Big Sur is one of the few communities left where every gas station (all three of them) is full-service. Don't expect cheap gas, though: everything delivered to Big Sur from the outside world costs more.

 Julia's Waterfall Trail. At the southern end of the Big Sur area is Julia Pfeiffer Burns State Park. With 3,580 acres to roam—and a less-crowded feel to it than the region's other parks—you'll find some excellent day hikes here. One of the most beautiful is the ¼-mile Waterfall Trail to 80-foot-high McWay Waterfall, which once plunged directly into the sea, but since the 1983 rains, when a landslide just north of here deposited large amounts of sediment in the cove, now falls instead onto the sandy beach below. As you walk the trail that winds from redwoods to chaparral on the cliff, 100 feet above the water, keep an eye open for California sea lions and sea otters that often appear in McWay Cove. At the end of the fairly level trail, bordered by sticky monkey flower with its orange trumpetlike flowers, clingweed (wild morning glory), and California sage, are benches shaded by bay laurel and redwoods with terrific views of the water below. (For information call 831/667-2315)

For Real Hikers. The serious hike rated number one by state park rangers we spoke to is also in Julia Pfeiffer Burns State Park. Called the Ewoldsen Trail, it's a 4-½-mile loop that's considered moderate to strenuous, starting in the redwoods by McWay Creek and climbing to incredible coastal views. The trail is 95 percent in the shade. Along the way you'll see one of the biggest redwood trees in Big Sur. When you get to the top, choose the trail marked "Viewpoint" and it will take you to a bluff overlooking the ocean, where California condors have been spotted. (For information call 831/667-2315)

A GOOD DAY IN BIG SUR

8–9:30am:	*Breakfast at Cafe Kevah.*
9:30–10am:	*Browse the Phoenix shop at Nepenthe for gifts.*
10–11am:	*Hike the trail to McWay waterfall.*
11–11:30am:	*Visit the Coast Gallery.*
11:30–12:15pm:	*Browse the Henry Miller Library and chat with the manager Magnus about Henry Miller.*
12:30–2:30pm:	*Lunch at the River Inn.*
3:30–6pm:	*Take a horseback ride through Molera State Park*
6:30–7:30pm:	*Change for dinner.*
8–10pm:	*Dinner at Deetjen's Big Sur Inn Restaurant.*

View **Big Sur Audio Driving Tour.** A wonderful way to know what you're seeing along Highway 1 is to take an audiotape tour as you drive. The Big Sur Land Trust has a great one, which you can order in advance for $9.95 by calling 831/625-5523, or via email at mail@bigsurlandtrust.org. Rich with history, culture, and personal anecdotes of early residents in their own voices, this guided tour of the region comes in a "driving south" version and also a "driving north" version, so when you order, specify which one you want.

RESTAURANTS

BIG SUR RIVER INN ★

The Big Sur River Inn is exactly the kind of restaurant you would expect to find in a mountain community—a large, rustic cabin (circa 1934), built and furnished entirely with rough-hewn woods, warmed by a large fireplace surrounded by comfy chairs, and occupied by jeans-clad locals sharing the day's news over beers at the corner bar. In the summer most everyone requests a table on the shaded back deck, which overlooks a picturesque stretch of the Big Sur River. Since the restaurant caters to the inn's guests, it's open morning till nightfall. Breakfast is all-American (eggs, pancakes, bacon, omelets, and such), as are lunch and dinner. The menu offers a wide range of choices: pasta, burgers, chicken sandwiches, salads, fish 'n' chips, and a whole lot more. Recommended plates are the Black Angus Burger with a side of beer-battered onion rings, or a big platter of the Roadhouse Ribs served with cowboy beans. Wash either down with a cool glass of Carmel Brewing Co. Amber Ale, and you're ready to roll. *Hwy 1 at Pheneger Creek, Big Sur; 831/667-2700; $; AE, DC, DIS, MC, V; no checks; breakfast, lunch, dinner every day; beer and wine; no reservations; www.bigsurriverinn.com; on Hwy 1, 2 miles north of Pfeiffer–Big Sur State Park.*

CAFE KEVAH ★

View If your idea of communing with nature is a comfy chair, a leafy salad, and a view of the rugged coast, then grab a seat on the deck of the Cafe Kevah, located one flight of stairs below the fabled—and high-priced—Nepenthe Restaurant. Breakfast is served all day—omelets, burritos, huevos rancheros—and lunch offers spicy chicken brochette, grilled salmon with salsa verde, quesadillas, and Caesar salads. It's an especially good place for breakfast, less crowded then than at lunch time. The staff are extremely friendly and helpful. The clincher, though, is the location: perched 800 feet above the glimmering Pacific, the cafe's deck has a phenomenal view of the Big Sur coastline. *Hwy 1, in Nepenthe complex, south of the Post Ranch Inn, Big Sur; 831/667-2344; $; AE, MC, V; no checks; breakfast, lunch* *every day (pastries and coffee in late afternoon); beer and wine; no reservations; on Hwy 1, 3 miles south of Pfeiffer–Big Sur State Park.*

DEETJEN'S BIG SUR INN RESTAURANT ☆

Deetjen's Big Sur Inn Restaurant, which has garnered a loyal following, serves good Euro-California cuisine that takes advantage of local produce and seafood. The setting is rustic-romantic, with white painted wood walls, dimly lit old-fashioned lamps, and antiques in every nook. A wood-burning stove provides heat on chilly winter nights. The small menu varies seasonally and features half a dozen starters including spinach goat cheese soup, a warm poached pear stuffed with Stilton cheese and walnuts on a bed of mixed baby greens. Several entrees are offered, among them a fresh pasta selection that changes nightly. The most robust fare includes coq au vin, roasted rack of lamb with a panko crust, and a prime New York steak served with macadamia-nut risotto with red wine butter and a smoked cheddar gratin. *On Hwy 1, 4 miles south of Pfeiffer–Big Sur State Park, Big Sur; 831/667-2378; $$; MC, V; checks OK; breakfast, dinner every day; beer and wine; reservations required.*

NEPENTHE RESTAURANT ☆☆

 This venerable Big Sur institution recently celebrated its 50th anniversary and still draws in the crowds. Located 800 feet above the ocean, Nepenthe commands views of the Big Sur coastline that will make you gasp. It is a friendly, family-owned and -managed place, and therein lies part of its appeal. Originally a log cabin that housed Lolly and Bill Fassett and their five children, it became Nepenthe when they realized that the only way to keep their family amply fed was to open a restaurant. The log cabin remains, but over the years Nepenthe has grown to encompass the entire bluff it rests upon. The restaurant boasts a full bar, and two outdoor areas offer lots of room for alfresco dining. Even after warnings about overpriced meals, locals insist visitors to Big Sur should try Nepenthe at least once. The fare tends toward standard American with a twist. Starters include Cajun poached shrimp and Castroville artichoke; entrees include a choice of fresh fish, steaks, and broiled or roast chicken. Burgers and salads should keep kids and vegetarians happy. Be sure to check out Nepenthe's Phoenix Gift Shop on your way out. This magical upscale store harbors wonderful imported treasures, indoor fountains, garden sculpture, elegant women's clothes, books, jewelry, kids' toys, and locally made soaps, lotions, and body oils. *Hwy 1, Big Sur; 831/667-2345; $$; AE, MC, V; no checks;*

In 1944, Orson Welles bought a Big Sur log cabin that had belonged to the Trails Club for his wife, Rita Hayworth, as a romantic retreat. But they never lived there and sold it in 1947. It is now Nepenthe, the restaurant with a soaring view over the valley.

lunch, dinner every day; full bar; reservations required for parties of 5 or more; www.nepenthebigsur.com; 27 miles south of Carmel.

SIERRA MAR ★★★

 High on the ridge, the Sierra Mar Restaurant at Post Ranch Inn is a gorgeous, cliff-hugging restaurant that has been hailed as one of the best on the Central Coast. It serves a sophisticated brand of California cuisine in a serene expanse of wood, brushed metal, and glass that lets you drink in the incredible views along with the costly wine. When you can wrest your eyes from the ocean and focus on the four-course prix-fixe dinner menu, which changes daily, you might see such sumptuous starters as pine-smoked squab with ginger and cilantro; mussel soup with saffron and potatoes; and perhaps a salad of lettuces (organic, of course) mixed with shaved fennel, oranges, Parmesan, and a Campari vinaigrette. Main courses include such bounty as roast rack of venison with glazed chestnuts and huckleberries, truffled fettuccine with asparagus and English peas, and roasted guinea fowl with potato gnocchi and pearl onions. Finish off your feast with a plate of assorted house-made sweets—proof positive that politically correct need not mean diet deprived. *Hwy 1 at Big Sur; 831/667-2800; $$$; AE, MC, V; local checks only; lunch, dinner every day; full bar; reservations recommended; 30 miles south of Carmel.* &

The Big Sur International Marathon, held annually on the last Sunday in April, has been named the best marathon in North America; 831/625-6226; www.bsim.org.

LODGINGS

BIG SUR CAMPGROUND AND CABINS ★

If $650 for a room at the Post Ranch Inn is a bit out of your price range, see if you can score one of the 13 adorable little A-frame cabins here, which start at about $155. Roughing it you're not: each wood cabin comes with cozy country furnishings, wood-burning ovens, full kitchens, sleeping lofts, and even a patio. Several of the units sit along the Big Sur River, and each has a private bath and fireplace. In the summer, tent cabins are also available—with beds and bedding provided—for $50 per night, or you can bring your sleeping bag and rough it at the 81 year-round campsites set in a large redwood grove. Guests often while away the day swimming or fishing in the river (steelhead season runs November 16 to February 28, on weekends, Wednesdays, and holidays only). Amenities include a store, laundry, playground, basketball courts, and inner-tube rentals. *Hwy 1, Big Sur; 831/667-2322; $–$$; MC, V; no checks; about 3 miles south of Andrew Molera State Park.*

DEETJEN'S BIG SUR INN ★

Don't blink or you'll miss this charming cluster of ramshackle cabins as you head around the curve on Highway 1 just south of Ventana. During the '30s and '40s, travelers making the long journey up or down the coast used to drop in and stay the night with Grandpa Deetjen, a Norwegian immigrant. No doubt weary of houseguests, he constructed a cluster of redwood buildings nestled in Castro Canyon with 20 rooms to accommodate them. Grandpa's idea of comfort was a bit austere, but then again, he never expected to charge $75 to $195 per night. Located in a redwood canyon, most cabins are divided into two units, each with dark wood interiors, hand-hewn doors without locks or keys (they can be secured with the hook and eye from within, though), and nonexistent insulation. Some have shared baths, and many are cozy in a rustic sort of way, but they're definitely not for everyone. If you stay in one of the two-story units (some with fireplaces or wood-burning stoves), be sure to request the quieter upstairs rooms. The cabins near the river offer the most privacy. Grandpa's Room #13 has a bed built just under a large window overlooking the creek, and also has a pedal organ that belonged to the old gentleman. *Hwy 1, Big Sur; 831/667-2377; $$; MC, V; checks OK; on Hwy 1, 4 miles south of Pfeiffer–Big Sur State Park.*

POST RANCH INN ★★★★

 Discreetly hidden on a ridge in the Santa Lucia Mountains, architect Mickey Muennig's redwood complex was completed in April 1992. Muennig supposedly camped out on the property for five months before setting pencil to paper for his design, which had to conform to the strict Big Sur Coastal Land Use Plan. He propped up six of the inn's units (known as the Tree Houses) on stilts to avoid disturbing the surrounding redwoods' root systems and sank others into the earth, roofing them with sod. The inn's deceptively simple exteriors are meant to harmonize with the forested slopes, while windows, windows everywhere celebrate the breathtaking vista of sky and sea that is Big Sur's birthright. Inside, the lodgepole construction and wealth of warm woods lend a rough-hewn luxury to the rooms. Earth tones, blues, and greens predominate, extending the link between the buildings and their environment. "Environment," in fact, is a word you'll hear a lot around this place, which was named after William Post, one of the area's early settlers. The Post Ranch Inn is one of the new breed of eco-hotels, where the affluent can indulge in sumptuous luxury and still feel politically correct. The water is filtered; visitors are encouraged to sort their paper, glass, and

HACIENDA

Picnic under the trees or wander the rose gardens at the Hacienda Restaurant, Lounge and Guest Lodge, designed by architect Julia Morgan and built by William Randolph Hearst as a ranch house. Located on Fort Hunter Liggett off Highway 101 in Jolon, the charming mission-style inn has rooms from $28–$50 per night (831/386-2900 for reservations). Stop in to the restaurant for lunch or dinner, or enjoy live music and dancing in the lounge (831/386-2262). While in the area, explore the nearby Mission San Antonio (831/385-4478), built in 1771 and still active as a parish church.

plastic garbage; and the paper upon which guests' rather staggering bills are printed is recycled. Despite this ecologically correct attitude, the folks behind the Post Ranch Inn haven't forgotten about the niceties of life. The 30 rooms have spare—but by no means spartan—decor, including fireplaces, massage tables, king-size beds, and sideboards made of African hardwoods (nonendangered, naturally). Designer robes hang in the closets and whirlpool tubs for two adorn the well-equipped bathrooms. In the lobby and public areas, stereo systems fill the air with ethereal new age music. A continental breakfast and guided nature hikes are included in the room rates; the massages, facials, herbal wraps, and yoga classes are not. *Hwy 1, Big Sur; 831/667-2200 or 800/527-2200; $$$$; AE, MC, V; checks OK; 30 miles south of Carmel.* &

RIPPLEWOOD RESORT ★

With its 16 spartan cabins clustered along a rugged section of Highway 1, Ripplewood Resort is a wonderful place to go with a large group of friends or just the two of you. Nothing is provided except linens and firewood, so bring your own plates, utensils, glasses, cookware, napkins, and corkscrew. Try to book cabins 1 to 9, which are set far below the highway on the river, where you can hear the water burbling. The popular units can be booked six months in advance. The Ripplewood Cafe is comfortable and pretty and serves a good breakfast and lunch. The muffins, sticky buns, and pies are house-made, and the cinnamon French toast is a big favorite. For lunch try the marinated bean salad or the grilled Jack cheese sandwich slathered with green chile salsa; beer and wine are available. *Hwy 1, Big Sur; 831/667-2242; $$; MC, V; no checks; on Hwy 1, about 1 mile north of Pfeiffer–Big Sur State Park.*

VENTANA INN AND SPA ★★★★

🗺 Set on the brow of a chaparral-covered hill in the Santa Lucia Mountains, this modern, weathered cedar inn is serene and contemplative. Its spacious 59

"Please do not lean bicycles against the daisies," says the sign at the funky cluster of buildings that make up the charming Gorda Springs Resort by the Sea on Highway 1 just south of Big Sur. The collection includes cabins to rent (805/927-4600), a food and sundries market, an antique shop, and the engaging Whale Watchers Cafe.

rooms, decorated in an upscale country style and divided among 12 low-rise buildings, look out over the plunging forested hillsides, wildflower-laced meadows, and roiling waters of the Big Sur coast. Three houses are also available to rent; the rooms in the Sycamore and Madrone Houses have large private balconies and some of the best views of the ocean. Several rooms have fireplaces, hot tubs, and wet bars; rates climb in accordance with the amenities offered. A sumptuous breakfast is included. The inn's other big draw is Cielo Restaurant ("heaven" in Spanish), which delivers panoramic patio views of 50 miles of coastline at prices that can be equally breathtaking. Although critics have been unanimous in praising its aesthetics, a revolving-door parade of chefs has kept them uncertain about the quality of the food since Jeremiah Tower's star turn here years ago. The current chef, Jerry Regester, serves rustic, "New American" style dishes such as seared ahi tuna with asparagus, porcini mushroom, and leek sauce; lavender-grilled lamb chops; or oak-grilled Angus New York steak. *Hwy 1, Big Sur; 831/667-2331 or 800/628-6500; $$$–$$$$; AE, DC, DIS, MC, V; checks OK; 28 miles south of Carmel, 2 miles south of Pfeiffer–Big Sur State Park.* &

THE SAN SIMEON COAST

This section of the shore looks a little like Wyoming with a coastline. The dramatic open ranch scenery reveals more surprises the farther south you drive. There are cow-studded pastures, pristine beaches, windswept cliffs, and tree-shaded country roads. The area's diversity is part of its appeal: you can bask in sunshine at ocean's edge, bicycle through lush vineyards, ride horses along rural back roads, and shop a boulevard of chic boutiques—all in one day. Glorious vacation destinations are sprinkled throughout the sometimes funky beachfront towns. The coastline itself has a distinct personality: sunny white-sand beaches segue into rocky, cliff-lined shores, then give way to calm, picturesque bays. No matter how many visitors it gets, the San Simeon coastal region always retains something of the frontier flair of pioneer ranchers. Although the area is best known for Hearst Castle, other destinations are tucked into the inland mountains and valleys, where citrus orchards and vineyards beckon to the discerning traveler.

ACTIVITIES

Elephant Seals Close Up. Just south of the Piedras Blancas Lighthouse and about 12 miles north of Cambria is a rocky shoreline dotted with huge snoozing, mating, molting, or barking elephant seals, depending on when you visit. These enormous creatures—mature males grow a schnozz that looks like an elephant's trunk—can literally weigh a ton, and this is one of the best places in the state to see them close up. Whatever month you come, seals will be there, providing the opportunity to eavesdrop on their always intriguing and frequently noisy society. The most active time is mating season in December, when females who have just given birth to the pups conceived the previous year almost immediately conceive again. Mothers and pups hang out on shore for several months, then the moms split and the young ones are left to teach themselves how to swim. In the summer, other seals return for molting.

SAN SIMEON

Before you get to Hearst Castle, cross Highway 1 to the sheltering bay where W. R. Hearst's father in the 1880s built a wharf, pier, and mission-style warehouses for the operation of what was then a massive cattle ranch. His son would later use the port to bring in the voluminous building materials and furnishings for the castle, including crates of exotic animals for his private zoo (the zebras you see grazing with cattle alongside the highway are remnants of that short-lived endeavor).

ACTIVITIES

Sebastian's General Store. This former general store, now a historic landmark, has recently undergone a change. The store opened at the point in San Simeon in 1852 and was moved to this location in the 1870s. It sold rope, soap, grocery staples, and lace among many other items, serving the former whaling industry and the thriving general shipping port that supplied the 1880s cattle ranch operation owned by W. R. Hearst's father. Recently Neil Hansen, great-grandson of the man who founded it, lovingly restored the historic building with plans to reopen it as a coffee bar and gift shop with a whaling theme. Tucked into the same cluster of buildings is the tiny San Simeon post office, so you can mail your Hearst Castle postcards when you drop in for a latte. (442 San Luis Obispo–San Simeon Rd)

San Simeon State Park. This long sandy stretch of beach runs for 2 miles from San Simeon Creek to Santa Rosa Creek. You can walk alongside streams and watch birds or hike the trail closer to the shore. The park is intersected by Highway 1, which separates the beach and the camping areas. Of the two campgrounds, San Simeon Creek Campground has the most amenities; it's on a grassy area near the beach, with toilets and showers. Washburn Campground is on a hilltop 1½ miles from the beach; it has no shade and no showers. One of the best parts of the park is Moonstone Beach, where you can pick up white, translucent moonstone agates. For campsite reservations (required Apr 15–Sept 1) call 800/444-7275 or visit www.reserveamerica.com; other times of year the campsites are on a first come first served basis.

"*I've read about everything I could find on William Randolph Hearst, and the best book I've ever read about him is titled* The Chief: The Life of William Randolph Hearst, *written by David Nasaw.*" —Dave Babcock, Hearst Castle guide

W. R. Hearst Memorial State Beach. This small 2-acre park, on a hill overlooking a half-moon-shaped beach protected by a cove, is just across the highway from Hearst Castle. The beach has the best swimming in the area, along with picnic tables, a fishing pier, and rest rooms.

Kayaking and Sportfishing at San Simeon. Paddle out and see the sea otters snoozing in kelp under the shade of San Simeon's cliffs. From May to October you can rent a kayak by the hour, half day, or full day with the California Kayaks Co., located at Virg's Landing at W. R. Hearst Memorial State Beach, across the road from Hearst Castle. Guided tours are also available, and they rent boogie boards and wet suits too. Call for reservations at 805/927-1744, or visit www.californiakayaks.com. All-day fishing trips for rock cod leave daily from Virg's Landing at 6:30am (805/927-4676).

Hiking the San Simeon Trail to Whitaker Ranch. The Bluff Trail (easy; 2 miles round trip) is the best way to get out to San Simeon Point. Access to the trail is directly across from the entrance to Hearst Castle; park outside the state beach and walk west through the picnic area to the beach. The trail affords good views of the coastline to the south and San Simeon Bay, the fishing pier, and even Hearst Castle. Other bluff access points lie along Highway 1, including a gate at 2.1 miles north of the entrance to Hearst State Beach and a viewing spot at 3.3 miles. Check the tidal situation; low tides offer better beach access.

Hearst Castle. If you have time to see only one museum or monument on your trip on the Central Coast, make it Hearst Castle, named this country's best monument by readers of *Conde Nast Traveler* magazine. The lavish palace that publishing magnate William Randolph Hearst never called a castle, but always referred to as "the ranch" or "the Enchanted Hill," sits high above the coastline, and at a distance it does look like a fairy-tale castle. It's opulently and almost haphazardly furnished with museum-quality treasures purchased by Hearst, a man of indiscriminate taste and inexhaustible funds who spent years traveling to Europe, buying up complete interiors and art from ancestral collections. Touring the house you'll see carved ceilings from Italian monasteries, fragments of Roman temples, lavish doors from royal castles, and a breathtaking collection of Greek pottery carelessly displayed among equally priceless volumes in the library. The estate boasts two swimming pools—one indoor, one outdoor—whose grandiose opulence must be seen to be believed. Besides viewing the palatial grounds and interiors, visitors learn about Hearst's Hollywood connection and the countless celebrities who were weekend guests. Now operated as a State Historic Monument by the Department of Parks and Recreation, the landmark Hearst Castle can be seen only by guided tour; four separate itineraries (plus a night tour— see sidebar) cover different areas of the estate. First-timers should take the Experience Tour, which includes the National Geographic movie titled *Hearst Castle Building the Dream,* combined with Tour Number 1, which includes the Neptune pool, the indoor Roman pool, rooms in the Casa Del Sol guest house, and five expansive rooms in the Casa Grande (main castle). You'll see a large sitting room where Hearst's famous Hollywood guests gathered before dinner, the refectory or dining room, and the

In spring and fall Hearst Castle offers a special treat. The Evening Tour is a chance to feel the thrill of being a guest at one of Mr. Hearst's 1930s parties. Living History docents in costume wander throughout the property, play poker, and gather for cocktails in the Assembly room, and a movie star may sit playing the grand piano as a butler carries a tray of drinks. The tour is a little over two hours, and reservations are a must; 800/444-4445.

morning room, stocked with Spanish antiques and Flemish tapestries. If you love art, architectural form, and libraries, take Tour Number 2; if the years-long construction and development of the whole mountaintop project fascinate you, take Tour Number 3. Gardeners will want to take Tour Number 4, which includes the botanical gardens, a hidden terrace, and the Casa del Mar, the most elaborate guest house, where Hearst lived in his final years. Many visitors take two or even three tours a day, but be aware that all tours involve climbing many steps (it is on a hill, after all) and can be tiring. Call or go to the web site (see below) for information on tours for those with limited mobility. It's sometimes possible to buy tour tickets after you arrive at Hearst Castle, but it is smart to make reservations in advance if possible, particularly if you are coming in the busy summer period. There is plenty of free parking; nearby at the visitor center you board tour buses that take you the 5 miles up to the castle, where your tour guide awaits. Consult the web site (www.hearstcastle.com) or contact Hearst Castle (750 Hearst Castle Rd; 800/444-4445) for information on tour schedules and advance ticket purchases (day tours $10–$14 adults, $5–$7 kids; evening tours $20 adults, $10 kids).

RESTAURANTS

RAGGED POINT INN ★★

This is a great place to get out of the car and walk the short cliff trail that looks down on the frothing surf, get a cup of coffee at the outdoor Espresso Bar, or have a meal at the Ragged Point restaurant. The whole complex, including the nearby motel resort, offers a million-dollar view and a dramatic cliff-top location. The dining room is classic California redwood architecture with plenty of view-enhancing windows, and there's a partially enclosed patio for alfresco dining when the weather allows. The menu is California cuisine, with hearty American favorites and gourmet European touches. The signature dish is garden-fresh rosemary pasta in a cream sauce with sun-dried tomatoes, onions, and cayenne pepper, which you can order topped with shrimp, sea scallops, or chicken, or vegetarian style. At lunchtime there's a variety of gourmet sandwiches. You'll want to be here during daylight to enjoy the scenery, so plan on lunch or a reasonably early dinner (the dining room serves lunch until 4pm, with dinner starting at 5pm). Ragged Point also serves up a hearty and satisfying breakfast, when the menu offers yummy Belgian waffles with apple cinnamon sausage. *19019 Hwy 1, Ragged Point; 805/927-5708; $$; AE, DIS, MC, V; local checks only; breakfast, lunch, dinner every day; beer and wine; reservations recommended; www.raggedpointinn.net; 15 miles north of Hearst Castle.* &

LODGINGS

BEST WESTERN CAVALIER OCEANFRONT RESORT ★

This is by far the nicest of the good-value hotels and motels on Highway 1 just south of Hearst Castle, and it's the only oceanfront property. The landscaping is a bit bare but the views are grand. Composed of a handful of buildings sprawled across a gentle slope, the hotel offers a wide range of accommodations. Each room has warm robes and—surprise—a pair of binoculars lying on the bed, great for watching sea otters and shorebirds. Every room—whether you choose a basic double or opt for extras such as a fireplace, ocean view, wet bar, or oceanfront terrace—features a stocked minibar, hair dryer, computer jack, and cable TV with VCR (rentals are next door). Two outdoor pools are shielded from the wind—but not from the exceptional view, thanks to glass walls—and guests are invited to huddle around cliff-side bonfires each evening. There is an in-house restaurant offering such dishes as veal scaloppine with roasted garlic–tomato fettuccine and baked trout with almonds, scallions, and orange zest. Guests will keep discovering extras, including an exercise room, coin laundry, and telescopes set up for whale or porpoise watching. Though travelers focusing on Hearst Castle are probably the only ones who'll choose to stay along this motel-heavy stretch, the Cavalier is top-notch in its class. *9415 Hearst Dr,*

"This San Simeon Cove is our secret. I love to walk with my dog here along the East-West Ranch Trail on cliffs overlooking this coast. Another place I really like is the Cayucos drugstore, where they have a real old-fashioned soda fountain."
—Harry Fowler, former radio host and 15-year resident of Cambria

Get information on visiting the Hearst Castle area and referrals to lodging through the San Simeon Chamber of Commerce (250 San Simeon Avenue #3A, 805/927-3500).

San Simeon; 805/927-4688 or 800/826-8168; $$; AE, DC, DIS, MC, V; checks OK; on Hwy 1, 3 miles south of Hearst Castle. ♿

CALIFORNIA SEACOAST LODGE ★

Canopy beds, Dresden blue fabrics, wing chairs with matching lampshades—hardly what you'd expect tucked among the nearby motels. This cozy Country French inn in a motel configuration is also close to Hearst Castle, and although the rooms have no ocean view, you can walk to the beach, and there is a small pool just off the lobby. You'll never awaken thinking you're in an impersonal chain hotel here: some rooms have fireplaces or whirlpool tubs to add a romantic mood, and a complimentary continental breakfast is served each morning in the sunny parlor. For shopping or dining, Cambria is only a 10-minute drive away. Between September and May, off-season rates offer substantial bargains. *9215 Hearst Dr, San Simeon; 805/927-3878 or 800/451-9900; $$; AE, DIS, MC, V; no checks; on Hwy 1, 3 miles south of Hearst Castle.* ♿

RAGGED POINT INN & RESORT ★

Perched on a grassy cliff high above the ocean, this modern woodsy complex offers views as spectacular as any farther north in pricey Big Sur. Part of an upscale rest stop complex that includes a gas station, mini-mart, gift shop, snack bar, and the Ragged Point Inn restaurant (see review, above), the motel itself has been upgraded. Each of the spacious 22 rooms features an oceanfront balcony or patio, along with separate heating controls for getting cozy on blustery nights. The furnishings are both contemporary and comfortable, and the motel is set back a ways from the other roadside facilities, so you can count on silence and seclusion. Foxes and raccoons are often spotted scurrying around the grounds. Take the walking trail out to the bluff, where you can look down on the ocean and sometimes see sea otters bobbing among the kelp. San Simeon and Cambria are a 25-minute drive south, but the restaurant is good enough to eat all your meals here if you want. Ask for an upstairs room to get the best view and the most privacy; the first-floor rooms, however, are a good value and also have views other hotels would brag about. *19019 Hwy 1, Ragged Point; 805/927-4502; $$; AE, DIS, MC, V; checks OK; 15 miles north of Hearst Castle.* ♿

CAMBRIA

Cambria is almost terminally cute. What saves it is genuine small-town friendliness, several fine restaurants, and shops offering goods of very high quality, including art, crafts, household items, boutique clothing, and fine gifts. The town's bread and butter are visitors to Hearst Castle, but it would stack up well against any romantic escape destination in California. Both chic and countrified, this sophisticated little village combines the best elements of both Northern and Southern California. The town's name reportedly compares the natural beauty of the area to the lush, rolling countryside of Wales, whose ancient name was Cambria. The town has two sections: the East Village and the West Village, both full of restored Victorians, art galleries, antique stores, boutiques, and exceptional restaurants, nestled among pine-blanketed hills. Across the highway, however, Moonstone Beach (named for the translucent milky stones that wash ashore) is lined with inns of wildly varying designs, from Tudor to modern, offering an opportunity to sleep alongside the breaking surf and stroll windswept beaches populated by seals and sea lions. For an introduction to the area, stop by the Cambria Chamber of Commerce (767 Main St; 805/927-3624; www.cambriachamber.org).

ACTIVITIES

Shopping. Cambria, with its rich jumble of shops full of high-quality art and antiques, is a stroller's paradise—a bit funky here, coolly sophisticated there, with many pocket gardens and window boxes bursting with flowers. This close-knit community has always attracted artists, and the term "museum quality" is frequently bandied about. The finest handcrafted studio glass, from vases to presentation bowls to affordable jewelry to investment-scale sculpture, can be found at the Seekers Collection & Gallery (4090 Burton Dr; 805/927-4352; www.seekers glass.com). It has the largest collection of art glass on the West Coast, displaying pieces handmade by more than 250 artists. Nearby, at Moonstones Gallery (4070 Burton Dr; 805/927-3447; www.moonstones.com), you'll find a selection of works ranging from woven crafts to jewelry (with and without moonstones), indoor fountains, and an exceptional selection of wood carvings and other crafts. The Otter Trading Co. (4044 Burton Dr; 805/927-3130) has resort wear, shells, and a marvelous selection of glass-bead jewelry at low prices. Oliver's Twist (4039 Burton Dr; 805/927-8196) has glass vases, large sculptures, and antique Japanese and Chinese chests and boxes. Visiting Heart's Ease (4104 Burton Dr; 805/927-5224; www.hearts-ease.com) is like exploring a rambling garden shed full of seeds, birdhouses, antiquarian books, and loose scented herbs to buy by the scoop, such as sandalwood, citrus, and cambria rose. They also have teas such as lavender green tea and things to steep yourself in too, such as aromatic eucalyptus bath salts.

Find the Farm. About 10 minutes east of Cambria, on a rambling country road, sits Linn's Fruit Binn (on Santa Rosa Creek Rd; 805/927-8134), a family farm known statewide for freshly baked pies and other goodies. The Linns' cash crop is the olallieberry, a tart blackberry hybrid used in pies, preserves, salsas, teas, mustards, candies, and anything else they dream up. The most popular pies are apple-olallieberry and rhubarb; pies can be sold frozen for easy transport home. Their goods are also available in town at Linn's Main Binn restaurant (2277 Main St; 805/927-0371; see review in Restaurants, below).

San Simeon Trail. This moderate, 3.3-mile loop offers quite a contrast to the beach routes, and is a don't-miss hike when you visit Castle country. The trek includes a wooden boardwalk that is wheelchair accessible for about half a mile from the parking lot. After leaving the wooden boardwalk, go right through the gate to hike the trail. It starts in seasonal wetlands, crosses a marsh, moves through Monterey pine forest, a fern gully, coastal scrub, and grassland, and ends in a riparian woodland that once was part of an old Western ranch owned by the Whitaker family. The trail winds around the Washburn Campground after a moderately steep elevation change of 200 feet to Poopout Hill. There, the views include a lush meadow to the east and rolling hills and the Pacific Ocean to the west. The trail then descends to Whitaker Flats, where there have been sightings of mountain lions in recent years. Watch for the trail markers, as it's easy to make the wrong turn, but just remember it's all downhill after the Washburn Campground. The Whitaker family lived here for nearly a century, and interpretive panels, although very sun-bleached, tell the family's rich history. Be careful of the poison oak. The trail begins at the Washburn day-use area parking lot on the east side of Highway 1, half a mile south of the entrance to the San Simeon Creek State Campground.

Hiking the Coastal Trail. The Coastal Trail, including the Moonstone Beach Trail (easy; 4½ miles round trip), spans the coastline from San Simeon Creek south to Santa Rosa Creek. There are several access points to the beach along the route, some with old wooden stairs (be careful, some are in poor condition). At low tide you can walk the beach and look at the massive collections of driftwood and other goodies that wash up on the shore here. On the trail above the beach, you'll pass along "motel row" on the east side of Moonstone Beach. The place can be as busy as an anthill at certain times of year, especially summer, but it can be very quiet and serene during off-peak times, and when it's cooler and foggy, which is

In the summer the Pewter Plough Playhouse (824 Main St; 805/927-3877) offers excellent stage plays on weekends for a modest price (approximately $15–$20), gives free dramatic readings one Thursday evening a month, and has jazz performances Thursday through Saturday evenings.

a lot. At 1 mile north, you'll hit the old highway bridge spanning Leffingwell Creek. There's a picnic area and rest room stop above the creek at Leffingwell Landing, the old site of a pier used in the 19th century. There's also a tide pool area, and benches overlook the shoreline. At low tide, hikers can extend the hike on the sand spit created by San Simeon Creek. Twice monthly, tides fall below normal levels here, and those are the best times to comb the beach for unique rocks and driftwood, a regular pastime. Start the hike at Santa Rosa State Beach parking area, 2¼ miles south of San Simeon Creek Campground off Highway 1.

For an introduction to the area, visit the Cambria Chamber of Commerce (767 Main St; 805/927-3624; www.cambria chamber.org).

Hiking the East-West Ranch Trail. This easy, 2-mile round-trip trail in Cambria is a favorite with locals and regular visitors. It's on private land, but for now it's open space and a real treat to hike. A more secluded coastline hike than the Coastal Trail, it has none of the commercialism of the Moonstone Beach Trail. Birds soar on the air current above the cliffs and there are some unique benches constructed of driftwood and huge stones, rope and wood bridges, and charming lean-tos built by students and local artists who helped the Land Conservancy shore up the area. This is a pleasant walk, and you can easily fall into conversation with locals out for a healthy stroll or being pulled along by their pooches. To reach the trail, take the Windsor Street turnoff from Highway 1 across from the Cambria West Village exit. Follow Windsor Street past Shamel Park (a picnic area with tables and barbecues, rest room, and outdoor shower and beach access) to where it enters what appears to be a private development. Drive in and keep going a few hundred yards until the road dead-ends against a raised bank. The trailhead is clearly marked. The East-West Trail connects to Windsor Street on the other side; it's a turnaround hike rather than a loop.

RESTAURANTS

THE BRAMBLES DINNER HOUSE ★

The 126-year-old former home's red wooden exterior with white shutters and a white picket fence out front give the impression that you might be dropping in on someone's farmhouse for dinner, and the small rooms inside with low ceilings and china on the walls reinforce that feeling. It's a family kind of place. The specialty is prime rib, but there are French, Italian, American, and Greek offerings on the menu, the last thanks to the Greek influence of owner Nick Kaperonis. Dolmas (stuffed grape leaves) and saganaki (fried cheese) share billing with fresh salmon, oysters Rockefeller, chicken cordon bleu, and rack of lamb. Since the dining room's romantic retro atmosphere alone isn't enough to compete

*What's an olal-
lieberry? It's a
crossbred fruit
that is two-thirds
blackberry and
one-third red Euro-
pean raspberry.*

with the culinary excellence elsewhere in town, Brambles stays on top with the freshest fish and beef, expert preparation, and fair prices; they've also augmented the menu with some lighter Mediterranean fare such as eggplant fettuccine with tofu. End with one of the tempting chocolatey desserts. The early bird dinners are a great value (every day 4–6pm, Sat 4–5:30pm) but you may find yourself competing for a table with busloads of tourists. *4005 Burton Dr, Cambria; 805/927-4716; $$; AE, DIS, MC, V; local checks only; dinner every day, brunch Sun; full bar; reservations recommended; www.bramblesdinnerhouse.com; 2 blocks south of Main St.* &

LINN'S MAIN BINN ★

This is just the kind of place you want to find on a family trip: unassuming, welcoming, and offering a specialty worth traveling to find. The steaming chicken potpies and the Yankee pot roast are delicious. Other winners are homemade daily soups, hearty sandwiches, and fresh-from-the-farm salads; at breakfast, sweet treats like berry-covered waffles and pancakes prevail. But don't miss the legendary berry pies, especially the olallieberry. The olallieberry bread pudding is also transcendent. The in-town outlet for the popular Linn's Fruit Binn, this casual all-day restaurant also carries straw hats, decorative housewares, gifts, and a selection of Linn's food products such as fancy fruit butters and berries in port wine. Every town should have a spot like this, where a reliably good meal doesn't have to be an event and where you'll feel equally welcome stopping in for just a slice of warm pie and a glass of ice-cold milk. *2277 Main St, Cambria; 805/927-0371; $; AE, DIS, MC, V; checks OK; breakfast, lunch, dinner every day; beer and wine; no reservations; 1 block east of Burton Dr.* &

OLD STONE STATION ★

The Old Stone Station is a rambling stone-and-wood restaurant that looks as if it has been on the main street of town forever, and part of it was—as the old Marathon gas station with the flying horse sign out front. A couple of years ago chef Carl Vanicky and his dad, Ray Done, decided to use the former structure's old river stones and wood and rebuild the place as a restaurant. Inside, the rooms are warm with knotty pine walls and open beams, and the father-son duo even handmade the redwood and pine tables. Steak and seafood are the specialties at dinner, when the menu offers steamers, barbecued oysters, and crispy prawns, plus grilled filet mignon wrapped in bacon and an 8-ounce grilled top sirloin served with barbecue sauce or teriyaki style. At lunch the favorite is Chinese chicken salad made with authentic Asian ingredients and a secret killer dressing. Outside, the seafaring rope and wood benches hanging on the wall seem to defy gravity, and the plaque declaring "On this site in 1897 Nothing Happened" tends to lure you inside, since the place clearly has a personality. *713 Main St, Cambria; 805/927-4229; $$; MC, V; checks OK; breakfast Sun, lunch, dinner every day; beer and wine; reservations recommended for dinner; in the West Village on Main St at Cornwall St.* &

ROBIN'S ★★

"Cooking from around the world" is the slogan at this adventuresome and eclectic cafe that's been a local favorite for many years. Step up on the porch of the stucco bungalow with its red tile roof and you feel immediately welcome. Located in Cambria's East Village, Robin Covey's charming eatery has a cozy, casual, almost hippie ambience, and a menu that runs the gamut from exotic Mexican-, Thai-, or Indian-tinged recipes to simple vegetarian salads, pastas, and sandwiches. Recent offerings included a Thai eggplant dish and a Caribbean seafood stew. Other great choices are tandoori prawns; roghan josh, a North Indian lamb dish in a richly spiced nutty yogurt sauce accompanied by sweet-tangy chutneys; and Singapore chicken satay. Much of the menu is somewhat health oriented, giving many diners the justification to indulge in one of Robin's to-die-for desserts like lemon cheesecake or vanilla custard bread pudding with apricots and golden raisins in Grand Marnier sauce. You can eat inside or on the sunny patio, or order any item to go for a picnic in the nearby hills. *4095 Burton Dr, Cambria; 805/927-5007; $$; MC, V; local checks only; lunch, dinner every day; beer and wine; reservations recommended; www.robinsrestaurant.com; 1 block south of Main St.* &

SEA CHEST OYSTER BAR & SEAFOOD RESTAURANT ★

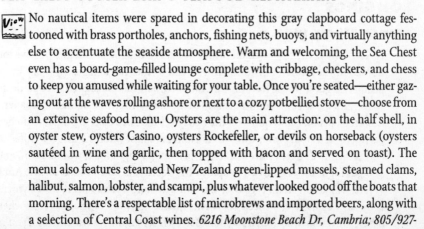 No nautical items were spared in decorating this gray clapboard cottage festooned with brass portholes, anchors, fishing nets, buoys, and virtually anything else to accentuate the seaside atmosphere. Warm and welcoming, the Sea Chest even has a board-game-filled lounge complete with cribbage, checkers, and chess to keep you amused while waiting for your table. Once you're seated—either gazing out at the waves rolling ashore or next to a cozy potbellied stove—choose from an extensive seafood menu. Oysters are the main attraction: on the half shell, in oyster stew, oysters Casino, oysters Rockefeller, or devils on horseback (oysters sautéed in wine and garlic, then topped with bacon and served on toast). The menu also features steamed New Zealand green-lipped mussels, steamed clams, halibut, salmon, lobster, and scampi, plus whatever looked good off the boats that morning. There's a respectable list of microbrews and imported beers, along with a selection of Central Coast wines. *6216 Moonstone Beach Dr, Cambria; 805/927-*

4514; $$; no credit cards; checks OK; dinner every day during summer, after Labor Day closed Tues; beer and wine; no reservations; west of Hwy 1 at Windsor Blvd. &

THE SOW'S EAR CAFE ★★★★

Gourmets in the know head for this humble-sounding place, considered the very best in town. One of Cambria's tiny old cottages, now sandwiched in a row of shops, has been transformed into a warm, romantic hideaway right on Main Street, where the best tables are in the fireside front room, lit just enough to highlight its rustic wood-and-brick decor. Pigs appear in oil paintings, small ceramic or cast-iron models adorning the shelves, and the restaurant's Americana woodcut sow logo. A new owner has been savvy enough not to change much and disturb the magic, and chef Richard Carpenter still rules in the kitchen. You'll find contemporary California cuisine, but the number-one dish is the chicken-fried steak with Grandma-style gravy plus chicken and dumplings. Other standouts are salmon prepared in parchment, local swordfish with lemon-sesame glaze, and grilled pork loin glazed with chunky olallieberry chutney. Although dinners come complete with soup or salad, do share one of the outstanding appetizers—the calamari is melt-in-your-mouth, and marinated goat cheese perfectly accompanies the restaurant's signature marbled bread baked in terra-cotta flowerpots. The wine list is among the area's best, featuring outstanding Central Coast vintages, with a large number available by the glass. If you have only one nice dinner in town, make this the place. *2248 Main St, Cambria; 805/927-4865; $$; DIS, MC, V; no checks; dinner every day; beer and wine; reservations recommended; www. thesowsear.com; ½ block east of Burton Dr.* &

LODGINGS

BRIDGE STREET INN ★

Next to a little white church on Bridge Street is a delightful and inexpensive inn housed in the church's historic 110-year-old former parsonage. The cozy European-style guest house has three private bedrooms and a shared six-bed dorm space, and the decor is country charm to the max, with white figured wallpapers, flowered curtains, and quilts on the beds over blue bed skirts. A shared kitchen permits you to make your own dinner, and breakfast (muffins, bagels, coffee or tea) is included. Rates start at $20 per person per night for the bunk room and $40 per night for one or two people in the bedrooms. The cordial owner, Anne Wyatt, will take a credit card over the phone to hold a reservation, but payment is by cash or traveler's check only. This quaint inn sometimes has room when others are booked, so even if you don't have a reservation, it's worth a try if you're in town and need a room for the night. It wins our vote for best lodging value on the Central Coast. *4314 Bridge St, Cambria; 805/927-7653; $; no credit cards; no checks; bridgestreetinn@yahoo.com; www.bridgestreetinncambria.com; on Bridge St at Main St in Cambria's East Village.*

CAMBRIA PINES LODGE ★★

As you drive up the steep hill from town, the road curving into a thick woods dense with Monterey pines, it's hard to believe an important lodging could be so far away from the action below. But that's part of the charm of Cambria Pines Lodge. Equal parts vacation lodge and summer camp, the lodge is composed of 31 different buildings, from simple, old-fashioned cabins to larger rooms in two-level buildings (pack light if you stay in these units, since no rooms are on exact ground level and you'll have to drag your luggage up or down stairs). At the heart of the resort is the main lodge, built in the early 1990s around the great stone hearth of the original 1927 building (destroyed by fire). It all has a welcoming, communal feel. Nearly all the rooms have fireplaces; contemporary furniture, coffeemakers, and cable TV. The only swimming pool on the village side of town is on these grounds—an indoor Junior Olympic–size pool heated for year-round use, plus a sauna and whirlpool. The massage facility in a nearby building is run by a separate business. Inside the main lodge, there's a moderately priced restaurant and large fireside lounge with occasional live music. When you check in be sure to get a coupon for the continental breakfast buffet, included in the rate. Ask about their wine tour in their own van. *2905 Burton Dr, Cambria; 805/927-4200 or 800/445-6868; $–$$; AE, DIS, MC, V; checks OK; www.cambriapineslodge.com; take Burton Dr uphill from the center of town.* &

FOGCATCHER INN ★

The FogCatcher's faux English style—featuring thatched-look roofing, flower-lined brick paths, and rough-hewn stone exteriors—fits right into the architectural jumble along inn-studded Moonstone Beach, even though this is one of the newer properties here. Its 60 rooms are contained in a U-shaped group of buildings arranged like a village; many have unencumbered views of the crashing surf across the street, while some gaze oceanward over a sea of parked cars, and others are hopelessly landlocked. Rates vary wildly according to the quality of view, but all rooms have identical amenities. Inside you'll find a surprising attention to comfort, especially considering the FogCatcher's prices, which can drop dramatically midweek and off-season. The recently redecorated rooms with new wallpapers, carpets, drapes, beds, and TVs are immaculately maintained. The style is comfy-cottage, including oversize pine furniture, wicker desks, and four-poster beds with overhead lace ruffles and feather duvets. Each room is made cozier by a gas fireplace and also boasts a microwave oven, coffeemaker, stocked refrigerator (on the honor system), and a hair dryer and iron. The rate includes a 15-item expanded continental breakfast. Unlike many comparably priced Moonstone Beach lodgings, the FogCatcher also has a heated swimming pool and whirlpool. *6400 Moonstone Beach Dr, Cambria; 805/927-1400 or 800/425-4121; $$–$$$; AE, DIS, MC, V; checks OK; www.fogcatcherinn.com; west of Hwy 1 at Windsor St.* &

J. PATRICK HOUSE ★★

The J. Patrick House is not far from the Cambria Pines Inn, in a pine-filled residential neighborhood overlooking Cambria's East Village. It was recently bought by innkeepers John and Ann O'Connor, who have changed its focus and decor from country coziness to country elegance, with cherry woods, crystal lamps, and other touches. The result is refined and welcoming. The main house is an authentic two-story log cabin, where each afternoon John and Ann host wine and hors d'oeuvres next to the living room fireplace, and where each morning they serve breakfast by windows overlooking a garden filled with hummingbirds, Chinese magnolias, fuchsias, white and pink Japanese anemones, flowering Jerusalem sage, primrose, and bromeliads. All rooms have been recently recarpeted, and the O'Connors plan to freshen things every two years. The eight guest rooms, most of which are in the adjacent carriage house, are named for Irish counties. Each features a private bath, wood-burning fireplace, feather duvets, and bedtime milk and cookies. The room named Clare, the only one in the main log house, offers privacy, with lace-covered windows looking out on the forest and gardens. A large wood-burning fireplace is located at the foot of a king-size bed with a beautiful brass and white iron headboard. There is a fireplace in the living room as well, and a full private bath. The Galway, in the carriage house, has a beautifully crafted 1840s solid maple queen rope bed, a wood-burning fireplace, a full bath, and a window seat framed by a lavish pink climbing rose. John creates the gourmet breakfasts, which might include homemade granola, fat-free yogurt, muffins, and a featured item such as a soufflé or banana-stuffed French toast, from his extensive repertoire. In fact, he takes special care that no guest has to have the same breakfast twice during their stay. *2990 Burton Dr, Cambria; 805/927-3812 or 800/341-5258; $$; DIS, MC, V; checks OK; jph@jpatrickhouse. com; www.jpatrickhouse.com; take Burton Dr uphill from the center of town.*

OLALLIEBERRY INN ★★

A beautiful 1873 Greek Revival house sits like a prim dowager on Main Street at the edge of the East Village in Cambria, within strolling distance of the best shops and restaurants, but in a calmer zone a bit away from the bustle. In the front yard, a 118-year-old coast redwood tree planted when the house was built shades the inn and its secret gardens. New owners/innkeepers Marjorie Ott and Marilyn and Larry Draper plan to extend the olallieberry theme with artisan-made stained-glass windows featuring the luscious dark fruit. A complete breakfast is included, such as Alaskan sourdough pancakes with hash-brown eggs. In the afternoon, wine from the local Paso Robles winery Arciero is served with crackers, the inn's famous curry pâté, and a popular olive spread. A warm artichoke dip baked in a sourdough bread ball is also served, plus fresh vegetables with dip and tropical salsas. Cookies or cakes are put out earlier in the afternoon. Like the home's parlor and breakfast room, guest quarters are teeming with antiques, floral wallpaper, and Victorian lace. Six rooms are in the main house; though all have private baths, three of the baths are across the hall rather than en suite. The nicely renovated carriage house has two spacious rooms overlooking a creek; another has a view of trees and hills. The Creekside suite has a hide-a-bed and can accommodate up to four people. Six rooms have fireplaces. The most charming room is Room at the Top, a sunny nook where you can relax fireside in a white wicker chaise or soak in the antique claw-footed tub. Ask about off-season packages with local restaurants. *2476 Main St, Cambria; 805/927-3222 or 888/927-3222; $$; AE, MC, V; checks OK in advance, clearing 7 days prior to arrival; olallieinn@olallieberry.com; www.olallieberry.com; from Hwy 1, turn east on Main St.*

HARMONY

This town seems to be all of one short block long. Along Highway 1 just a few minutes south of Cambria, the sign says "Harmony, California, Population 18," and the hamlet indeed seems not much larger than a postage stamp. Highway 1 used to pass right through the center of town along what's now known as Old Creamery Road, named for the once-vital dairy operation that provided milk, cream, and butter throughout the county; William Randolph Hearst even used to stop in to stock the weekend larder on his way up to San Simeon. The old creamery building now houses a few gift shops and a U.S. postal station. Far from languishing as a 19th-century ghost town, Harmony has an enduring appeal among folks from all over. There is a glass artist, a potter, and other shops for gifts, and you can buy a souvenir Harmony snowdome. Feeling romantic? You can even get married in the town's tiny wedding chapel.

ACTIVITIES

Shopping for Arts and Crafts. Like its neighbor Cambria, Harmony also has an arts and crafts movement, and most visitors stop off here to shop at one of three serious galleries, all on the same street. Inside the barnlike Phoenix Studios (10 Main St; 805/927-4248) you can watch the resident glassblowers create superbly designed vases, lamps, and bowls. Their organic patterns are smooth, iridescent colors have a sophisticated art nouveau style. Next door is Backroads (2180 Old Creamery Rd; 805/927-2919), a gallery displaying mainly small items like jewelry, glassware, and handmade paper goods by regional artists. Across the street, the cavernous Harmony Pottery Studio/Gallery (Old Creamery Rd; 805/927-4293) displays ceramic artwork ranging from inexpensive painted coffee mugs to elegant glazed platters and vases and everything in between.

Wine Tasting. While in Harmony, drive up the hill from the tiny hamlet to Harmony Cellars (3255 Harmony Valley Rd, 805/927-1625), a family-owned winery offering premium wines at affordable prices. Their Chardonnay has won a gold at the California State Fair—in fact, every one of their wines has won an award of some kind.

PASO ROBLES

Early on, Paso Robles was known for its hot mineral springs. The mission padres often brought their sick here to be healed by bathing in the thermal waters. More recently, the tawny rolling hills around Paso Robles (Spanish for "pass of oak trees") were dotted with cattle and framed with orderly almond orchards. But today every hill is stitched with grapevines, and wineries with tasting rooms appear almost around every curve. Part of the up-and-coming Central Coast wine country, Paso Robles currently boasts almost 40 wineries (see the wineries sidebar in this chapter). The town is also proud of its faintly checkered past: it was established in 1870 by Drury James, uncle of outlaw Jesse James (who reportedly hid out in these parts). In 1913, pianist Ignace Jan Paderewski came to live in Paso Robles, where he planted zinfandel vines on his ranch and often tickled the ivories in the Paso Robles Inn.

ACTIVITIES

A Historic Ramble through Town. Paso Robles is blessed with a well-preserved turn-of-the-century sleepy downtown that could have leapt from the script of *The Music Man.* At the center of town is City Park (Spring and 12th Sts), a green gathering place—complete with festival bandstand—anchored by the 1907 Carnegie Historical Library (805/238-4996), a Classical Revival brick masterpiece that today houses an exhibit of area maps, early photographs, and historical documents. Several downtown side streets are lined with splendid historic Victorian, Craftsman, and Queen Anne homes, all shaded by grand trees. Drive along Vine Street between 10th and 19th Streets for a superb peek into the past, including the Call-Booth House (1315 Vine St; 805/238-5473), a carefully restored Victorian on the National Register of Historic Places, which is now an art gallery featuring local painters and artisans.

TOURING PASO ROBLES WINERIES

Wine touring in Paso Robles is reminiscent of another, unhurried time; here it's all about enjoying a relaxed rural atmosphere and driving leisurely along country roads from winery to winery. Three major wine events are held here every year: the Zinfandel Festival in March, the Wine Festival in May, and the Harvest Wine Affair in October. For a wine touring brochure and information on events and area wineries, contact the Paso Robles Vintners & Growers (800/549-WINE; www.pasowine.com). Meanwhile, any time of year is fine for dropping by the following wineries.

Eberle Winery: *Winemaker Gary Eberle is sometimes called the "grandfather of Paso Robles's wine country" by the local vintners who honed their craft under his tutelage. A visit to Eberle includes a look at its underground caves, where hundreds of aging barrels share space with the Wild Boar Room, site of Eberle's monthly winemaker dinners. (Hwy 46 E, 3½ miles east of Hwy 101; 805/238-9607; www.eberlewinery.com)*

EOS Estate Winery at Arciero Vineyards: *Follow the checkered flag to the 650 acres of wine grapes owned by former race car driver Frank Arciero, who specializes in Italian varietals like Nebbiolo and Sangiovese. The facility includes a self-guided tour, race car collection, spectacular rose garden, and picnic area. (Hwy 46 E, 6 miles east of Hwy 101; 805/239-2562 or 800/249-WINE; www.eosvintage.com)*

Justin Vineyards & Winery: *At the end of a scenic country road lies the boutique winery of ex-Angelenos Justin and Deborah Baldwin, whose best wine is Isosceles, a sophisticated Bordeaux-style blend with splendid aging potential. Since 1987 the Baldwins have commissioned a different artist each year to interpret their gorgeous Tuscan-style property for the label, and the results are on display throughout the complex. (11680 Chimney Rock Rd, 15 miles west of Hwy 101; 805/237-4150; www.justinwine.com)*

Meridian Vineyards: *Meridian is the largest local producer, the Central Coast's best-known label, and where you'll get the most polished, Napa-like tasting experience. The grounds are beautiful, featuring a man-made lake surrounded by rolling hills. (Hwy 46 E, 7 miles east of Hwy 101; 805/237-6000; www.meridianvineyards.com)*

Tobin James Cellars: *With a Wild West theme based on the unpredictable personality of colorful winemaker Tobin James (who claims with a wink that he must be a descendant of the James Gang), this winery is fun and unpretentious. Don't think he's not serious about his craft, though—Tobin James's Zinfandel and late-harvest Zinfandel are both award winners. (8950 Union Rd; at Hwy 46 E, 8 miles east of Hwy 101; 805/239-2204)*

York Mountain Winery: *The first winery to be established in Paso Robles, York Mountain stands on land originally deeded by Ulysses S. Grant. Inside the 100-year-old stone tasting room, look for a dry Chardonnay with complex spice overtones, and reserve Cabernets made from hand-selected grapes. (7505 York Mountain Rd; off Hwy 46 W, 7 miles west of Hwy 101 in Templeton; 805/238-3925)*

Pioneer Museum. The Paso Robles Pioneer Museum (2010 Riverside Ave, near 21st St across the railroad tracks; 805/239-4556) is worth a visit for insight into the heritage of a working frontier town. The small museum is filled with donated artifacts presented as a series of life-size dioramas illustrating the town's history, ranging from Native American settlements and vintage ranching equipment to a primitive turn-of-the-century medical-surgical office. One explains the life of renowned Polish pianist Ignace Jan Paderewski, who relieved the neuritis in his hands at a local hot sulfur springs bathhouse. He became so enchanted with the area in the process that he bought an old rancho, planting walnuts and zinfandel grapes. Another room is a re-creation of the old Clark Smith sporting goods store, with vintage bikes, tennis rackets, moose heads, and boat motors. One densely packed space shows an early radio station. A large attached facility showcases a 1923 Model T Touring Car and a deep blue 1911 Maxwell touring car with brass lamps, bought new in Paso Robles, that still runs.

Shopping for Antiques. Antique hounds have been flocking to Paso Robles since long before the wine country explosion, and downtown still proves fertile hunting ground for treasure seekers. The best are the giant mall-style stores representing dozens of dealers each; you can easily spend hours in just one building. Two reliable choices are Antique Emporium Mall, with 55 vendors (1307 Park St; 805/238-1078), and Great American Antiques Mall, which has 40 vendors (1305 Spring St; 805/239-1203). For more information, contact the Paso Robles Chamber of Commerce and ask for its Guide to Antique Shops (1225 Park St; 805/238-0506 or 800/406-4040; www.pasorobleschamber.com).

Lake Park Zoo. A charming small zoo known as the Lake Park Zoo, or Charles Paddock Zoo after its founder, is located near the coastal town of Atascadero, on Highway 41. There are bears, monkeys, ostriches and a beautiful Indian tiger, plus many other animals that will fascinate children in a tidy, well-tended environment set in gardens next to a large shady park that's great for picnics. Call 805/461-5080 for information. Rates are $3 for adults and $2 for ages 3 to 15; open every day 10am–5pm in summer; 10am–4pm in winter.

RESTAURANTS

BISTRO LAURENT ★★

You'll think you've wandered into a small village in France when you come upon the Bistro Laurent. Although it was inevitable that fine dining would follow here on the heels of fine wine, chef Laurent Grangien nevertheless created quite a stir when he opened this cozy yet chic bistro in a town unaccustomed to innovations like a chef's tasting menu. With his extensive French cooking background and his Los Angeles restaurant experience (at the well-respected Fennel), Grangien offers a California-tinged style of French cuisine while maintaining an unpretentious atmosphere that locals have come to love. Banquette-lined walls make virtually every table in the historic brick building a cozy private booth, and there's alfresco dining on a romantic patio. While you peruse Bistro Laurent's impressive list of Central Coast and French wines, you'll enjoy a complimentary hors d'oeuvre that changes daily (goat cheese toasts, perhaps, or a croustade of mushrooms with red wine vinaigrette). Menu highlights include traditional bistro fare such as roasted rosemary garlic chicken, pork loin bathed in peppercorn sauce, or ahi tuna in red wine reduction, depending on the season. Adventurous diners will choose the four-course tasting menu, which changes nightly to reflect the chef's current favorite ingredients or preparations, with a glass of wine paired to each course. During lunchtime, the shady patio magically becomes its own separate restaurant, dubbed Petite Marcel, and serves a simple, weekly changing provençal menu that may include two or three salads, simple pizzas, and a meat and a fish item. *1202 Pine St, Paso Robles; 805/226-8191; $$; MC, V; no checks; dinner Mon–Sat; Petite Marcel, lunch Mon–Sat (spring–fall only); beer and wine; reservations recommended; at the corner of 12th St.* &

BUSI'S ON THE PARK ★

As the name promises, stroll across the lovely downtown City Park to the bordering Pine Street and you'll find Busi's, a local institution that doesn't stand on ceremony: it virtually shouts "Come on in!" This comfortable tavernlike joint will surprise you with the sophistication of its menu. Dinner entrees are served with your choice of soup or salad; among the options are fresh halibut with a Dijon and pistachio crust, baked in lemon and white wine and served with saffron basmati rice; and sautéed pork loin with fresh peach reduction sauce, with parsnip potato purée. For dessert you can choose from temptations such as Viennese torte for two and chocolate pave—dense chocolate and pistachio praline served with mixed berry coulis. Busi's on the Park is a perfect lunch or weekend brunch choice and is a good option for an affordable dinner as well. On Friday and Saturday nights the place jumps with live music. *1122 Pine St, Paso Robles; 805/238-1390; $$; AE, DIS, MC, V; checks OK; dinner every day; full bar; reservations recommended; between 11th and 12th Sts.* &

LODGINGS

ADELAIDE INN ★

Though clearly not in an elegant neighborhood—it's tucked among gas stations and coffee shops—this immaculate hotel is nicely isolated from its bustling surroundings. Lush, manicured gardens are screened from the street by foliage, a relaxing outdoor hot tub is secluded inside a redwood gazebo, and there's even a miniature golf course/putting green. The result is a surprisingly quiet, comfortable property tended with a loving care that's rare among lower-priced inns—and this place is truly a bargain: rooms start under $50 per night in high season. The accommodations are clean and comfortable, with an extra warmth that's a cut above standard motels; unexpected amenities include refrigerators, coffeemakers, hair dryers, and complimentary newspaper, plus work desks in some rooms and dataports in all rooms. No wonder it's popular with business travelers as well as families. The property is constantly being upgraded with new carpeting, curtains, and other niceties so everything always looks fresh. The center of the complex is an outdoor heated pool. Morning fruit and muffins are provided in the lobby. *1215 Ysabel Ave, Paso Robles; 805/238-2770 or 800/549-PASO; $; AE, DC, DIS, MC, V; no checks; www.adelaideinn.com; at 24th St just west of Hwy 101.* &

PASO ROBLES INN ★

The Paso Robles Inn has some rich history. People once came by stagecoach to dip in the hot springs here. Designed by famed architect Stanford White and built in 1891, the "absolutely fireproof" structure burned to the ground in 1940, except for the separate ballroom, which in 2001 was rebuilt into meeting rooms and 12 bedrooms with whirlpool tubs, private patios, microwave ovens, and refrigerators; these rooms are roughly 1½ times the size of regular rooms. The rest of the inn was reconstructed in the 1940s, and its Spanish-style architecture and tile reflect the passion for Mission Revival that was in full swing at the time. The lobby and public rooms are a bit dark and old-fashioned, but the historic photos on the walls are interesting. In 1999 the hot springs on hotel grounds were redrilled and 18 new fireplace rooms with therapy spas were added. A stroll through lushly landscaped grounds leads guests to a footbridge over the creek meandering through this oak-shaded property and to 68 bungalow-style motel rooms with convenient carports. Well shielded from street noise, these units are simple and plain, but many guests consider them charming and nostalgic, although they are not cheap. Don't bother to stay here if the only rooms available are those with numbers beginning with 1 or 2—they're small, decorated in bleak motel style with free-form swipes of brown paint on the walls, and close enough to the street to be noisy. A large heated pool near the creek makes for great after-noon dips, and the dining room (with cocktail lounge) serves three diner-style meals daily. *1103 Spring St, Paso Robles; 805/238-2660; $–$$$; AE, DC, DIS, MC, V; no checks; between 10th and 12th Sts.* &

SUMMERWOOD INN AND WINERY ★★

Across from its own Summerwood Winery, about a five-minute drive from the center of town, this AAA four-diamond bed-and-breakfast is a fine place to base yourselves for a wine-tasting tour of nearby Paso Robles area wineries. Though the main building—a white clapboard cross between Queen Anne and Southern plantation style—looks old, it was actually built in 1994. This means that guest rooms are extra-spacious and bathrooms ultramodern, though the entire inn is furnished with formal English country antique reproductions. The winery's vine-planted acres are just steps from the inn's back patio and visible from every room's private balcony. Each of the nine rooms is named for a wine (Syrah, Bordeaux, Chardonnay, etc.) and has a gas fireplace, balcony, color satellite TV, telephone, terry bathrobes, and bedside bottled water. Luxury is achieved through small, thoughtful touches; you'll find fresh flowers accompanying everything from the Godiva chocolate on your pillow with turndown service to the early-morning cof-fee-and-scones spread on the sideboard downstairs. The room rate includes full breakfast, afternoon wine and hors d'oeuvres, and late-night cookies. If you're looking for a romantic splurge, the Moscato Allegro Room features an in-room whirlpool-for-two, and the top-floor Cabernet Suite is as rich and decadent as an aged wine, with sumptuous furnishings, a seven-headed shower, and an ultrapri-vate patio with a view. *2130 Arbor Rd, Paso Robles; 805/227-4673; $$–$$$$; AE, MC, V; checks OK (at time of reservation); at Hwy 46 W, 1 mile west of Hwy 101.* &

SAN MIGUEL

San Miguel, on old Highway 101 8 miles north of Paso Robles, is a tiny one-street town with a few small businesses. The main reason to come here is to see the Mission San Miguel Archangel, founded in 1797, and the nearby Caledonia Adobe.

ACTIVITIES

Mission San Miguel Archangel. San Miguel grew up around its Mission San Miguel Archangel (on old Hwy 101; 805/467-3256), founded in 1797; the mis-sion burned to the ground in 1806 and was rebuilt in its current form in 1816. It is still run by the Franciscan order as a functioning church, and it's not uncommon to see brown-robed friars going about their daily business on the grounds. Several rooms are set up as if it were still the early 1800s, such as the padre's quarters, containing a kitchen, dining room with built-in cabinets, living room with books and bottled minerals, and a bedroom with a fireplace, sheepskin-covered windows, and a gray hat worn by early Franciscans. Less extensively restored on the outside than many other missions in the state, San Miguel's has a highly decorated interior with a well-preserved church sanctuary, which was painted in lovely pastel shades of pink and blue by area Native Americans under the supervision of Spanish designer Estevan Munras. The walls and woodwork glow with these luminous colors, untouched since their application in 1820. The walls are six feet thick, and the width of the church was determined by the length of the timbers overhead. Be sure to look down to see the graves of early friars on the sanctuary floor. Behind the altar, with its statue of San Miguel (St. Michael), is splendid tile work featuring a radiant Eye of God.

Rios-Caledonia Adobe. You can't see the mission from Highway 101 but you can see this historic adobe (700 Mission S; 805/467-3357) that was once part of the mission's grounds and later served a number of uses, from schoolhouse to mattress factory to tailor shop, and then a stagecoach stop and tavern. Pick up a self-guided tour brochure at the gift shop in the building next door. The adobe was built in 1835 of hand-hewn timbers, and in its life as the Caledonia Inn and tavern it hosted such notorious people as the Dalton Brothers and Frank and Jesse James. The small two-story adobe's interiors are filled with furniture and household items from the 1800s. The (free) museum and gift shop are open 10am–4pm daily.

TEMPLETON

Located just a few minutes south of Paso Robles, Templeton came to life as a classic boomtown in 1886 with the arrival of the Southern Pacific Railroad, which spawned a land rush, creating many farms from the old Rancho Paso de Robles. As in so many coast towns, in 1897 a great fire burned down most of the business district and the town was rebuilt. Templeton still sports a true Old West flavor, with wooden boardwalks and antique-style signage. It's a farm town that continues to reflect its past: the grain elevator of Templeton Feed & Grain is still the centerpiece of downtown business, and across the street, period storefronts house modern establishments.

ACTIVITIES

Chocolate Curiosities. At Herrmann's Chocolate Lab and Ice Cream Parlor, Marcia Herrmann makes chocolate boots and horse heads (and other equine parts), plus chocolate kits such as the Hospital Survival Kit, complete with chocolate aspirin, Band-Aids, and tongue depressors, and similar kits with tools of the trade for electricians, handymen, firefighters, and teachers. With enough notice, she can make up a custom set tailored to your interests, and they ship anywhere. This shop makes wine-flavored chocolates for several premium wineries in the area; it's also the only place around where you can buy both garlic chocolates and hot or mild chili chocolates. Another specialty is "Alicia" chocolates, created by Marcia's granddaughter, made of white chocolate with Oreo cookie pieces and raspberry ganache. Marcia and husband Fritz are friendly and love to talk with visitors: this is a good first stop in town. (422 South Main St; 805/434-3007)

The Templeton Museum. This tiny museum, located in the tidy white Albert Horstman House (610 Main St; Fri–Sat 1pm–4pm) has walking tour maps of the town, as well as artifacts and photos of its glory days. The tour map describes 51 sites, from the still-operating Blacksmith Shop to the Fellowship Hall built by Swedes in 1914 as a meeting and social hall to the Shoe & Harness Shop built in 1886. The Templeton Feed & Grain was built in 1913 as a garage, became a grain mill in the 1930s, and is the largest mill within 100 miles.

Saddle and Tack Shop. Reinforcing the feeling you've stumbled into the past, California Classics makes and sells saddles, bridles, and everything else made of leather, horsehide, and horsehair, for Western horses, ranch work, and riding. They craft beautiful saddles and have a custom silversmith on staff to decorate them. Also of interest: huge cast-iron Dutch ovens for cooking on the trail. One 45-quart monster with the name "Grub Rustlers" stamped on it can reportedly make a peach cobbler for 90 people. (520 Main St; 805/434-0987)

RESTAURANTS

MCPHEE'S GRILL ★★

Yes, this place is out in the boonies, but your palate will thank you for making the drive. Locating his hip grill in Templeton's first building, and the only one to survive the 1897 fire, chef/restaurateur Ian McPhee has created an eatery that manages to perfectly balance the town's rural Americana with big-city culinary eclecticism. An old-fashioned pressed-tin ceiling complements sponge-painted walls adorned with English livestock prints and stenciled barnyard animals. Through the open kitchen, chefs can be seen busily preparing McPhee's most popular dishes. Appetizers include Kung Fu Baby Back Ribs with barbecue sauce, and ruby grapefruit and Maytag blue salad with spicy nuts and port wine vinaigrette. Among the entrees are roasted-garlic and goat-cheese-stuffed chicken with basil pesto and garlic mashed potatoes, and the ancho chili–apricot glazed double pork chop with sweet potato french fries.

Fresh fish specials, offered daily, include dishes like macadamia-nut-encrusted salmon. McPhee's wife, June, presents delectable desserts, from berry crisps and tarts to chocolate decadence and a lemon curd tart with fresh berries and whipped cream. An impressive list of Central Coast wines, many available by the glass, ensures a perfect match for your meal. *416 Main St, Templeton; 805/434-3204; $$; MC, V; checks OK; breakfast, lunch Mon–Sat, dinner every day, brunch Sun; beer and wine; reservations recommended; between 4th and 5th Sts.* &

THE ESTERO BAY COAST

The Estero Bay Coast begins at Point Estero on the north and follows a scalloped pattern down past the cliffs and beaches of Cayucos to the almost enclosed Morro Bay, with its long sand spit running nearly parallel to the shore, then on south to the windy cliffs of Montana de Oro State Park in Los Osos.

CAYUCOS

Roughly 5 miles north of Morro Bay and just 15 miles south of Cambria lies Cayucos, a small town that has retained its Old West feel and remains an authentic California beach town. A boardwalk and old-style storefronts give it a look of a Ponderosa on the Pacific. People come here for the beach, night fishing on the pier, or to eat at Hoppe's Garden Bistro.

ACTIVITIES

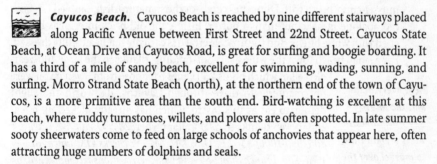 **Cayucos Pier.** The 940-foot Cayucos Pier was built in 1875, and the Pacific Steamship Company's ships stopped here to pick up dairy products. Later, abalone and sea lettuce were shipped from the pier. The pier is wheelchair accessible and lit at night for fishing. It's a great place for a walk, or to sit on one of the benches to gaze at the Pacific. There's picnicking in a wind-protected area next to the pier.

Cayucos Beach. Cayucos Beach is reached by nine different stairways placed along Pacific Avenue between First Street and 22nd Street. Cayucos State Beach, at Ocean Drive and Cayucos Road, is great for surfing and boogie boarding. It has a third of a mile of sandy beach, excellent for swimming, wading, sunning, and surfing. Morro Strand State Beach (north), at the northern end of the town of Cayucos, is a more primitive area than the south end. Bird-watching is excellent at this beach, where ruddy turnstones, willets, and plovers are often spotted. In late summer sooty sheerwaters come to feed on large schools of anchovies that appear here, often attracting huge numbers of dolphins and seals.

 Kayak and Bike Rentals. Cayucos Outfitters rents kayaks, gives lessons, and leads tours off Cayucos and Morro Bay. Watch their beach cam at www.gcf-surf.com. to check out what's happening on the beach. They also rent bikes for cruising the town and the beach. (151 Cayucos Dr; 805/995-2600)

For information on the Western-style beach town of Cayucos, call the Chamber of Commerce at 805/995-1200.

 Polar Bear Dip. At noon on New Year's Day every year, on the south side of the pier, 3,000 to 5,000 people take part in the Cayucos Polar Bear Dip. Some dippers go in and immediately retreat, but others even swim around the pier. The water is very cold, and maybe that's why people dress in costume to, er, bear it. The gentleman who leads the charge into the water always comes dressed in top hat and tails, teenage boys have come dressed as hula dancers, and families have appeared as a bunch of crabs or a pack of polar bears. Restaurants are open, there is live music, and certificates are given at the end to all those who are wet and not wearing a wet suit to keep warm. Call the Chamber of Commerce for more information at 805/995-1200. If you'd rather celebrate when it's warmer, the town has a Fourth of July celebration that draws 10,000 to 15,000 people and includes an old-time parade open to all, a street fair, and fireworks from the pier.

RESTAURANTS

HOPPE'S GARDEN BISTRO ★★

Wilhelm Hoppe once had two fabulous restaurants in Morro Bay but he closed them both and relocated to tiny Cayucos. In fall of 2000 he opened this lovely indoor-outdoor restaurant in a historic building with lush gardens just off the town's main drag. The lunch menu offers such dishes as a goat cheese and red pepper omelet with chives, a warm salmon terrine with garlic aioli, or apple-wood-roasted brisket with horseradish sauce. At dinner, choose from the likes of seared king salmon glazed with honey and sesame, fresh local swordfish with a mussel-curry broth with Dungeness crab, or the signature dish, sautéed Cayucos red abalone in hazelnut-mango butter. Inside, the old brick interior is brightened with white linens, and the upscale crowd is casually but beautifully dressed. For a small beach town the wine list is outstanding, thanks to the large 100-year-old cellar, which holds 250 wines to choose from. Even if you were not planning to drive through Cayucos, it's worth the slight detour to eat at this bistro, which has already picked up a legendary rep thanks to its popular owner. *78 N Ocean Ave, Cayucos; 805/995-1006; $$; AE, DIS, DC, MC, V; checks OK; lunch, dinner Wed–Sun, brunch Sun; beer and wine; reservations recommended; on N Ocean Ave near Cayucos Dr.* &

MORRO BAY

Held every October, the Morro Bay Harbor Festival is a great time to marvel over the professionally-created sand sculptures, enjoy boat tours, and snack on seafood specialties. For more information call 805/772-1155 or 800/366-6043.

Vast and filled with birds and sea mammals, scenic Morro Bay is named for the peculiarly shaped Morro Rock anchoring the mouth of the waterway, one of nine remaining extinct volcanic rocks, called the Nine Sisters, along the coast. This ancient towering landmark, whose name comes from the Spanish word for a

Moorish turban, is inhabited by the endangered peregrine falcon and other migratory birds. Across from the rock, a monstrous oceanfront electrical plant mars the visual appeal of the otherwise pristine bay. In the summer the town is overrun with sunburned tourists, and no one would call it an elegant seaside village, but it's unpretentious, and outside the town proper are some wonderful hiking trails.

Morro Rock is a 23-million-year-old volcanic plug dome outcropping that is a registered California Historical Landmark.

ACTIVITIES

 Play Chess in a Big Way. Morro Bay Boulevard leads right to the harborfront Embarcadero and Centennial Park, site of a giant chess board (the second biggest chess board in the United States), with 3-foot-tall redwood pieces. The "board" is 16 feet square and the chess pieces weigh from 18 to 20 pounds each. The Morro Bay Chess Club offers games on the giant board every Saturday from noon to 5pm, and visitors are welcome to compete. For information on renting the pieces and making reservations for other times, contact the Morro Bay Recreation and Parks Department (805/772-6278).

A Day at the Beach. If you're only going to be in Morro Bay for a day or a few hours, there are a number of parks in which to enjoy quick picnics, a swim in the bay, or even some fishing. Coleman Park, at the Embarcadero and Coleman Drive, has barbecues, fishing, and swimming in Morro Bay. Keiser Park at Atascadero Road and Highway 1 offers barbecues and cool places to relax. At Morro Rock City Beach, at the foot of Coleman Drive, you'll find barbecues, fishing, swimming, and surfing in the bay. Bayshore Bluffs Park, at the west end of Bayshore Drive, offers a bluff-top picnic area with a path to the beach. And finally, Tidelands Park, at Embarcadero between Olive and Fig, has good fishing plus swimming in the bay. Morro Bay touts itself as a place "where the sun spends the winter," but no matter the season, the views of the Pacific, the great seafood, and the sunset make it a must stop for any traveler in the area. Call the Morro Bay Harbor Department for information (805/772-6254).

Morro Bay Aquarium. Tucked behind a touristy storefront on Embarcadero is the Morro Bay Aquarium. This humble operation with its tanks displayed in a dank and grim basementlike room won't be putting Sea World out of business any time soon, but it is officially sanctioned to rehabilitate injured and abandoned sea otters, seals, and sea lions. During their stay, all the animals learn to perform tricks for a morsel of fishy food. (595 Embarcadero; 805/772-7647)

Getting on the Water. Water recreation is a mainstay in Morro Bay's bustling marina, and you can venture out on a kayak tour from Kayak Horizons (551 Embarcadero; 805/772-6444). Tiger's Folly II Harbor Cruises (805/772-2257) takes guests on one-hour cruises of the harbor in a grand riverboat to see wildlife, the Great Blue Heron rookery, and the working fishing harbor. Sunday it offers a champagne brunch tour (1½ hours, reservations required). The boat is docked at the Harbor Hut Restaurant at 1205 Embarcadero.

Fishing. The Central Coast has been called the world's largest fish trap, and Virg's Sportfishing is the best way to get at the fish in the great outdoors. Virg's offers a variety of trips from Morro Bay, including half-day, three-quarter-day, full-day (overnight), and even two-day runs. They have seven boats and a full-service tackle store. The biggest and best boat is the *Admiral*, at 90 feet long. Albacore tuna—ranging from 30 to 60 and 70 pounds—are the main attraction here; when they're running, usually July to October, they attract anglers from throughout California. There can be excellent salmon fishing here as well. Also, the landing has shallow-water rock cod and lingcod trips. However, recent regulation changes have restricted rock cod fishing, so check with the landing about closures; www.virges.com. The landing has its own bait boat, *Billy Boy*, which usually provides live bait for the fleet. ("Near the Rock," 1215 Embarcadero; 805/772-1222 or 800/ROCKCOD)

Shopping. Morro Bay has many touristy T-shirt shops, but tucked among them is the fabulous Shell Shop (590 Embarcadero; 805/772-8014), which has the largest selection of shells anywhere on the West Coast. In a charming bungalow on Main Street, One Door Down (736 #A Main St; 805-772-5399) offers antiques, gifts, and collectibles for the house and garden. Latitudes (591 Embarcadero; 805/772-1451) has beautiful jewelry that will remind you of the sea—black pearls, shell shapes, mother-of-pearl, and other marine adornments.

Morro Bay State Park. Located near the shoreline of Morro Bay, with tidal flats, hiking trails, and three vital bird-nesting areas, this 2,749-acre park encompasses the lagoon shoreline and the hills behind the beach. Each site has a picnic table and barbecue grill. The campground provides drinking water, flush toilets, showers, and a dump station, as well as a restaurant, marina, golf course, museum exhibits, ranger-led nature walks, and ranger programs. Morro Bay State

Park Campground has 115 sites for tents or RVs (no hookups; RV limit 31 feet), including 20 sites for RVs (electrical and water hookups; RV limit 24 feet). Reservations are recommended year-round. Stay limit is 14 days; open all year. Out of Morro Bay take Highway 1 for 1 mile south to South Bay Boulevard and go south to the fork, then right onto State Park Road. Or follow Main Street south from Morro Bay until it becomes State Park Road. (800/444-7275 for reservations; 805/772-2560 for information)

The long, curving 4-mile sand spit that protects Morro Bay is a great stretch to hike, but by the time you get out there, you may be too tired to walk back. Bay Taxi (at Virg's Landing; 805/772-1222) is the answer; they will take you and your picnic by water taxi out to the sand spit, or drop you off for a hike or a day of bird-watching.

Heron Rookery. The Heron Rookery Natural Preserve, north of White Point and next to Morro Bay, is a great place to see the mating, nesting, and nurturing behaviors of the great blue heron. Take State Park Road, or reach it by trail from the Morro Bay State Park Museum of Natural History; it's only a quarter-mile hike along the bay.

Museum of Natural History, Morro Bay State Park. Located in the State Park not far from the bird sanctuary and park marina, this truly charming museum has a great view of the bay, a spy glass with which to see Morro Bay Rock, and interesting displays explaining tides, ocean currents, and the life cycle of clams, among many other topics. The museum has just reopened after a $3 million modernization that created many state-of-the-art interactive exhibits. Docents offer a nature walk in the park, and videos on local marine and plant life help explain the natural environment. (State Park Rd; 805/772-2694; www.morrobaymuseum.org)

Sub-Sea Tours. These tours in a glass-bottomed boat leave from the Morro Bay Marina (805/772-9463). You will see marine mammals, fish, and plant life. Kids love this tour.

RESTAURANTS

THE GALLEY RESTAURANT ★

 The Galley is a popular fish restaurant with a great view of the Morro Bay Rock. Lunch at this family-friendly place includes fish and chips, chowder, and other seafood items, and at dinner people like to start with oysters Rockefeller and go on to grilled halibut, rock cod, or other seafood specialties. The decor is minimal, but there are lots of windows through which to gaze at the bay and the rock. Service is quick and cordial, and it's a good idea to come early or have a reservation, particularly in the busy summer season. *899 Embarcadero, Morro Bay; 805/772-*

For maps and local information, stop in at the Morro Bay Chamber of Commerce (880 Main St; 805/772-4467 or 800/231-0592; www.morrobay. org) for helpful information.

2806; $; AE, DIS, MC, V; checks OK; lunch, dinner every day; beer and wine; reservations recommended; Embarcadero at Harbor St. ⟨

WINDOWS ON THE WATER ★★

 Upstairs in the Marina Square shopping complex on Embarcadero, in the location that Hoppe's Marina Square once occupied, is this fine dining establishment with windows all around and spectacular views of the water. Chef Tyler Wiazed, who has cooked with famous chefs such as Wolfgang Puck, joined the staff in 2001. The most popular appetizer is crab cakes, and entrees include tombo-tuna–stuffed crab, halibut, and seafood fettuccine, a rich dish with scallops, shrimp, and lobster. The decor is heavy on woods, with grape themes everywhere, a nod to the extensive wine list (both local California wines and European vintages) that recently got this place mentioned in *Wine Spectator* magazine. For dessert, order the turtle, an individual pecan pie with warm caramel sauce and chocolate pooled under it, like a turtle swimming in a pond of chocolate. They also make their own ice creams and sorbets in flavors such as passion fruit and white chocolate–macadamia nut. In fact, they have made more than 400 flavors, although not all are available at once! *699 Embarcadero, Morro Bay; 805/772-0677; $$–$$$; AE, DC, DIS, MC, V; checks OK; lunch Fri–Sat, dinner every day, brunch Sun; full bar; reservations recommended; www.windowsonthewater.net; on Embarcadero in the Marina Square shopping center, 2nd floor.* ⟨

LODGINGS

GRAY'S INN & GALLERY ★

These rooms truly have the best view in town. Just a few yards below your deck are the sailboats and pleasure craft in the harbor, and you can easily chat with people as they go to and come from their boats. As these are the only lodgings right on the water, they are popular, so call for reservations as far ahead as you can. When you get there, enter through Gray's Gallery to check in. There are just three units, which are like small apartments—two on the first floor behind the gallery, and one upstairs. Each has a bedroom with a king-size bed plus a living room with a queen-size futon. All the units have a full kitchen, tub, and shower. *561 Embarcadero, Morro Bay; 805/772-3911; $$; AE, DIS, MC, V; checks OK; bobnjosi@aol.com; hometown.aol.com/~graysinn.*

THE INN AT MORRO BAY ★★★

When you drive into this shaded and manicured resort you may think you're in the wrong place, given the price you were quoted when you made your reservations. This is an exceedingly comfortable and affordable accommodation that's smart enough to let its splendid natural surroundings be the focus of attention. Two-story Nantucket-style buildings have contemporary interiors with tempered white wooden shutters, blond-wood cabinetry, polished brass beds with tan feather duvets and oversized pillows, and tan and white wainscoting. There is a sink in each room and a separate bath with tub and shower. A complimentary continental breakfast is delivered to your room. Rates vary wildly according to the view; the best rooms enjoy unobstructed views of Morro Rock plus convenient access to a bayfront sundeck, while those in back face the well-landscaped swimming pool, gardens, and eucalyptus-forested golf course at

If you need a short hike to get your juices flowing, try the 1½-mile Exercise Trail to Black Mountain, as it winds through rolling tree- and brush-covered hills to the highest point in Morro Bay State Park. Follow the signs as you enter the park.

Morro Bay State Park. Hiking trails lead conveniently from here through the state park, and you can take one of the complimentary mountain bikes on a spin at any time. Guests receive a discount on pampering treatments at the on-site Therapeutic Massage Center, and the hotel has a romantic bayside lounge and dining room, which serves California/Mediterranean cuisine and three meals daily. *60 State Park Rd, Morro Bay; 805/772-5651 or 800/321-9566; $$–$$$$; AE, DC, DIS, MC, V; checks OK; www.innatmorrobay.com; take Main St south past park entrance.* &

MARINA STREET INN ★

This warm and pleasant inn in a yellow old-fashioned captain's style house is run by former teachers Vern and Claudia Foster. There are great views from its bay windows, and the inn has four rooms decorated differently, all special. Our favorite is the Dockside Room, which has a four-poster bed, a matching bureau, nautical antiques, and an attached patio. In case you forget you're near the water, you can hear the foghorns from here. From the window you can see a bit of the ocean and bay, plus a fantastic view of Morro Rock. Another favorite, the Rambling Rose Room, is decorated in warm red and green colors, with Battenburg lace curtains and bedspread. A four-poster bed, armoire, and English writing desk add to the charm, and the attached patio looks out over the garden. The Garden Room has a romantic four-poster made of willow. Each morning a full gourmet breakfast is served in the dining room. *305 Marina St, Morro Bay;*

805/772-4016 or 888/683-9389; $–$$; AE, MC, V; checks OK; vfoster105@aol.com; www.marinastreetinn.com; corner of Main and Marina St. &

BAYWOOD PARK

Baywood Park is a tidy residential community along the estuary that connects Morro Bay with Los Osos and the Montana de Oro State Park.

LODGINGS

BAYWOOD INN BED & BREAKFAST ★

This romantic, cozy, and secluded bed-and-breakfast is a great place to base yourself if you intend to hike in nearby Montana de Oro State Park. You can also launch kayaks from the small wooden landing right across the street. Though the building was originally constructed for business tenants, its spacious interiors lent themselves perfectly to a remodel when owner Alex Benson bought it and created B&B suites, each furnished in a distinctive theme. From the knick-knacks and ruffles of Granny's Attic to the pale pastels of California Beach or the rough cedar beams and stone fireplace of the Appalachian, there's a room for every taste and preference. Our favorite is Quimper, a country French room with a tiled hearth and vaulted ceiling illuminated by a high window. Every room has a separate entrance, fireplace, microwave oven, coffeemaker, and refrigerator stocked with complimentary snacks and nonalcoholic beverages; many have bay views. Included in your stay is full breakfast each morning and a late-afternoon wine and cheese reception highlighted by a tour of many of the rooms. If you're looking for solitude, the Baywood Inn fits the bill. There are a couple of decent restaurants on the block, so you never really have to wander far. *1370 2nd St, Baywood Park; 805/528-8888; $$; MC, V; checks OK; innkeeper@baywooinn.com; www.baywoodinn.com; 2 blocks south of Santa Ysabel Ave.* &

> "Our favorite thing to do is to get up early in the morning, walk the mile out to Morro Rock, and watch the great blue herons and white egrets perched all over the rock or standing motionless in the shallow water near shore."
>
> —Christine Linhares, lifetime resident of Morro Bay

LOS OSOS

Located just south of Morro Bay and around the bird estuary, this quiet community is prime territory for bird-watching, hiking, and tide-pooling. Most people seek it out as the gateway to Montana de Oro State Park.

ACTIVITIES

 Hiking Montana de Oro State Park. South of Morro Bay in Los Osos is the 8,400-acre Montana de Oro State Park (805/528-0513), encompassing sand dunes, jagged cliffs, coves, caves, and reefs. Named "mountain of gold" by the Spanish for the golden poppies that carpet the hillsides each spring, the park contains trails for hiking, biking, and horseback riding as well as rest rooms and picnic facilities. Easily reached tide pools offer glimpses of starfish, anemones, crabs, and other residents. Stop first at the Visitor Center and Ranger Headquarters in the historic Spooner Ranch House for hiking maps and directions to trails, to learn the history of this former ranch, and to see videos of local and natural history, including displays on hawks, bobcats, and coyotes. The Bluffs Trail is an easy but breathtaking 4-mile round-trip hike atop the Montana de Oro State Park bluffs, the trail dipping down to tide pools, a true peak hiking experience. From Highway 101, exit Los Osos Valley Road and continue northwest for 12 miles to where the road turns south and becomes Pecho Valley Road, then continue to Montana de Oro State Park, and park at Spooner's Cove. Look for the trail that begins 10 yards south of the turnoff for the campground on the west side of Pecho Valley Road.

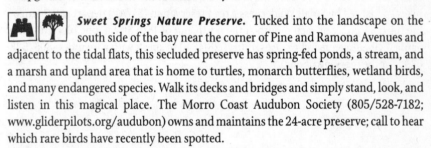 **Sweet Springs Nature Preserve.** Tucked into the landscape on the south side of the bay near the corner of Pine and Ramona Avenues and adjacent to the tidal flats, this secluded preserve has spring-fed ponds, a stream, and a marsh and upland area that is home to turtles, monarch butterflies, wetland birds, and many endangered species. Walk its decks and bridges and simply stand, look, and listen in this magical place. The Morro Coast Audubon Society (805/528-7182; www.gliderpilots.org/audubon) owns and maintains the 24-acre preserve; call to hear which rare birds have recently been spotted.

 Audubon Overlook. At the north end of Third Street off Santa Ysabel in Los Osos, the Audubon Overlook includes a view deck open from dawn to dusk. Rail, brant, and teal are often seen.

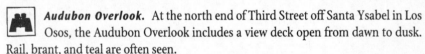 **Elfin Forest.** The Elfin Forest Natural Area, a unique 40-acre site on the southeastern edge of the Morro Bay Estuary, is a complex plant community with pygmy oak woodlands, coastal dune scrub, and a brackish marsh. Many species of birds, animals, reptiles, and amphibians live here. There is a 4,000-foot wooden boardwalk (wheelchair accessible) with two viewing decks overlooking the bay. To reach the forest from Highway 1, take the Los Osos–Baywood Park exit near Morro Bay, go right on Santa Ysabel Avenue in Los Osos, and

The Los Osos-Baywood Park Chamber of Commerce (805/528-4884) can help you choose where to stay and find hiking trails in the area.

GOLF

This part of the coast has golf courses with inspiring views of rich valleys, the coast, or the sea. Morro Bay Golf Course has often been referred to as "the poor man's Pebble Beach," and with good reason. With its tree-lined fairways and ocean views, especially on the sixth hole, the lush course has Pebble Beach–like charm at a lot less cost—one-tenth the fees at the famous course. Call 805/782-8060 for information. Hunter Ranch Golf Course (805/237-7444) is on Highway 46, east of Paso Robles. The 18-hole championship course has a four-star rating from Golf Digest, *a restaurant, and a clubhouse. One of the most challenging courses on the Central Coast is the 18-hole, par-71 championship course is Avila Beach Golf Resort (805/595-4000). Laguna Lake Golf Course is in San Luis Obispo on Los Osos Valley Road. The 9-hole course has a driving range with stunning greens and fairways (805/781-7309). Blacklake Golf Resort, off Hwy 101 in Nipomo between Santa Maria and Pismo Beach, is the only 27-hole golf resort in the area and features lakes, canyon, and oaks courses (805/343-1214).*

then turn right on 16th Street; the boardwalk starts at the end of 16th Street. Guided hikes sponsored by Small Wilderness Area Preservation (SWAP) depart at 9:30am on the third Saturday of each month at the north end of 15th Street, one block north of Santa Ysabel Avenue in Los Osos. (805/528-4540 to speak with a member; 805/528-0392 for the message phone)

THE SAN LUIS OBISPO COAST

The San Luis Obispo Coast area includes a wide range of coastal and inland agricultural lands, with towns as varied as the charming creekside university town of San Luis Obispo to the old working fishing port of San Luis Pier to the raffish beach towns of Avila Beach and Pismo Beach and the former ranching towns of Arroyo Grande and Santa Maria. In the past 20 years the area has become an important wine region, including the Edna Valley and Arroyo Grande Valley areas. One of the largest ranges of sand dunes in the world stretches for miles at Pismo Dunes and Oceano Dunes.

SAN LUIS OBISPO

San Luis Obispo is one of the prettiest towns on the coast. With two rivers running through it, a vibrant mission, and an art-filled downtown alive with music and events along the river walk, it's easy to spend several hours just wandering this enchanting place. While it appears quiet, many big-city transplants have flocked to live here. With its beautiful surrounding countryside, relaxed yet vital college-town atmosphere, charming neighborhoods of historic cottages, and developing wine region nearby, SLO—as the locals call it—has been growing by leaps and bounds. But even with the influx of new residents and commerce, SLO's downtown is wonderfully compact and perfect for exploring on foot, while the sparkling coastline is only minutes away.

ACTIVITIES

River Walk. Start at the mission or the Children's Museum and wander along San Luis Creek, where you'll come upon sculptures, musicians playing, and several informal restaurants with great views of the creek. You can stop along the way and listen to the water, or have a glass of wine on a deck overlooking the creek bank. There is also a small amphitheater where bands often perform.

The Mission. Like several other charming Central Coast towns, this one began life as a Spanish mission outpost. Founding friar Junípero Serra chose this valley in 1772, drawn by reports of friendly natives and bountiful food, and established Mission San Luis Obispo de Tolosa (782 Monterey St; 805/543-6850). The mission has the dubious honor of being the first to use the now-traditional red tile roof after its original thatched roofs repeatedly fell to the burning arrows of local Chumash Indians. The church sanctuary is simple, its high white walls adorned with

"When friends come to visit, I always suggest they hike Cal Poly Canyon. You reach it by going through the Cal Poly San Luis Obispo campus to where it backs up against the hills. As you hike higher you can look down on great views of both the campus and the town." —Steve Watkins, Paso Robles resident

hand-painted garlands, with heavy beams overhead. The altar is surrounded by green marble; behind it there's gold-painted detail, and high above, a large Eye of God beams down. The mission gardens are shady with orange and lemon trees and a huge olive tree. Daisies, foxgloves, and roses provide color, and mission bell lighting fixtures light the paths at night. The well-restored mission church, padres' quarters, and colonnade are in the heart of town, fronted by the pedestrian-friendly Mission Plaza, a pretty park that serves as SLO's town square for festivals and other events.

Walking Tours. The San Luis Obispo Chamber of Commerce (1039 Chorro St; 805/781-2777; www.VisitSLO.com) offers a helpful Points of Interest brochure. The brochure outlines three walking tours: a "Downtown District" walk, which includes the Ah Louis Store (800 Palm St), where Chinese laborers working on the railroad shopped; a "Historic Core Walk," which stops by the Hayes–Latimer Adobe (642 Monterey St); and a San Luis Creek Walk. While at the Chamber of Commerce, pick up its colorful "Visitors Guide," which is packed with useful information.

"I thinks what's great about San Luis Obispo is finding artful treasures in unexpected places—sculpture by the creek, lovely tile around the door of a business. Another fun thing: the first Friday of every month is Art After Dark, where all 13 galleries are open from 6 to 9pm and you can walk from one to another."
—Karen Kile, executive director, SLO Art Center

Farmers' Market. On Thursday nights everyone comes out for the Farmers' Market, a beloved local tradition. Emptied of auto traffic, Higuera Street fills with a colorful and festive assemblage of vendors and entertainers. Shoppers stroll through, clutching bags of luscious fruits and vegetables, fresh flowers, locally made arts and crafts, and warm baked goods. The sounds of Peruvian street musicians, old-fashioned brass bands, or lively dance troupes fill the air as the tantalizing aroma of oak barbecue wafts from sidewalk grills. Come hungry and graze your way through a classic SLO evening. (Higuera St, between Osos and Nipomo Sts; Thurs 6–9pm rain or shine)

Find the Public Art. The streets, gardens, buildings, and courtyards of San Luis Obispo are studded with public art pieces, from sculptures to fountains to murals, and you can find them by picking up a free guide to galleries and public art at the SLO Art Center (1010 Broad St; 805/543-8562) or any gallery. Many are found along the river walk and in the mission plaza area. A favorite is *Tequski Wa Suwa*, also called the *Child & Bear Sculpture Fountain*, by Paula Zima, located in front of the mission. At 1027 Marsh Street you'll find the *Stage Coach Wall Mural* by Hugh Sladen. Located right over the creek near the Mission Plaza Amphitheater is *Tankhead Fish* by John Augsburger.

Shopping. Luna Rustica Imports (1127 Broad St; 805/542-0825; www.lunarusticaimports.com) has colorful pottery, serving platters, pitchers, vases, jars, mirrors, and wall art as well as furniture, all from central and southern Mexico. Prices are direct-import and lower than elsewhere. The Nanette Keller Factory Outlet (745 Higuera St; 805/547-7933) has cotton and linen "sophisticated casual" women's wear. Clothes designed by Keller are usually sold in high-end boutiques and catalogs, but here in this well-organized shop that looks like a boutique itself, the prices are at least a third or lower than usual, and the selection is excellent.

San Luis Obispo Children's Museum. A favorite attraction for kids and parents, this museum helps youngsters learn about the past with an authentic reproduction Chumash cave dwelling and inspires their imaginations in a music room, computer corner, pint-size bank and post office, and more. The fire engine is the biggest hit with little guys, and the theater with its costumes is popular with all ages. (1010 Nipomo St; 805/544-KIDS)

San Luis Obispo Art Center. The Art Center is bustling with rotating exhibits of art and serious crafts, with friendly docents eager to answer your questions. It has three galleries with monthly shows usually dedicated to local and regional artists, and hosts frequent art demonstrations, workshops, and gallery openings at which the public is welcome. The first Friday of every month, the SLO Trolley runs a special loop service that stops at all galleries in town, including this one; call the museum for information. (1010 Broad St; at Mission Plaza; 805/543-8562; Tues–Sun 11am–5pm)

History Center and Museum of San Luis Obispo Country. After being closed for two years, this small museum in the dignified Carnegie Library Building, built in 1904 of granite quarried from nearby Bishop's Peak, reopened in 2001. The building was retrofitted by the great-grandson of the original builder. The main-floor exhibits focus on the life of a local woman and her family in the rancho period, displaying artifacts such as gowns and ranch tools to show what things were like 150 years ago in what was still a wild part of the West. (696 Monterey St; 805/543-0638; Wed–Sun 10am–4pm)

San Luis Obispo is the site of the mission-style Milestone Mo-Tel, as it was originally named, which opened in 1925 and is recognized as the first motel in the United States. Architect Arthur S. Hieneman copyrighted the word, a contraction of "motor" and "hotel." It was located here because it was roughly halfway along the then two-day journey from San Francisco to Los Angeles.

Bishop's Peak is the highest peak in the string of volcanic peaks called the Nine Sisters. Named for a bishop's miter or hat, it is 1,559 feet high; from its quarries came the rock that built the city foundations and buildings of San Luis Obispo.

 Biking San Luis Obispo County. This area is also a terrific region for bicycling, with scenic terrain for riders of all levels. Pick up the San Luis Obispo County Bike Map, a color-coded guide that includes mileage, terrain descriptions, and a list of local bike shops, at the Chamber of Commerce (1039 Chorro St; 805/781-2777).

Golf. Dairy Creek Golf Course is conveniently located next to El Chorro Regional Park. Dairy Creek, which runs along the front nine holes, and Pennington Creek, along the back nine, define the 6,548-yard course. It rises and falls 300 feet twice and has plenty of water hazards and bunkers. Fees are reasonable for the quality of the course. (2990-A Dairy Creek Rd; 805/782-8060; take Hwy 101 to the Morro Bay/Hwy 1 exit, go west along Hwy 1 5.5 miles to El Chorro Regional Park; enter park and look for entrance to the course)

Chalk Mountain Golf Course, 15 minutes north of San Luis Obispo, is situated in lush, ancient oak groves overlooking the southern Salinas Valley. The course features a meandering creek, rolling hills, and undulating greens. Rates are very reasonable compared to typical fees in Northern and Southern California. (10000 Elbordo Rd; 805/466-8848; from San Luis Obispo, drive north on Hwy 101 to Atascadero/Santa Rosa exit; follow the signs to Atascadero Regional Park and Golf Course)

RESTAURANTS

BIG SKY CAFE ★

While the first page of the menu says this is "New American cooking," stepping into the Big Sky Cafe is like stumbling on a Mexican village, with red-tile-roofed walls and a blue star-studded ceiling. The menu selection, however, is eclectic Caribbean-Creole. At breakfast they serve such lively items as Spicy, Smoky Chicken and Sausage Jambalaya Omelet and the Devil's Mess (spinach, spicy andouille sausage, herbs, and chiles). At lunch you can have a Zydeco Fried Chicken Salad, which comes with peppered walnuts, dilled cucumbers, and a mint-chile/fruit salsa/walnut ranch dressing. The Creole flavors go beyond jambalaya to the gumbo and authentically airy beignets. Jumping the Atlantic, try the Moroccan Dry Rubbed Chicken Breast with apricot-tomato chutney and almonds. The setting is comfy casual; creative paint treatments and weathered furniture enhance the Mexican/vaguely Southwestern ambience, accented by local art. Big plush booths and small wooden tables coexist happily and complement the long counter/bar. Big Sky is well known and well liked, as evidenced by the benches thoughtfully placed outside for customers who encounter a wait. *1121 Broad St, San Luis Obispo; 805/545-5401; $; AE, MC, V; local checks OK; breakfast, lunch, dinner every day; beer and wine; no reservations; between Higuera and Marsh Sts.* &

BUONA TAVOLA ★★

Situated next to the art deco Fremont Theater, this upscale dining room and its charming outdoor patio offer well-prepared Northern Italian cuisine in a setting that's fancy enough for special occasions but welcoming enough for the casually dressed. Checkerboard floors and original artwork adorn the warm, intimate interior, while lush magnolias, ficuses, and grapevines lend a garden atmosphere to alfresco seating out back. Begin by choosing one of the traditional cold salads on the antipasti list, then proceed to a main course menu that highlights delicious homemade pastas. Chef/owner Antonio Varia offers entrees such as agnolotti di scampi allo zafferano—half-moon purses pinched around a scampi filling, then smothered in saffron cream sauce; fresh fish such as fresh Norwegian salmon; and meat entrees such as costelette d'agnello, rack of lamb marinated with rosemary, sage, thyme, and garlic, and served with a rosemary-Dijon reduction sauce. For dessert try the deceptively simple crema di vaniglia—vanilla cream custard with caramel or chocolate sauce. The wine list is a winner, with traditional Italian offerings accented by stellar choices from the surrounding wine region. *1037 Monterey St, San Luis Obispo; 805/545-8000; $$; AE, DIS, MC, V; local checks only; lunch Mon–Fri, dinner every day; beer and wine; reservations recommended; between Osos and Santa Rosa Sts.* &

THE MISSION GRILL ★

 A winner thanks to both its location and its ambience, the Mission Grill is adjacent to the Mission Plaza and across from a splashing courtyard fountain. There is shady outdoor seating and a light California-style menu with Mexican influences. Charbroiled chicken with lemon pepper purée in marsala sauce is a good choice, as is the Sedona chicken salad with mandarin oranges, red onions, and tomatoes. Whatever is happening on Mission Plaza will entertain you as you eat. Dine here on Friday evenings in the summer and enjoy the free blues concerts staged nearby. *1023 Chorro St, San Luis Obispo; 805/547-5544; $; AE, MC, V; no checks; lunch, dinner every day, brunch Sun; full bar; reservations recommended; Monterey and Chorro Sts next to the mission.* &

A "Central Coast Antique Guide," which includes both a map and a detailed listing of antique shops and dealers, is available by writing the Antique Mall (1539 S Broadway, Santa Maria, CA 93454).

Save your pennies and rub shoulders with mellow students at the Vista Grande Restaurant on the Cal Poly campus. The public is welcome, (lunch every day, dinner Sat, brunch Sun; closed Sat in summer); they serve pasta, seafood, prime rib, and other wholesome dishes. (On the campus, off Grand Ave; call 805/756-1204 for dinner reservations)

SLO BREWING COMPANY

Hang out with the area's collegiate population at this local-brew-pub-makes-good success story. Its 14 homemade beers—the most famous are Pale Ale, Amber Ale, and Porter—have created such a buzz (no pun intended) that they're now nationally distributed. Located downtown in a historic 100-year-old brick commercial building, the Company offers a bar downstairs and a cavernous dining room upstairs. Illuminated by industrial skylights and filled with hardy wooden tables and chairs, the restaurant is comfortable, although it can get loud. The menu—burgers, deep-fried appetizers, and other pub basics—is far from gourmet, but quite satisfying with a tall cold one. All in all, this is a great place to meet friends, celebrate a sports victory, or grab a pre-movie bargain bite. *1119 Garden St, San Luis Obispo; 805/543-1843; $; AE, DIS, MC, V; local checks only; lunch, dinner every day; full bar; no reservations; www.slobrew.com; between Higuera and Marsh Sts.* &

LODGINGS

APPLE FARM INN ★★

The rooms are more elegant that you'd expect at this ultra-popular getaway right near Highway 101, and it is remarkably quiet. The entire complex—which includes a restaurant, gift shop, and working cider mill—exhibits an over-the-top Victorian-style cuteness, with floral wallpaper, fresh flowers, and sugar-sweet touches. No two guest rooms are alike, although each has a gas fireplace, large bathroom with plush terry robes, canopy or brass bed, and lavish country decor. Some bedrooms open onto cozy turreted sitting areas with romantic window seats, while others have wide bay windows overlooking the creek that rambles through the property. Morning coffee and tea are delivered to your room, or you can opt for breakfast in bed at an additional cost. Rooms in the motel-style Trellis Court are also beautifully decorated and have virtually the same amenities as those in the main inn (including fireplaces and cozy decor), but cost less and include a discount voucher for breakfast at the restaurant, a great value without sacrificing a bit of luxury. The complex has a heated outdoor swimming pool and whirlpool, and there's unlimited hot apple cider on hand in the lobby. Before you leave be sure to have one of the famous hot apple dumplings in the restaurant. There is sometimes a line at the restaurant, but the Apple Farm guarantees diners with reservations a maximum wait of 15 minutes or your meal is 50 percent off. *2015 Monterey St, San Luis Obispo;*

805/544-2040 or 800/255-2040; $$$; (main inn), $$; (Trellis Court); AE, DIS, MC, V; checks OK; www.applefarm.com; just south of Hwy 101. &

GARDEN STREET INN ★★⁴

The first time you step into this beautifully furnished and maintained inn, the whole effect is so grand you expect to be greeted by a butler. The gracious Italianate/Queen Anne bed-and-breakfast near downtown was built in 1887 and was fully restored in 1990, a monument to Victorian gentility and to the good taste of owners Dan and Kathy Smith. Each bedroom and suite is decorated with well-chosen antique oak armoires, opulent fabric or paper wall coverings, and vintage memorabilia. Choose one with a clawfooted tub, fireplace, whirlpool bath, or private deck—whatever suits your fancy. The Fields of Dreams room has a baseball theme, and the Concours d'Elegance suite has a tan damask spread, wing chairs, and black fireplace and a sitting room with art on the theme of classic cars. Breakfast is served in the morning room as the sun filters through original stained-glass windows, and each evening wine and cheese are laid out. The well-stocked library is always available to guests. *1212 Garden St, San Luis Obispo; 805/545-9802; $$; AE, MC, V; checks OK; innkeeper@gardenstreetinn.com; www.gardenstreetinn.com; between Marsh and Pacific Sts.* &

Every Friday night in the summer the SLO Downtown Association presents free concerts on Mission Plaza from 5:30 to 7:30pm. Most of the music could be categorized as blues or soft jazz. You can sit on the grass, bring a folding chair, or have dinner at one of the informal restaurants near the plaza and enjoy the sounds.

MADONNA INN ★

Take a break from good taste and step into this eccentric hotel of fantasy rooms where faux-rock waterfalls, velvet-flocked wallpaper, marbled mirrors, and deep shag carpeting are just the beginning. The 109 rooms are individually decorated in themes so unusual the Madonna Inn sells 109 different postcards—just in case your friends can't believe you slept in digs reminiscent of *The Flintstones*. Before you call for reservations check the web site for photos of every one of the unique rooms. Favorites include the all-rock Caveman rooms, featuring waterfall showers and giant animal-print rugs; among other over-the-top options are the Austrian Suite and English Manor, which look like they sound. Many guests of this Disneyland for adults request their favorite rooms annually, celebrating anniversaries or New Year's Eve, and the Madonna hosts hundreds of honeymooners each year. The rooms are spacious and very comfortable; if the loud decor doesn't keep you up, there's a very good night's sleep to be had. A surprisingly good coffee shop adjoins a delectable European bakery. Don't miss the Gold Rush dining room, an eyeful beyond description that's flaming with fuchsia carpet, pink leather booths, and gold cherub chandeliers. *100 Madonna Rd, San Luis Obispo; 805/543-3000 or 800/543-9666; $$–$$$$; AE, DIS, MC, V; checks OK; www.madonnainn.com; Madonna Rd exit off Hwy 101.* ᬇ

AVILA BEACH

Avila Beach is a bit like Rip Van Winkle, just waking up from a period when it was effectively asleep for three years. Thanks to an environmental tragedy from seepage of underground crude oil, the town had to be destroyed to be saved and was essentially leveled, especially along the waterfront. The cleanup is now complete, and the still-bare town is just starting to flourish with attractive seating, benches complete with bas-relief starfish so lifelike they look as if they might slither off, large rocks, and sculptures. Plans for restaurants and bars are in the works, and soon Avila Beach should spring back to the sunny and popular resort it once was, just a bit less funky.

ACTIVITIES

View **Drive through Sycamore Canyon.** Half the fun of Avila Beach might be getting here; from San Luis Obispo, scenic San Luis Bay Road leads toward the ocean. During the late summer and fall harvest seasons, take a detour into woodsy, sun-dappled See Canyon, where makeshift roadside fruit stands and U-Pick signs mark this apple-producing region. Continuing on, you'll come to Sycamore Mineral Springs Resort, a 100-year-old therapeutic hot springs that's also popular as a day spa.

Old San Luis Pier. Drive roughly a half mile from the Avila Beach wharf, along the rim of San Luis Obispo Bay with its azure, crescent-shaped natural harbor filled with bobbing sailboats. Follow its natural curve to the Old San Luis Pier for a day of sportfishing or a hearty fresh-caught meal. This is an old-time working pier with uneven heavy timbers, so don't wear high-heeled shoes. In the mornings, the wooden platform bustles with commercial fishermen unloading their daily catch of rock cod, halibut, crab, and the like, while pelicans and sea gulls vie with sea lions for undersize fish. In July, grandpas and their grandkids fish off the pier for mackerel, which practically jump onto your line. Eat at the Olde Port Inn (see review, below) at the very end of the pier or go sportfishing for rock cod, albacore, salmon, or halibut with Patriot Sportfishing (805/595-7200; www.patriotsportfishing.com).

Hike the Pecho Coast Trail to the Lighthouse. A 3½-mile hike on the Pecho Coast Trail takes you to the Point San Luis Obispo Lighthouse, built in 1889 in the Prairie Victorian Style, and the only remaining lighthouse of its type on the West

Coast. Organized by the Land Conservancy, the docent-led hike ascends steep cliffs up a trail that gains 440 feet of elevation. You must be fit, over 12 years old, a regular hiker, and wear hiking boots; it takes about half a day to do the round-trip hike. Hikes normally depart at 9am on specific dates, usually weekdays. Call for reservations (805/541-8735); they will give directions to the trailhead.

RESTAURANTS

OLDE PORT INN ★

It's possible to drive all the way out onto the working pier, but if the handful of parking spaces are filled you'll have to park on shore and wander out past sport-fishing outfitters and snack stands to reach this unique seafood restaurant. The family-run Olde Port Inn serves absolutely the freshest seafood, from the hearty fresh-catch cioppino (a house specialty) to the morning's fresh scallops and shrimp tossed in pasta to blackened fish to a combination fisherman's plate of the best seafood available that day. Dinners, sized for hungry dockworkers, include soup or salad, potatoes, vegetables, and plenty of warm sourdough bread. Though the upstairs dining room has a nice bay view through picture windows, request one of the glass-topped tables downstairs if you want a straight-down view of the churning waters below through a mirror-lined cutout. Gooey, decadent desserts include Butterfinger ice cream pie and a homemade peach cobbler that's well worth the extra calories. *Port San Luis, Avila Beach; 805/595-2515; $$–$$$; AE, MC, V; no checks; lunch, dinner every day; full bar; reservations recommended; www.oldeportinn.com; 4 miles west of Hwy 101 via Avila Beach Dr.* &

LODGINGS

SYCAMORE MINERAL SPRINGS RESORT ★★

This sprawling historic resort drew guests for decades thanks to its mineral springs, and it still does now, with upgraded decor and new accommodations called the West Meadow Suites. Discovered in 1886 by prospectors drilling for oil, the natural bubbling mineral springs provide relaxation and rejuvenation in an idyllic natural setting. Sycamore Springs feeds close to 75 private mineral baths on the property—many rooms have their own spa tubs on the attached deck or balcony, and two dozen more freestanding hot tubs are tucked away on the wooded hillside above the spa. Hot tub rentals for nonguests are available 24 hours a day, and a half-hour soak is included with any massage or facial. The spacious guest rooms, many of which have fireplaces, are in contemporary condo-style two-story buildings, reached via a long walking bridge arching over Avila

Beach Drive and San Luis Creek. The resort's Gardens of Avila restaurant isn't much to look at, but its outdoor setting shines and its fare is casually elegant, if slightly expensive. Seafood is prepared especially well, so you can't go wrong with one of the fresh-catch specials. Other offerings include red curry-coconut chicken potstickers, tiger shrimp in a Mediterranean ragout, and an excellent prime rib. All overnight guests receive a breakfast credit for the restaurant. *1215 Avila Beach Dr, Avila Beach; 805/595-7302 or 800/234-5831; $$–$$$$; AE, DIS, MC, V; local checks only; info@smsr.com; www.sycamoresprings.com; 1 mile from Hwy 101.* &

PISMO BEACH–SHELL BEACH

Pismo is about the beach. Forget about chic. Shorts, a T-shirt, sandals, a beach hat, and lots of sunscreen are all you need to pack. The native Chumash, who lived here as far back as 9,000 years ago, named Pismo Beach for the abundance of *pismu*, or tar, found in the sand. In the 1900s, with saloons, brothels, and a dance hall established, the town had become a tourist getaway for wild times, and that reputation was furthered during the Depression when Pismo Beach became a well-known source for illicit booze. Currently, it's merely a time-warp shrine to days when California beach towns were unpretentious places meant for just goofing off. Couples and families wander around town with no agenda except to soak up the sun. There is an upscale side to all this, but it's a bit north at Shell Beach, where the newer beachfront resorts can be quite elegant.

In the 1930s and '40s, a group of freethinkers and nudists made the dunes here their home. They called themselves "Duneites" and believed Oceano Dunes was a center of cosmic creativity. They also called the area Moy Mell, a Gaelic name meaning "where the spirits dwell."

ACTIVITIES

 Clams Are King. Here is where you'll find the acclaimed Pismo clam, which reached near extinction in the mid-1980s due to overzealous harvesting. If you'd like to get your feet wet digging for bivalves, you'll need to obtain a license and follow strict guidelines. Or come for the annual Clam Festival. Held at the pier each October since 1946, the weekend celebration features a chowder cook-off, sand sculpture contest, Miss Pismo Beach pageant, and competitive clam dig.

 Beach Buggies. You can rent beach cruisers or banana bikes for running the dunes at Beach Cycle Rentals (150 Hinds Ave, Pismo Beach; 805/773-5518).

Monarchs. Those butterflies get around—you can find them hanging out in Santa Cruz, Pacific Grove, and now here in Pismo Beach. If you're here between October and March, don't miss the monarch butterfly preserve on Pacific Coast Highway in nearby Grover Beach. The brilliantly colored monarchs nest in a grove of eucalyptus and Monterey pine, where an information board tells you about their unique habits. During cold weather (below 40°F), they remain densely clustered on tree branches, but on warm days you'll see their stately orange-and-black wings fluttering throughout the area as they search for flower nectar.

The pismo clam fed the Chumash Indians here as their main food source, but the clam population has dwindled terribly in the time since. Each person can still harvest ten clams a day if the claims are at least 4½ inches across. You may have to get wet to find them, as the larger ones are found beyond the low tide line, out in the surf.

The Dunes. Near Pismo Beach—and claimed by Oceano, Grover Beach, and even inland Nipomo—lies a stretch of extraordinary sand dunes. Walk along the shifting sands at Pismo State Beach (enter at Grand Ave) or, alternatively, visit the Pacific Dunes Ranch riding stable in Oceano (1207 Silver Spur Pl; 805/489-8100); they'll outfit you with a horse to match your riding ability and send you (alone or with a guide) along their private trail to the dunes, where you can gallop along the surf's edge or just mosey around. The Pismo dunes are also the only place in California where it's legal to drive on the beach—in the specially designated Oceano Dunes State Vehicular Recreation Area (805/473-7230), accessed via a ramp from Pier Avenue in Oceano. A 5½-mile sand highway at the ocean's edge parallels the mountainous dunes; you can take the family car onto the sand highway, but the dunes themselves are off-limits to all but four-wheel-drive and all-terrain vehicles. For information on guided hikes to the dunes, contact the Dunes Center in Guadalupe (805/343-2455; Fri 2–4pm, Sat–Sun noon–4pm). Also see the Guadalupe section listing in this chapter.

Hummer Rides. If you don't have your own off-road vehicle for running the dunes, you might want to sign up for a wild hummer ride with Pacific Adventure Tours of Oceano. The 1-hour tour explores the dunes and beach in their luxury four-by-four. (805/481-9330; www.pacificadventuretours.com; every day 9am–6pm; $39 adults, $20 ages 14 and under)

Biplane Rides. You can fly over the pier, dunes, or coastline in an Open Cockpit 450 Super Stearman biplane. Banner Airways, operating out of the Oceano Airport, offers a pier and dunes tour, a pier and dunes extended tour, a coast and lighthouse tour, and others. A helmet, leather flying jacket, and goggles are provided. (805/474-6491; Wed–Mon 9am–5pm; $69–$185)

RESTAURANTS

F. MCLINTOCKS SALOON & DINING HOUSE ★

This restaurant is the granddaddy of the F. McLintocks chain, where you will always find stick-to-your-ribs ranch-style meals in an Old West setting, with their own brand of fun added to the mix. Set in a 100-year-old former farmhouse (later the local speakeasy), this informal family-friendly place offers ocean views and abundant meals. Best known for oak pit-barbecued steaks and ribs, they also feature fresh local shellfish and a few oddball selections like chicken cordon bleu and liver and onions. Every dinner starts with onion rings and salsa, then salad, and includes sides of barbecue beans, garlic bread, and fried potatoes, plus ice cream or an after-dinner liqueur. Parents are relieved to know there is a kids' menu for smaller stomachs. The staff is spirited, which you can't help but notice when a waiter stands on a chair and pours water into your glass from 8 feet up, never spilling a drop. Other surprises include a butcher shop where you can take home their tasty cuts of meat. *750 Mattie Rd, Shell Beach; 805/773-1892; $$; DIS, MC, V; local checks only; late lunch Thurs–Sun till 3pm, dinner every day; full bar; reservations accepted Sun–Thurs only; www.mclintocks.com; at Hwy 101 (Shell Beach exit).* ♿

GIUSEPPE'S CUCINA ITALIANA ★★

The enticing aroma wafting from this always-crowded standout on Pismo Beach's Italian restaurant row is enough to lure you inside. Known countywide for consistently good home-style food, generous portions, and a friendly, casual ambience, Giuseppe's can get a little boisterous, but it retains a classy touch just a notch above the usual family-style pizza joint. White linen rather than red-checked tablecloths set the stage for a menu that offers both traditional southern Italian-style fare (pizza, lasagne, veal parmigiana), and trattoria-influenced California cuisine such as peppercorn-seared ahi tuna and individual gourmet pizzas. Dinners come with soup or salad; try the "alternate" salad, butter lettuce with creamy Gorgonzola. Appropriately, given its seaside location, Giuseppe's menu includes plenty of ocean fare—favorites include an appetizer of clams stuffed with shrimp, scallops, and lox, baked in the wood-fired oven and served with aioli. *891 Price St, Pismo Beach; 805/773-2870; $$; AE, DIS, MC, V; local checks only; lunch Mon–Fri, dinner every day; full bar; no reservations; at Pismo Ave.* ♿

For information on local attractions and events, visit the Pismo Beach Chamber of Commerce (581 Dolliver St; 805/773-4382 or 800/443-7778; www.pismochamber.com).

SPLASH CAFE ★

Splash Cafe is the kind of place people can wander into with sandy feet, wearing a damp bathing suit. They come looking for a great bowl of clam chowder, and this informal place does not disappoint. While Pismo Beach is famous for clams, they aren't sold commercially, so any chowder is made with imported bivalves. Although Splash is basically a burger stand with a short menu and just a few tables, locals agree its creamy New England–style chowder is the best in town, which explains why the place makes 10,000 gallons annually. If you like, you can order it in a sourdough bread bowl. If that's not enough of a meal, the menu also includes fish and chips, hamburgers, corn dogs, hot dogs, and other sandwiches. *197 Pomeroy Ave, Pismo Beach; 805/773-4653; $; MC, V; local checks only; lunch, dinner every day; beer and wine; no reservations; www.splashcafe.com; between Pomeroy St and the pier.* ☆

If your vehicle gets stuck in the sand dunes, try this: Drop your tire pressure on all four tires to 15 to 18 psi, dig out the sand from around the tires, recruit some friends to push as you keep the front wheels straight, and don't allow your wheels to spin, as you'll only dig in deeper.

LODGINGS

THE CLIFFS AT SHELL BEACH ★★

 What it lacks in personality, this efficiently luxurious cliff-top resort hotel makes up for in comfort. The lobby is a grand marble space, and guest rooms are light and airy, somewhat formally furnished in tan and black, with a sophisticated urban feel. Each room is also outfitted with extras like hair dryers, irons, and private balconies. Ask for a room on the fourth or fifth floors, which have been totally remodeled. Poolside beverages and snack service give more reason to recline by the heated swimming pool and whirlpool, which are shielded from the wind and situated to capitalize on the bay views. The Cliffs has its own spa, so a massage is a convenient reward after a workout at the on-site fitness center. A private staircase zigzags down to a prime, albeit small, strip of sandy beach—just stay aware that high tide comes nearly to the base of the cliffs. The adjacent Sea Cliffs Restaurant features an eclectic menu of grilled meats and fish accented by international flavors (a little Caribbean here, a little Pacific Rim there) and is more formal than it ought to be considering the area, though it does have a good selection of local wines by the glass. The Sunday jazz brunch was voted the best brunch on the Central Coast by a local publication. *2757 Shell Beach Rd, Shell Beach; 805/773-5000 or 800/826-7827; $$$–$$$$; AE, DC, DIS, MC, V; no checks; www.cliffsresorts.com; north of Spyglass Dr.* ☆

COTTAGE INN BY THE SEA ★★

You might think you have wandered into a British seaside resort in Cornwall when you see this cottage-style enclave with brown half-timber construction and a rounded thatch-style roof. There's even a vine-covered wishing well. Paths wind around the several buildings on their way to the beach. This is one of the newest inns on Shell Beach, although it looks completely established. The rooms are romantic but more dignified than cloying, with reproductions of antiques, curtains with Roman shades, wallpaper with little roses, armoires, and wrought-iron beds. Each room has a fireplace, a microwave oven, coffeemaker, iron and ironing board, and a small refrigerator. Room rates are based entirely on the view, with non-view rooms beginning under $100 on weekdays. There are an inviting sundeck and a small glassed-in pool, and a spa right on the bluffs overlooking a dramatic stretch of the Pacific. The complimentary continental breakfast is served in the breakfast room or on the patio. *2351 Price St, Pismo Beach; 805/773-4617 or 888/440-8400; $–$$$; AE, DIS, DC, MC, V; no checks; www. cottage-inn.com; on Price St just off Hwy 101.* &

KON TIKI INN ★

While the Kon Tiki Inn looks from the freeway like an uninspired three-story condo hotel, in fact it is one of the most personal and friendly places to stay in Pismo Beach. From the minute you enter it's clear this is a family-owned establishment, and people care that you have a good stay. The name is a bit of a mystery. This is also the best value in town. The rooms have all had recent makeovers, with new furniture, wall coverings, and carpets. Furniture is simple, in light woods, and the beds have a sun design carved in the headboard. The new bedspreads and curtains have fish designs in either blue or green. Rooms are modest in size, yet each has an oceanfront balcony or patio, refrigerator, TV with free HBO, a convenient in-room vanity separate from the bathroom sink, and stationery on the bureau. Some rooms have fireplaces. If the weather turns raw once the sun sets, individual heaters quickly and quietly toast your room. Outside, vast lawns slope gently toward the cliffs, broken only by the wind-shielded, kidney-shaped heated swimming pool flanked by twin whirlpools. This humble hotel—which is privately owned and does no advertising—has several advantages over most along these Pismo cliffs, including a sandy beach with stairway access, lack of highway noise, and ground cover that discourages gatherings of pesky sea gulls. The adjacent Steamers oyster bar and seafood grill restaurant, managed by F. McLintocks, has just been refurbished, and hotel guests go there for their continental breakfast each morning in the Admiral's Room. *1621 Price St, Pismo Beach; 805/773-4833 or 888/KON-TIKI; $–$$; AE, DIS, MC, V; local checks only; kontiki@ kontikiinn.com; www.kontikiinn.com; 8 blocks north of the pier.* &

SEAVENTURE RESORT ★★

[View] This heavenly beachfront find is the only upscale local resort not on Shell Beach. Located right on Pismo Beach, it offers exceptional pampering without a trace of pretentiousness. Each room is decorated in a soothing blend of deep greens, with thick carpeting, white plantation-style furnishings, and a gas-burning fireplace. With the beach directly below, private balconies or decks are welcoming enough, but in addition almost all rooms have irresistible private hot tubs with soft leatherette rims. Whether the night is foggy or clear, slide into the spa tub, and the invigorating yet ethereal experience is worth the entire cost of the room—or slip into mindlessness with a rental movie from the hotel's video library. Mornings, a continental breakfast basket is delivered to your door. Another nice amenity: the free use of beach cruiser bicycles or multipassenger beach surreys. Free beach chairs and beach towels are also a plus. If you're still having problems relaxing, SeaVenture has an on-site therapeutic massage center, and the restaurant offers dinner room service and a lovely brunch. *100 Ocean View Ave, Pismo Beach; 805/773-4994 or 800/662-5545; $$–$$$$; AE, DC, DIS, MC, V; checks OK; seaventure@fix.net; www.seaventure.com; from Price or Dolliver Sts follow Ocean View Ave to the beach.* &

ARROYO GRANDE

Francisco Zeba Branch was bear hunting in 1832 when he first came across the Arroyo Grande Valley. The bears are gone, but Arroyo Grande still keeps its small-town atmosphere and Old West heritage. Visitors mainly seem drawn to the many antique stores that line Branch Street, the village's main drag, but most also stop for ice cream at Burnardo'z (114 W Branch St; 805/481-2041), an ice cream parlor with plank floors, a few wooden booths, and a model train running around overhead near the ceiling. The annual gathering that began in 1983 as a small-town ice cream social has grown into Memorial Day weekend's Strawberry Festival, which draws a quarter of a million people.

ACTIVITIES

Walking Tour. Contact the Arroyo Grande Village Improvement Association (805/473-2250; www.arroyogrande.com) for information on a self-guided walking tour of historic sites that includes the Swinging Bridge across Arroyo Grande Creek. It's worth visiting the web site just to see the swinging bridge actually swing.

Swinging Bridge. Turn off Branch Street at Short Street, park in the public lot, and you'll find a slender green metal swinging bridge spanning Arroyo Grande Creek. It sways gently as you cross. Built in 1875 by the Short family, whose property lay on both sides of Arroyo Grande Creek, the bridge is 171 feet long, hangs

VISIT ARROYO GRANDE WINERIES

Often overshadowed by the Central Coast wine regions in Paso Robles and the Santa Ynez Valley, the wineries around Arroyo Grande are slowly but surely coming into their own. Ancient volcanoes created soil rich in granite and tufa, which, combined with cooling ocean breezes, makes for a long, fruitful growing season. The Edna Valley/Arroyo Grande Valley Vintners Association (5828 Orcutt Rd, San Luis Obispo; 805/541-5868; www.thegrid.net/vintners) is an excellent source for wine country information, including a map of the wine region.

Claiborne & Churchill Winery: *Specializing in the dry Alsatian Riesling and Gewürztraminer varietals, Clay Thompson's boutique winery might be best known for its unusual straw-bale construction. Though the foot-thick walls have been stuccoed over for looks, you can peek through a "truth window" and see the straw beneath. (2649 Carpenter Canyon Rd/Hwy 227, San Luis Obispo; 805/544-4066)*

The **Edna Valley Vineyard's** *beautiful tasting room also has an impressive selection of Provençal pottery and wine-country gifts; stand at the wine bar to get the best panoramic view of the valley below. Outside are demonstration vines that illustrate the art of grape growing. (2585 Biddle Ranch Rd, San Luis Obispo; 805/544-5855; www.EdnaValley.com)*

Laetitia Vineyard & Barnwood Winery *offers superior sparkling wines, along with a selection of Burgundy-style whites. Stylish gourmet oils and specialty foods bear the Laetitia label as well. (453 Deutz Dr, Arroyo Grande; 805/481-1772)*

The **Talley Vineyard** *tasting room is an 1860 two-story adobe house atop a quiet, peaceful hill amid the grapevines of this out-of-the-way winery. Talley's Pinot Noir grapes are hand tended and aged only in French oak, resulting in a locally respected wine whose small production always sells out quickly. (3031 Lopez Dr, Arroyo Grande; 805/489-0446)*

40 feet high over the creek, and is shaded by trees. There's a small park where you can walk along a path just above the creek. Not far from the bridge are the most charming public bathrooms on the coast—their exterior is smothered in ivy.

Heritage House. The 1895 Victorian Heritage House and Museum displays photographs and artifacts from Arroyo Grande's history as farmland, railroad route, and occasional outlaw hideout. (126 S Mason St; 805/481-4126; Sat 11am–3pm, Sun 1–4pm)

Schoolhouse. On the other side of the swinging pedestrian bridge is a cheer-ful little one-room yellow schoolhouse and museum with the words "Santa Manuela 1901" just under the roofline. Inside, the museum is set up just as if the school were still open and the kids were out at recess.

Strawberry and Harvest Festivals. The annual gathering that began in 1983 as a small-town ice cream social has grown into Memorial Day weekend's Strawberry Festival (805/473-2250), which draws a quarter of a million people to locations around town for game and craft booths, music, and entertainment, plus every strawberry treat imaginable. Contact the Chamber of Commerce (805/489-1488) for more information on the Arroyo Grande Harvest Festival, which is smaller, and pure hometown. There are baby contests, artists' booths, pie-eating contests, a beauty pageant, demonstrations by the Future Farmers group, and a farmers market. (805/481-5038; www.arroyograndeharvest.org)

RESTAURANTS

THE BRANCH STREET DELI ★

You can walk in and order at the counter at this popular, friendly place, then take your goodies out to a lovely open patio. Famous for their tri-tip sandwich, they also have deli subs that include your choice of two meats and one cheese on a French roll, hot wraps, red potato salad, a chicken Caesar salad, and good sweet things such as Ghirardelli brownies and giant chocolate chip cookies. On Friday and Saturday nights in the summer they have a rollicking (but not hard rock) live band on the patio, where you can sit and eat and sip a microbrew. *203 E Branch St, Arroyo Grande; 805/489-9099; $; AE, MC, V; no checks; breakfast, lunch every day, dinner Mon–Sat; beer and wine; no reservations; Branch St at Short St.* ⚐

KLONDIKE PIZZA ★

Kids love this Alaskan-themed pizza restaurant. Free peanuts are served while you wait for your order, and you're welcome to toss the shells on the floor. Decor is heavy on Alaskan memorabilia such as moose heads, snowshoes, Eskimo art, hockey sticks, maps, and Alaskan flags. The most popular pizza is the Denali, named for a Tanaina Indian word meaning "the big one" or "the great one." There's outdoor seating, and on Saturday nights there are sing-alongs for the fam-ily. *104 Bridge St, Arroyo Grande; 805/481-5288; $; AE, DIS, MC, V; local checks only; lunch, dinner every day; beer and wine; no reservations; on Bridge St near Branch St.* ⚐

SANTA MARIA

The largest city in the region, Santa Maria is a bustling community of aerospace and farm employees, drawn by both nearby Vandenberg Air Force Base and the wealth of profitable agriculture throughout the Central Coast valleys. Although tourism has never been a big attraction, the area is famous for Santa Maria–style barbecue, the featured grub at all festive occasions, both public and private. In the early days of huge ranchos, the rancheros, the vaqueros (cowboys), and their families and friends would gather midday under the towering oaks to enjoy Spanish barbecues. The recipe is simple: sirloin tri-tip steak is seasoned with salt, pepper, and garlic, then cooked over the hot coals of a red-oak fire. The red oak is important; unlike Southern-style barbecue, which hides underneath tangy glazes, the Santa Maria variety is all about simple seasoning and the freshness of the meat, which must be served immediately after cooking. Customary accompaniments are sweet-and-spicy barbecue piquinto beans, garlic toast, salsa, and green salad.

LODGINGS

SANTA MARIA INN ★

Originally opened in 1917, the Santa Maria Inn does indeed have a historic side. One entire wing of rooms occupies the original building, as does the hotel's Garden Room restaurant, a reasonably good place completely upstaged by its vintage decor. What was formerly an outdoor promenade is now an enclosed porch, and there's also a cozy taproom. To the other side is a newer, six-story tower with oversize guest rooms, somewhat sparsely furnished. The original wing offers very small rooms (with large closets); unfortunately, all the original bathroom tile here was demolished in a careless renovation. Perhaps retaining more original detail would've been enough to make up for small space and no air-conditioning, but most guests do prefer the tower. On weekends, group events can sometimes make the place noisy with revelers in the halls and walkways. Beyond the garden lies a swimming pool and heated spa. *801 S Broadway, Santa Maria; 805/928-7777 or 800/462-4276; $$; AE, DC, DIS, MC, V; checks OK; north of Stowell Rd.* &

GUADALUPE

This small, modest, windblown town on Highway 1 is known mostly for its Rancho Guadalupe Dunes County Park, which boasts the highest dune on the West Coast. Guadalupe is also known for its Santa Maria–style barbecue (see Far West Tavern review, below).

ACTIVITIES

 Dunes Center. The Guadalupe-Nipomo Dunes Preserve spans 18 miles of the Central Coast and bills itself as "one of the last unspoiled coastal dune complexes." It's also home to over 1,400 animal and 244 plant species, and the best way to learn about them is to take an interpretive walk through the Dunes Center (1055 Guadalupe St; 805/343-2455; www.dunescenter.org; Fri–Sun noon–4pm). Topics of the walks range from the World of the Western Snowy Plover to Dune History to a Dunes Word Walk that involves pausing along the way to read poetry.

Oso Flaco Lake Natural Refuge. Among all these dry, windswept sand dunes, it seems odd to find a freshwater lake, but Oso Flaco freshwater habitat has been set aside to protect the unique life forms that inhabit the wetland and open sand communities, including endangered plants and birds such as the western snowy plover and the least tern. Dozens of species of waterfowl visit the lake each year, and willow thickets provide habitat for many other birds. An elevated walkway helps you see it all. The refuge is located in the Oceano Dunes State Vehicular Recreation Area. Reach it from the north by taking southbound Highway 101 to the Pismo Beach/Highway 1 exit, stay on Highway 1 (also known as Dolliver Ave) through the city of Pismo Beach and Oceano and continue 20 miles toward Guadalupe; watch for Oso Flaco Lake Road, and then turn right and follow the road. For more information call State Park Dispatch, 805/473-7220.

In fall of 1769, Don Gaspar de Portola and his men were the first non-natives to explore the dunes. They killed "un oso flaco" or skinny bear along the way, which gave the area its name.

RESTAURANTS

FAR WESTERN TAVERN ★

It may be out of the way, but this famous barbecue eatery has been praised in *Gourmet* magazine and on the Discovery Channel, and it's a frequent winner of the Santa Maria Style Barbecue Cook-off. Operating in a reclaimed Old West theater (whose entire lobby is now a raucous barroom), the restaurant packs 'em in for every variety of steak and chop, each given the traditional barbecue treatment and presented in a cowboy-size portion. They age their beef for over a month, and their chefs hand-cut each steak. Sirloin tri-tip, rib-eye, or New York steaks are seasoned with a dry rub of salt, pepper, garlic, and parsley, then thrown on a sizzling red oak fire until perfectly done. The specialty is the Bull's Eye Steak, a rib-eye cut. The menu also includes Alaskan king crab legs, scampi, lobster, lamb chops, and a daily pasta dish. Appetizers run the gamut from a deep-fried sweet

A THREE-DAY TOUR OF THE SOUTH CENTRAL COAST

Day One. *Get an early start at San Simeon's Hearst Castle to avoid the midday crowds. After touring this landmark, drive a bit north to enjoy lunch on the dramatic cliffs at Ragged Point Inn, followed by a leisurely afternoon walking the Bluff Trail or strolling the antique stores and boutiques of Cambria's Main Street. Have dinner by the welcoming fireplace at the Sow's Ear Cafe, then walk the path at Moonstone Beach as the sun sets. Bed down in one of Cambria's charming B&Bs, such as the Olallieberry Inn.*

Day Two. *After breakfast, head down scenic Highway 1 toward San Luis Obispo, where you can explore the historic mission and stroll the creek-side walk. Take a lunch break at the mellow Mission Grill or the eclectic and colorful Big Sky Cafe in the heart of town. When you're ready, continue to funky Pismo Beach and check into an oceanfront room at luxurious SeaVenture Resort. If the weather's nice, take a predinner stroll on the pier, perhaps stopping for a bowl of clam chowder. Or proceed directly to dinner at popular Giuseppe's Cucina Italiana.*

Day Three. *Leave the beach behind for a day of wine touring in the idyllic Santa Ynez Valley. Stop first in tiny Los Olivos for lunch provisions, then ramble leisurely from winery to winery. When you get hungry, buy a bottle of wine and enjoy the picnic grounds at a vineyard such as Gainey, Sunstone, or Zaca Mesa. Later on (perhaps after an afternoon nap), make your way to the Danish storybook town of Solvang for a relaxed dinner at Cabernet Bistro. Spend the night at the cozy Chimneysweep Inn before heading to Santa Barbara for a few days.*

tumbleweed onion to crisp mountain oysters. Breakfast here invariably involves meat, served with the classic Santa Maria sides—barbecue beans, salsa, and potatoes. The dining room would make a good Western movie set, its 19th-century saloon ambience enhanced with red velvet wallpaper, fuzzy cowhide draperies, enormous mounted steer heads, and plenty of cowboy hats. If you've got a hankering to sample the legendary Santa Maria–style barbecue, this is the place to come. Kids eat free Monday through Wednesday with each paid adult, so bring the little rancheros. *899 Guadalupe St, Guadalupe; 805/343-2211; $$; AE, DIS, MC, V; local checks only; breakfast every day, lunch Mon–Sat, dinner every day; full bar; reservations recommended; on Hwy 1 at 9th St.* &

THE SANTA BARBARA COAST

From the all-but-lost town of Los Alamos to the flower fields of Lompoc and its exquis-
itely preserved mission, to the latter-day living theme park of Danish Solvang and on
through the charming rediscovered villages of Ballard, Los Olivos, and Santa Ynez,
this region never fails to charm. Contrasts are striking: the majestic wonder of the San
Marcos Pass, the golden cities of Santa Barbara and Montecito, the beaches with fabulous surfing breaks known the world over—no wonder this coastal region is known
as one of the most magical parts of California. It was named by explorer Sebastian Vis-
caino, who discovered it on December 4, 1604, a day of remembrance here. Father
Junípero Serra, who founded missions throughout California, established the Presidio
here in 1782, and Santa Barbara Mission's founding followed in 1786. The land was
largely ranches and farms.

What Santa Barbara has that no other California coastline has is a stretch of beach
that runs east and west. The city and shoreline face south, splashed in sunshine from
dawn to dusk. The area from Point Arguello to Point Conception is called "the Corner,"
for the way it separates Southern and Central California. And in a sense, when visitors
go beyond Point Arguello, there is no question they are in Southern California. Above
here, the north-south coastline is fed by the cold, nutrient-rich Alaskan current. As with
the cities farther south, Santa Barbara's unique east-west coastline is heated by the
warm water that works its way north from Mexico.

East of the city are the peaks of the Santa Ynez Mountains. The Santa Barbara back-
country is a special place all in itself. There are deep canyons, sandstone cliffs, forested
ridges, and beautiful meadows with streams and ponds.

Contact the Santa Barbara Conference and Visitors Bureau (1601 Anacapa St,
Santa Barbara, 93101; 805/966-9222 or 800/676-1266; www.santabarbaraca.com)
and ask for a Visitors Guide and a map/visitor information brochure. When in town,
drop by the main Chamber of Commerce Visitors Center office at 1 Garden Street near
the ocean (805/965-3021) for additional maps, guides, and personal help. It's open in
summer 9am–6pm Mon–Sat, Sun 10am–5pm; winter hours are shorter.

GETTING THERE

US Highway 101 is the main artery into Santa Barbara from the north and south. As
for airlines, most of the major carriers offer service to Santa Barbara Municipal Airport (805/967-7111). Amtrak (800/872-7245) has stations and ticket offices in Carpinteria, Goleta, Guadalupe, Lompoc, Santa Barbara, Santa Maria, and Solvang. And
Greyhound Bus information is available at 800/231-2222.

LOS ALAMOS

Founded in 1876, Los Alamos became a Wells Fargo stagecoach stop in 1880 with the inauguration of the old Union Hotel. The town remained a traveler's stop and local gathering place well after the demise of the stagecoach route. When the streamlined Highway 101 was completed in the 1960s, it circumvented little Los Alamos, and now you can't even see the place from the freeway. The town reinvented itself as an authentic Old West attraction, complete with wooden boardwalks, a historic hotel and bed-and-breakfast (the restored Union Hotel and Victorian Mansion), and the Old Days festival and barbecue each September. The growth of the surrounding wine country has also helped, since many vineyards are within easy driving distance. Several antique stores have sprung up along the main drag, including the enormous Los Alamos Depot Mall (in the old Pacific Coast railroad station at the south end of town; 805/344-3315), a 17,000-square-foot warehouse with a good selection of antiques and collectibles, especially furniture. Don't be surprised to find yourself asking that all-important question, "Will it fit in the trunk?"

LODGINGS

UNION HOTEL ★
VICTORIAN MANSION ★★★

Staying in either of these fantasy lodgings may be the highlight of your trip, and will certainly give you stories to tell for years. The Union Hotel was built in 1880 as a hotel and stagecoach stop, burned down in 1893, and was not rebuilt and reopened until 1912. More than 25 years ago, it was carefully restored to its original decor, using old photographs to ensure an exact re-creation. The feeling at this wonderful wacky place is a cross between going to Grandma's house and visiting the Munsters. Climb the faded crimson-carpeted stairs to the boarding-house-style rooms upstairs, then later descend and parade into the dining room through swaths of ruby drapes, or push the swinging doors into the formerly hard-drinking Union Saloon across the lobby, where one wall is lined with old barn wood, and a moose head looms amid old tools and washboards. The bar is now open only on special occasions, as the regulars got too rowdy for guests to get much sleep. The parlor-lobby has overstuffed velvet wing chairs and a coffee table made from a claw-footed bathtub. The curved wooden reception counter has delicate Queen Anne ball-and-dowel lacy fretwork overhead. Upstairs, where well-worn carpet runners and creaky hardware reinforce the illusion of living in history, there is a library sitting area, and most of the rooms share a couple of baths (although every room is equipped with in-room sinks). A single shower room is the hotel's only concession to modernity; the few rooms with private bath have only a tub—claw-footed, of course. Even though a few antiques may be missing a part, and the paint may be bubbling up on the wall here and there, the charm of this place is truly infectious. The main reason is the current owner, Christine Williams. With a merry look in her eye and an easy laugh, she revels in the place, adding continually to the inn's collection of antiques, and planning Stagecoach Murder Mystery evenings with relish, from scripts she wrote herself—about strangers arriving on a stage. Try to book a room here on a night when one is planned, usually the last Saturday of every month. The afternoon you arrive, you can select a historic-style 1880s outfit, have it quickly fitted, and rent it for the night so you are dressed for the part—anything from dandy to retired madam. With every stay breakfast is included—a generous family-style feast of eggs, bacon, pancakes, muffins, juice, fruit, and coffee. The hotel's dining room also serves dinner on weekends; the menu always offers steaks and seafood dishes such as salmon with cucumber dill sauce. As if the Union Hotel weren't enough, next door stands the lemon-yellow Victorian Mansion, an ornate mix of Queen Anne and Victorian elements with outrageous theme rooms. Try the Roman Room, with its bed built into an oversize chariot, a hot tub reached by 8-foot-high formal marble steps suitable for an ancient temple, and a selection of gladiator movies such as *Ben Hur*, *Julius Caesar*, and *Spartacus* for the built-in VCR. "It's hard to get people to check out!" says Williams of these special rooms. Each has a fireplace, a hot tub, a chilled bottle of champagne upon arrival, and a secret door through which breakfast appears each morning. Sleep in the '50s Room and you'll bed down in a vintage Cadillac at a drive-in movie, watching *Rebel Without a Cause* and *Picnic*. You get the picture. *362 Bell St (Hwy 135), Los Alamos; 805/344-2744 or 800/230-2744; $$; (Union Hotel); $$$$; (Victorian Mansion); AE, DIS, MC, V; no checks; www.union hotelvictmansion.com; Hwy 135 at Hwy 101.*

LOMPOC

Known as the City of Murals for its local history depiction on downtown walls, this town in the fertile, flat "Valley of the Flowers" is also famous for the surrounding vast flower fields, which supply more than half the world's seeds. Since the early 1900s, flower farmers—beginning with W. Atlee Burpee, whose name would eventually grace seed packets in potting sheds throughout the world—have been cultivating flowers for seed here, and today nearly 2,000 acres of the valley floor are planted with more than 30 different kinds of blossoming plants.

Minutes from Lompoc, Vandenberg Air Force Base offers free two-hour tours every Wednesday, covering the base's rocket launch sites, Space Launch Complex 2, and a Heritage Museum full of Cold War artifacts. Call 805/606-3595 a few weeks ahead for reservations.

ACTIVITIES

Seeing the Flower Fields. It's possible to drive right between fields of flowers bursting with color during peak blooming season between May and September, acres colorful and fragrant with sweet peas, larkspur, petunias, delphiniums, asters, marigolds, and zinnias. Take Highway 1 South, turn west on Ocean Avenue to Bailey, then right on Bailey to Central Avenue. Continue weaving your way back and forth past the fields, between Central and Ocean Avenues. Union Sugar Road is the last road through the fields before returning to town. The Lompoc Chamber of Commerce (111 S "I" St; 805/736-4567 or 800/240-0999; www.lompoc.com) publishes a map to guide you to the various fields and to a designated Observation Point in town that offers a panoramic look at the patchwork valley floor. In June the annual Lompoc Valley Flower Festival (805/735-8511) begins with a colorful downtown parade and continues with many bus tours through acres of brilliant blooms. (You can also follow a self-guided tour.) Festivities continue with a carnival, flower show, arts and crafts fair, and more.

Murals Project. While you're in Lompoc it's worth admiring the results of the Lompoc Murals Project, an ongoing effort in which enormous murals depicting Lompoc's heritage and natural history have been executed on building extensions scattered through downtown. Often painted by nationally renowned muralists, these public works of art currently number around 40. The titles of murals include *The Flower Industry*, *The History of Agriculture*, a *Salute to Aerospace and Nearby Vandenberg Air Force Base*, and the *Great Lompoc Gold Rush*. A two-block stretch of buildings in Old Town is known as "Mural Alley." For a map and guide to each mural's subject matter, contact the Chamber of Commerce (111 S "I" St; 805/736-4567).

The Best-Restored Mission. The chain of missions begun by Father Junípero Serra while this region was under Spanish rule were built a day's horseback ride apart, partly to secure the area for Spain and partly to claim it for God. Lompoc's Mission La Purisima (2295 Purisima Rd; 805/733-3713; open every day 9am–5pm; $2 per car) is widely accepted as the best restored and most educational surviving example of these 18th-century colonial outposts. Founded in 1787 along El Camino Real (aka the Royal Road), the original Spanish road from Mexico, La Purisima had literally melted from neglect and the elements until it was completely reconstructed by the state and the Civilian Conservation Corps in the 1930s from adobe bricks made in the old manner. Even the plants are native and might have grown here during the mission era. Woolly brown sheep, long-horned cattle, and drying cowhides slung over a wooden rack all show what life was like for the padres and their Indian charges. The brick and stone vats with ovens underneath for rendering tallow stand in testimony to how the mission survived financially. Guided tours are given daily at 10am and 1pm.

From March through September, Mission La Purisima hosts monthly Mission Life Days, when costumed docents provide a living history lesson in tortilla baking, candle dipping, soap making, and other once-essential chores. Many schoolchildren visit then, but it's a magical time for anyone to experience this outpost, so just gaze over the heads of the kids and imagine life before highways and cell phones.

BUELLTON

Buellton, a small stop on Highway 101, is famous mainly for its pea soup but also for a couple of other, newer curiosities. Except for the ubiquitous billboards touting the trademark green concoction, you might blink and miss it. Many motorists make this a highway rest stop on the way to a larger town or take this exit to reach the Danish fantasy town of Solvang or the Los Olivos wine country, both roughly five minutes away.

ACTIVITIES

Ostrichland. Driving along Highway 246, accustomed to seeing cattle in the fields, motorists can find it a neck-jerking surprise to see real ostriches demonstrating their spastic stride and grazing in the distance on grasslands as far as the eye can see. Soon you come to the unassuming Ostrichland headquarters, consisting of a shed like a fruit stand and a pen of emus, a must-see stop. Maybe it's the chance to feed the friendly emus (in the ostrich family but smaller) with food from a dispenser for a quarter, or perhaps it's the chance to buy a deep green emu egg or a fresh ostrich egg, which scrambles up equivalent to two dozen chicken eggs, or score some frozen ostrich meat, a low-fat protein source. Or maybe it's the chance to watch the ostriches roam beyond a Cyclone fence in the near distance. Whatever the attraction, it's irresistible, especially for children. There usually aren't any adult ostriches kept within reaching distance of visitors because ostriches love jewelry and are wont to reach over and pluck your earrings or necklace right off your body—you might even lose your diamond nose stud. Disneyland it's not, but it's the kind of old-fashioned classic roadside attraction that is disappearing in the state.

Just west of Buellton lies the new wine-growing appellation Sta. Rita Hills, with 19 vineyards and 4 wineries. At Babcock Winery & Vineyards take the Discovery Tour, which includes an overview of the vineyard and cellar, barrel or vertical tasting, and sips of current releases on the estate vineyards (805/736-1455).

RESTAURANTS

THE HITCHING POST ★

Would you believe the *New York Times* and *Gourmet* magazine have blessed this steak house in the middle of nowhere, calling it one of the best in the country? Looking for all the world like an ordinary roadhouse, it offers oak-fired barbecue steaks, lamb, pork, turkey, seafood, and smoked duck, not to mention grilled artichokes with smoked tomato mayonnaise. These robust meals are served with the restaurant's own label of Pinot Noir, made and bottled at Au Bon Climat/ Qupe wineries. The bar also functions as a tasting room for house-produced wines. The restaurant is dark and rustic, a real man's kind of place, with photographs of real and would-be cowboys on a trail ride in the 1940s. Owner Frank Ostini's family has been in the business of serving up Santa Maria–style grilled meats since they bought the original Hitching Post in Casmalia, the year he was born—50 years ago. His brothers now run that one. Frank has had the Buellton version, which he thinks of as "Hitching Post 2," for 15 years. If you get hooked on the steaks you can later order and have them sent to you, seasoned and already grilled, on two-days' notice. The staff cooks them rare, packs them up, and ships them overnight, with instructions on how to reheat them. *406 E Hwy 246, Buellton; 805/688-0676; $$; AE, MC, V; checks OK; dinner every day; full bar; reservations recommended; on Hwy 246, east of Buellton.* ♿

PEA SOUP ANDERSEN'S

For some, pea soup is an acquired taste, but it's worth a try here in this virtual shrine to the dish. Opened in 1924 by Anton and Juliette Andersen as a little roadside cafe, the original restaurant was called Andersen's Electrical Cafe in honor of its newfangled electric range, but it was soon renamed for Juliette's specialty, which was gaining statewide popularity. And what about those trademark pea splitters? The cartoon pair of workmen wielding hammer and chisel were originally drawn for a magazine feature depicting "little-known occupations," but were licensed to Andersen's in 1946. You can pose outside the chain's original restaurant with your face filling a carnival-style life-size wooden cutout of one of the two for a photo (kids love this). Except for a rambling souvenir and foodstuffs gift shop and a bakery counter, Andersen's itself is simply a familiar coffeeshop kind of place where split pea soup is always on the menu. *376 Avenue of the Flags, Buellton; 805/688-5581; $; AE, MC, V; no checks; breakfast, lunch, dinner every day; full bar; no reservations; splitpea@silcom.com; www.silcom.com/~splitpea; at Hwy 246.* ♿

SOLVANG

You can get more information on the area by picking up a glossy Destination Guide at the Solvang Visitor Bureau (1511-A Mission Dr; 805/688-6144 or 800/GO-SOLVANG; www.solvang usa.com).

While this all-Danish town looks like a facade, it isn't. It was settled by Danes who moved here from Michigan, many of them dairy farmers, and the values are still homespun Danish, even as the town has evolved into a tourist mecca. The town fathers decided to capitalize on their Danish roots more than 50 years ago, and gradually another and another house or business was built in the Danish style, eventually stirring interest from future visitors. In what is now one of the state's most popular tourist stops, everything that can be Danish is Danish: The houses have half-timber construction, leaded windows, and thatched or copper roofs. You've never seen so many windmills, cobblestone streets, and wooden shoes or so much gingerbread trim. You'll come to appreciate the fastidiousness, though—the public rest rooms are in charming structures that look like small cottages, and they're spotless. As you walk the town, look up to see statues of storks gracing many rooftops, a sign of good luck. At night, the village truly does radiate a storybook charm, as twinkling lights in the trees illuminate sidewalks free of the midday throngs.

ACTIVITIES

Around Town. Solvang is a great walking town, so park the car and stroll to make sure you don't miss any bakeries or gift shops. Or hop aboard the 1915 replica street trolley car—called a honen in Danish—pulled by two huge goodnatured palomino Belgian draft horses, that makes a regular loop through town during the summer and on weekends. Or you might prefer to pedal your way around town in one of Surrey Cycles' fringe-top surries, which accommodate from 2 to 11 people. They also have tandem bikes and tow cycles, and mountain bikes for exploring the surrounding hills and wine country—pick up a winery map from them before you go. (475 First St, #8, behind the park; 805/688-0091)

Danish Museums. Solvang (whose name means "sunny field") offers pleasant lessons in Danish history, which you can learn with a quick visit to the small Elverhoj Museum (1624 Elverhoj Wy; 805/686-1211; open 1–4pm Weds–Sun). Set in a traditional handcrafted Scandinavian-style home, the museum consists of fully furnished typical Danish rooms and artifacts from Solvang's early days. Most intriguing are promotional pamphlets distributed in Nebraska and Iowa nearly 100 years ago to lure more Danes to sunny California. In the center of town, upstairs from the Book Loft and Kaffe Hus, you'll find the Hans Christian Andersen Museum (1680 Mission Dr; 805/688-2052; open 10am–5pm every day). The gallery is filled with memorabilia pertaining to the rather lonely Andersen, father of the modern fairy tale and Danish national hero. In addition to rare and first editions of his works and prints of book illustrations, the displays include manuscripts, letters, photographs, and a replica Gutenberg printing press.

Walk to a Waterfall. Drive south of Solvang on Alisal Road for roughly 3 miles and find beautiful Nojoqui Park, where you can follow the signs to the trailhead, then walk along a shady wooded path to Nojoqui Falls. It's an easy hike, under half a mile each way, so even those in less than perfect shape can do it easily. For information check out the park's web site at www.sbparks.com.

Shopping. Although many of the shops here have items that are Scandinavian or Danish in flavor but made in China, there are a few places to find authentic Danish collectibles and crafts. Gaveaesken (433 Alisal Rd, Ste F; 805/686-5699), which means "gift box" in Danish, is one of the nicest, selling Danish glass and pottery, table linens, and colorful cardboard mobiles—delicate handmade cutouts of farm and flower scenes, crafted in Denmark. While not everything here is Danish, owner Marianne Larsen shows great taste in the collectibles, teapots, vases, and other fine gift items she offers. For antiques, head for the Solvang Antique Center (486 1st St; 805/686-2322), which has silver, clocks, jewelry, and thousands more fine objects from 65 antique dealers, in 7,000 square feet of space. If you fall in love with those pristine blue Danish dresses with sparkling white pinafore aprons that many of the women in shops and restaurants wear, drop in at Elna's Dress Shop (1673 Copenhagen Dr; 805/688-4525; www.elnas.com), where in addition to selling nice conservative women's clothes, they offer handmade Danish costumes for children and women, available in five colors. They ship anywhere.

Theater Under the Stars. Each summer the Pacific Conservatory of Performing Arts (805/922-8313; www.pcpa.org) produces several plays for an audience relaxing in tiers of seats under the stars. The five performances in the selection usually include musicals and dramas. Several restaurants will make up a picnic to take along and enjoy while sitting on the grass before the show begins. Productions are at the 720-seat amphitheater on the east side of Second Street, to the north of Molle Way.

Danish Days and Other Festivals. Danish Days (805/688-6144) is the title of a three-day festival of Old World customs and pageantry held during September. There's a parade, demonstrations of traditional Danish arts, dancing by the Solvang Dancers, and a raffle to win a trip to Denmark. Of course, plenty of *aebleskiver* (Danish apple fritters) are served up along with the fun. February's Flying Leap Storytelling Festival (805/688-9533) grows in popularity each year, featuring everything from nationally renowned storytellers to local folks swapping impromptu tales in the park or ghost stories in the school barn.

Mission Bells amid Windmills. On the edge of town on Alisal Road is a historic building without windmills, roof storks, or other Danish frills—the Spanish Mission Santa Ines (1760 Mission Dr; 805/688-4815; www.oldmission@santa ines.org), built of adobe by Native Americans in 1804, destroyed by the earthquake of 1812, partially rebuilt, and then burned in 1824 in a violent Native American revolt. Santa Ines never regained its initial prosperity or its harmonious existence. Today little of the original mission remains, but the structures you see painstakingly replicate the originals. The chapel, still in use for daily services, features the ornate painting and tile work typical of Spanish missions. The grounds also include the well-restored and well-maintained monks' garden. A self-guided tour costs $3; pick up the brochure and pay in the gift shop.

Wine Tasting the Easy Way. If you want to taste wines on your stroll around Solvang and not worry about sipping and driving, there are two in-town wine-tasting emporiums. Wine Country (1539 Mission Dr; 805/686-9699) is a tasting room featuring bottlings from over 75 Central Coast wineries, many of which do not have their own tasting rooms. Stop in here to sip and buy or pick up a wine trail map for visiting other wineries later. They also have wine-related gifts and premium cigars. The Plam Vineyards–Mission Meadow Winery tasting room (Copenhagen Dr and 1st St; 800/978-PLAM; www.plam.com) offers tastings of their current Napa Valley wines and in 2003 expects to open a wine-tasting facility in their new Mission Meadow Winery vineyard near Solvang.

RESTAURANTS

BIT O' DENMARK ★

It's nearly impossible to visit Solvang without sampling the Danish fare that traditionally fills the groaning smorgasbord table, and Bit o' Denmark has the freshest and highest-quality spread around. It's the oldest restaurant in town, housed in Solvang's oldest building. Constructed in 1911, the two-story wood-frame structure served first as a college and later as a church before it welcomed its first diners in 1929. Inside, pleasant farmhouse tables are scattered throughout, and collections of blue-and-white china adorn every wall. The traditional all-you-can-eat smorgasbord (offered at both lunch and dinner) includes red cabbage, roast pork, mashed potatoes, Danish salami, gravlax, marinated herring, pumpernickel, boiled eggs, salads, Jell-O molds, and more. The regular menu includes Scandinavian fare such as roast beef with red cabbage and applesauce and *frikadeller* (Danish meatballs), sautéed golden and drenched in brown gravy. At breakfast (weekends only) you'll enjoy Solvang's famous *aebleskiver*—apple dumplings baked in an aebleskiver pan, turned with a knitting needle, and served with powdered sugar and raspberry jam. Casual and convenient, Bit o' Denmark is sometimes too popular—in other words, expect crowds when tour buses are parked outside the front door. *473 Alisal Rd, Solvang; 805/688-5426; $$; AE, DIS, MC, V; no checks; breakfast Sat–Sun, lunch, dinner every day; full bar; reservations recommended; between Copenhagen and Mission Drs.* &

CABERNET BISTRO ★★

This little pocket of France will delight gourmets. Chef/owner Jacques Toulet comes from a family of restaurateurs in the Pyrenees. He developed a fine reputation in Los Angeles when he and his brother opened their own restaurant, Les Pyrenees, in Santa Monica in the 1970s. A few years ago Jacques and his wife, Diana, moved to the Santa Ynez Valley and opened Cabernet Bistro. Open beams, antiques, and light pink tablecloths make the dining room elegant but relaxed. The menu offers veal Escoffier with morel mushrooms, T-bone steak, and fresh swordfish, as well as quail and rack of lamb. The signature dish is duck; you can order duck à l'orange, duck amaretto, duck with peppercorn sauce, duck with cherries, and duck cassis, and those aren't the only duck options. In fact, they sell 2,000 orders of duck a year, even in this town known for Danish pancakes. For dessert order the creamy almond praline cake, invented by Jacques for Diana on their wedding anniversary. *478 4th Pl at Copenhagen Dr, Solvang; 805/693-1152; $$–$$$; AE, DIS, MC, V; no checks; dinner Thurs–Tues; beer and wine; reservations recommended; www.cabernetbistro.com.* &

CAFE ANGELICA ★

If you ask local residents of Solvang where to have dinner, they're likely to recommend Cafe Angelica, and it's no wonder. This casually elegant place (blessedly un-Danish in decor) has fine Mediterranean food, and it's located in the middle of everything, close enough to the outdoor theater to have dinner here first and stroll over just before the play begins. Inside, there are tile floors, simple tables and chairs, and white linens. The menu's leanings are Italian, with such dishes as chicken marsala, various pastas, and garlic used liberally throughout. The house specialty, chicken Angelica—a chicken breast stuffed with blue cheese, pine nuts, and sun-dried tomatoes—is terrific. Owner Sean McCoy says they have only a tiny freezer, as produce and meats are brought in fresh every day. If you don't want a whole meal, you can eat à la carte or even just a salad if you like, or sit outside and have a glass of wine. It can in fact be a bit warm inside when the restaurant is full, and the breeze on the patio is pleasant, although the view of the driveway and the sidewalk is not terribly scenic. The McCoys also own the Ballard Store Restaurant in nearby Ballard. *490 1st St, Solvang; 805/686-9970; $$–$$$; AE, MC, V; local checks OK; lunch, dinner every day; beer and wine; reservations recommended (especially on theater nights); on 1st St at Mission Dr.* &

PAULA'S PANCAKE HOUSE ★

There's often a wait, but the line goes quickly at this popular eatery. The breakfast menu includes Danish sausage and eggs and wafer-thin Danish pancakes served plain and simple, sweet and fruity. Buttermilk and whole-wheat honey pancakes can be topped with fresh fruit or chopped pecans. Paula's French toast is made with dense sourdough bread. There's every omelet you can imagine, plus egg dishes served with country or Danish sausage. Paula's, friendly and casual, is right on Solvang's busiest street, so you can eat on the patio and watch the world go by. Breakfast is served all day, and there's also a lunch menu with burgers, sandwiches, homemade soups, and Santa Maria–style chili with ham, all of which go down smoothly with an ice-cold beer. Champagne is also available to turn any breakfast into a mind-tingling mimosa morning. *1531 Mission Dr, Solvang; 805/688-2867; $; AE, DIS, MC, V; local checks only; breakfast, lunch every day; beer and wine; no reservations; at 4th Pl.* &

LODGINGS

ALISAL GUEST RANCH & RESORT ★★

Families love this old-time upscale ranch resort. Part of a working cattle ranch, the rustic yet quietly posh retreat is ideal for anyone who wants an Old West–style vacation. But you certainly won't be asked to pitch hay or groom horses—it might interfere with your golf game, guided horseback ride, or poolside lounging. Alisal is Spanish for "alder grove," and the ranch is nestled in a vast, tree-shaded canyon, offering 73 guest cottages, some simple and others fancier, equipped with wood-burning fireplaces, refrigerators, and covered brick porches ideal for sitting and soaking up the scenery. There aren't any in-room TVs or phones to spoil the serenity, but restless visitors will never tire of the resort activities, which include hiking trails, tennis, croquet, bicycling, and fishing in the Alisal's private lake, where sailboats, pedal boats, and canoes sit ready for use. Guests typically are nearly all families, and parents can pursue their interests while the kids participate in crafts lessons, swim in the pool, boat on the lake, or take guided horseback trail rides. There is even an adults-only lounge to retreat to, with a computer hookup and a big-screen TV. Wildlife abounds on the ranch's 10,000 acres, so don't be surprised to see eagles, hawks, deer, coyotes, and mountain lions. Golf here is top-notch, with two championship 18-hole courses, both offering impeccably maintained fairways accented by mature oak, sycamore, and eucalyptus trees. The River Course, also open to the public, winds along the Santa Ynez River and offers spectacular mountain vistas. Resident PGA and LPGA pros are on hand for instruction. As if a visit here weren't sybaritic enough, breakfast and dinner, featuring fresh local ingredients and a wide range of choices, are included, and during the day a poolside snack bar and a golf-course grill make it entirely possible to never leave this peaceful getaway. Most people don't. In the evening the upscale ranch-style Oak Room lounge features live entertainment in a comfortable setting. *1054 Alisal Rd, Solvang; 805/688-6411 or 800/4-ALISAL; $$$$; AE, MC, V; checks OK; info@alisal.com; www.alisal.com; 3 miles south of Mission Dr.* &

CHIMNEY SWEEP INN ★★

This half-timber inn and its cottages set in a storybook garden with little bridges could force anyone to say "Awww!" It also happens to be one of the best values in town if you choose a room in the main lodge, especially during the week. Rooms are each decorated differently but some have four-poster, coaster, or canopy beds, a wing chair, and fresh print fabrics. All have real charm. There are also cable TVs and in-room coffeemakers. Lodge guests can use the gazebo-covered hot tub with patio and rock fireplace adjacent to the courtyard. The clock tower has fireplace rooms and suites, in a price range in between the lodge and the cottages. The fairy-tale cottages are like little homes and feature private spa and patio, kitchen, living room with fireplace, king bed with a down comforter, and proximity to the charming garden courtyard interlaced with winding streams and paths. The inn is in the middle of the town, surrounded by Danish bakeries, restaurants, museums, and shops, but as it's off the main drag of Mission Drive, it is quieter than some Solvang hotels. *1564 Copenhagen Dr, Solvang; 805/688-2111 or 800/824-6444; $–$$$$; AE, DIS, MC, V; chmny@silcom.com, www.chimney sweepinn.com; between Atterdag Rd and 4th St.*

INN AT PETERSEN VILLAGE ★

Prominent on Mission Drive, anchoring a small plaza of shops, cafes, and cobblestone paths, this boutique inn eschews ubiquitous Danish kitsch in favor of a more elegant Old World style. Mahogany lines the lobby and hallways, rich carpeting muffles the passing of tour groups, and strategically placed antiques lend

a touch of class. Each of the 39 rooms is different, but all are decorated in a sub-
dued country motif with print wallpaper, canopy beds, and high-quality antique
reproductions. Some overlook the bustling courtyard, while others face the scenic hills. The smaller rooms have private balconies, and the more spacious ones
have noisier outlooks. But it's the impressive little touches that set this hotel
apart: bathroom lights on a dimmer switch, lighted magnifying mirrors, and free
coffee/tea service in your room. You also get wine and hors d'oeuvres each
evening and complimentary desserts while a pianist tickles the ivories in the
piano lounge. The reasonable rates here include a generous breakfast buffet.
*1576 Mission Dr, Solvang; 805/688-3121 or 800/321-8985; $$; AE, MC, V; no checks;
www.peterseninn.com; just east of 4th Pl.* &

ROYAL SCANDINAVIAN INN ★★

Solvang's largest hostelry is this full-service hotel neatly tucked away from the
town's congested main drag, close to the mission. Attractive and recently redec-
orated, the Royal Scandinavian's lobby is rich with deep jewel colors and used
brick and wood-paneled walls. Rooms have also been updated, and there is a
recently added fitness center. Guest rooms are furnished in vaguely Danish coun-
try decor, and all areas are kept trim and scrupulously clean. Most rooms look
out onto the lovely Santa Ynez Valley and the hills beyond; some have private bal-
conies overlooking the courtyard and a beautifully landscaped and maintained
heated swimming pool and whirlpool. There's an all-day restaurant and a cock-
tail lounge. The hotel is within easy walking distance of village attractions, and
it offers some terrific golf and breakfast packages featuring play at the nearby
Alisal River Course. The inn is popular with convention and tour groups, so it
can be fully booked at times. *400 Alisal Rd, Solvang; 805/688-8000 or 800/624-
5572; $$; AE, DC, DIS, JCB, MC, V; checks OK; sroyal@silcom.com; www.solvang
rsi.com; between Mission Dr and Oak St.* &

BALLARD

You won't have to ask yourself "Are we there yet?" when you get to Ballard. On the
drive to this tiny hamlet situated midway between Los Olivos and Solvang, you'll be
charmed by the sight of the Quick Silver Horse Ranch with its miniature Shetland
ponies gamboling about in pastures along Alamo Pintado Road. The smallest town in
the region has a main street roughly a block long; once you arrive, look to one side of
the block at the popular Ballard Store restaurant, and to the other to see the Ballard
Inn. Go about a block in either direction and you'll find Ballard's other two treasures:
the Ballard School (School St between Cottonwood and Lewis Sts) is an archetypal "little red schoolhouse" with a wooden steeple accented by white gingerbread trim. Built

in 1883, it's been in continuous use and is now a kindergarten; Ballard youngsters spill out the front door, *Little House on the Prairie*–style, at morning recess. And Mattei's Tavern, an old stagecoach stop near Route 246, doesn't look as if it's missed a beat—or changed too much—in the last century.

RESTAURANTS

THE BALLARD STORE ★★

The refined sleek exterior of this building lit with oversize coach lamps gives no clue that it was once a general store. Built in 1939, the former market/gas station was purchased in 1971 by John and Alice Elliott, who began serving French/continental cuisine to a farming community unaccustomed to such gentility. It rapidly gained a fine reputation, and when they retired in 2000, after 30 years, its loss was greatly mourned. Happily, Sean and Danielle McCoy, owners of Cafe Angelica in Solvang, bought it early the next year, and after some renovations reopened it for dinner and Sunday brunch. The interior is slightly formal, with open beams, high-back chairs, and the refined ambience of a place where dining is an event. There are large fireplaces in both the restaurant and the bar. Chef Dennis Everett serves regional and European fine cuisine, including bouillabaisse, rack of lamb, grilled steaks, and fresh seafood. Starters often include baked artichoke hearts and oysters Rockefeller; among the entrees are New York steak, filet mignon, macadamia-crusted halibut fillet with kiwi-Chardonnay sauce, and veal marsala. They are able to flambé just about anything at tableside, and they do, including spinach sea scallop flambé and bananas Foster. The roving martini cart is famous; it rolls right to your table and the server makes your martini to order as you watch.

The McCoys recently opened their Cottage Caffe, a coffeehouse adjacent to the restaurant, serving coffee drinks, scones, and other breakfast goodies, and lunch items such as the famous Ballard Store homemade soups, salads, and sandwiches. Families will love the enclosed play area for children. *2449 Baseline Ave, Ballard; 805/688-5319; $$–$$$; AE, MC, V; local checks only; dinner Tues–Sun, brunch Sun; full bar; reservations recommended; on Baseline Rd just off Hwy 246, east of Alamo Pintado Rd.* &

LODGINGS

THE BALLARD INN ★★★

It wouldn't be surprising if this old-fashioned-looking inn with its welcoming porch popped up as a backdrop on a Country Time lemonade commercial; it's that folksy looking. Actually, the two-story gray and white inn was built less than

10 years ago. Country details abound, from the wicker rocking chairs that decorate the inn's wraparound porch to the white picket fence and the carefully tended rosebushes. Inside, there is usually a fire warming the giant hearth that serves both the lobby and the inn's restaurant. The downstairs public rooms, including an enormous, sunny parlor, are furnished with a comfortable mix of antiques and reproductions, hand-hooked rugs, bent-twig furniture, and vintage accessories. Upstairs, each guest room is decorated according to a theme from the valley's history or geography. Some have fireplaces and/or private balconies. The Farmhouse Room has a quilt depicting country folk and cabins, leafy stenciling near the ceiling, country pine furniture, and a wing chair, with a deep blue-green carpet like a grassy field. Wall decor runs to pitchforks and scythes. The most romantic room is the Green Room, where the bed's painted headboard has a depiction of the balcony scene from *Romeo and Juliet*. The best (and most expensive) is the Mountain Room, a minisuite decorated in rich forest green, with a fireplace and a private balcony. Included in the rate are a gracious wine and hors d'oeuvres reception each afternoon, evening coffee and tea, and a delicious full breakfast each morning; be forewarned, however, that a 10 percent service charge for the staff is added to your bill. Cafe Chardonnay is the inn's own restaurant, tucked into a cozy room downstairs by a crackling fire. The short, often inspired menu can include grilled meats, seafood pastas, and catch-of-the-day specials. Dinner might start with baked goat cheese salad garnished with kalamata olives, move on to roasted and grilled prime rib of pork with a glaze of caramelized shallots and port wine sauce, and end with a chocolate raspberry crème brûlée. *2436 Baseline Ave, Ballard; 805/688-7770 or 800/638-2466; $$$–$$$$; AE, MC, V; checks OK; innkeeper@ballardinn.com; www.ballardinn.com; just east of Alamo Pintado Rd.* &

LOS OLIVOS

While at first glance this looks like a typical small Western town, look again. Los Olivos is a town that wants to keep its country bones but also has a world-class spa, restaurants that appear in *Gourmet* magazine, an inn that attracts the most famous faces in Hollywood and the bodies to go with them, and galleries that sell paintings by artists whose work also sells in New York. Still, Los Olivos runs for only three blocks, and it has no stoplight, just a flagpole with a kind of steering wheel at eye level. A couple of the restaurants are engagingly informal, and a wooden boardwalk

The third Saturday in August of every year Los Olivos has a Quick Draw and art auction, where well-known artists shown in local galleries race the clock to complete a drawing, painting, or sculpture in 45 minutes; then the artworks are auctioned off. It's followed by a barbecue in the park (805/688-1222).

does contribute to a mild Wild West atmosphere. Although this tiny dot on the map has starred as a backward Southern hamlet in such TV shows as *Return to Mayberry*, Los Olivos sits squarely at the heart of the local wine country—and it boasts all the upscale sophistication you'd expect from a place that attracts big-city transplants and cosmopolitan tourists. Next to wine touring and dining, the favorite pastime here is shopping.

ACTIVITIES

Buying Art and More. Los Olivos has more than its share of art galleries and antique shops. Call ahead to one of the galleries to see if there will be an opening, which here typically spills out into courtyards and gardens and boardwalk. Gallery Los Olivos (2920 Grand Ave; 805/688-7517) is for serious collectors of regional artists; Judith Hale Gallery—actually two galleries (2890 and 2884 Grand Ave; 805/688-1222)—showcases a wide range of paintings and Navajo crafted silver jewelry; and Persnickity (2900 Grand Ave; 805/686-8955) is a darling niche filled with antique linens and laces, bath products, and pillows.

RESTAURANTS

LOS OLIVOS CAFE ★

This bustling and informal cafe has seating inside or on its trellis-shaded wooden porch. Inside, the simple cafe resembles an Italian country kitchen. Lunch consists mainly of Greek, Chinese, or curried chicken salads and Mediterranean sandwiches prepared in the gourmet deli (also a great place for buying a picnic lunch). Favorites include the smoked turkey on a roasted baguette with oven-dried tomatoes, radicchio, and creamy aioli and a roasted vegetable sandwich with a smoky undertone that calls out for a glass of wine. At dinner the short menu consists of chicken (marsala, piccata, cacciatore, or parmigiana); several light and savory pastas such as linguine al pesto or puttanesca Milano—linguine with tomatoes, capers, kalamata olives, and garlic; and specialty pizzas such as the Santorini, with roasted eggplant, red peppers, feta, and garlic on a pesto base. You can't go wrong by starting with the roasted vegetable appetizer served with smoked mozzarella and olive tapenade. Always packed at lunch, Los Olivos Cafe is also a pleasantly casual place for dinner. The wonderful wine list features only local wines, from wineries such as Babcock, Fess Parker, Buttonwood, and Firestone: you can choose from 26 local reds and 18 whites. *2879 Grand Ave, Los Olivos; 805/688-7265; $; DIS, MC, V; local checks only; lunch, dinner every day; beer and wine; reservations recommended; www.los olivoscafe.com; south of Alamo Pintado Ave.* ♿

MATTEI'S TAVERN ★

There are no pretensions here. Italian-Swiss immigrant Felix Mattei built this roadside hostelry and tavern in 1886 to accommodate travelers who had arrived in Los Olivos by narrow-gauge train and were preparing for the mountainous journey to Santa Barbara via stagecoach. Today the rambling white Victorian, submerged in wisteria, has successfully retained its historic charm, even to the door handle, which wobbles so that it seems it might come off in your hand. You can still make out the words "Santa Barbara Stage Office" in faded gilt paint over one door. The tavern stopped accepting overnight guests in the 1960s, and Mattei's is well known throughout the county for rollicking fun and good food. Choose to eat in the Mattei family's formal dining room with its red wallpaper and large chandelier, on the white-wicker enclosed sun porch, or inside the former water tower, looking up through the skylight at nesting owls atop the structure. The green checked tablecloths and warm welcome at the door make this a down-home kind of place. The straight-talking menu is American with some savvy twists, such as *boeuf camouflage*, described as "a really good beef stew made with prime top sirloin. . . . We don't always have it, but if we do you should order it." The Fettuccine Mattei comes with sun-dried tomatoes, Parmesan, pesto, and pine nuts, and the signature soup is a dill-tinged tomato bisque. On Friday and Saturday nights, Mattei's famous prime rib is served. Dinners, all of which are generous, include soup or salad and sides. *Hwy 154, Los Olivos; 805/688-4820; $$; MC, V; local checks only; dinner Weds–Sun; full bar; reservations recommended; west of Grand Ave.* ♿

Wilderness art by artists who have drawn or painted out in the wild is shown at the Wildling Art Museum in Los Olivos (2329 Jonata St, behind Mattei's Tavern; 805/688-1082). It has changing exhibitions and activities relating to art and nature.

PANINO ★★

For the best gourmet sandwiches in the wine country, head to this charming little cafe just a stone's throw from the flagpole that marks the center of Los Olivos. You can dine at simple bistro tables on the garden patio (cooled by a fine mist during the hotter months) or pack an upscale picnic lunch for a day of wine touring, bicycling, or boating. Choose from 31 sandwiches—all served on fresh-baked Italian-style breads—including grilled chicken with sun-dried tomatoes, fresh basil, and provolone; Genoa salami with kalamata-olive tapenade, basil, and roasted red peppers; smoked salmon with Caprino goat cheese, capers, and olive oil; or English Stilton with Asian pear on fresh walnut bread. Several Mediterranean salads are also available, and the shop is great at arranging easy-to-carry box lunches complete with all the necessary utensils. *2900 Grand Ave,*

Los Olivos; 805/688-9304; $; no credit cards; checks OK; lunch every day; beer and wine; no reservations; at Alamo Pintado Ave. &

LODGINGS

FESS PARKER'S WINE COUNTRY INN & SPA ★★★

What is it about wearing a coonskin cap that gives a person impeccable taste for the rest of his life? It's a mystery, but Fess Parker, who appeared weekly on television in the 1950s as Davy Crockett, soon found a higher calling: creating exquisite resorts and high-end restaurants. His finest effort is this wine country inn and spa in Los Olivos. It's tiny by most standards—only 21 rooms—but Parker knows that small and exclusive counts. A favorite retreat of Hollywood luminaries, the inn is tucked into the streetscape on both sides of Grand Avenue in two attractive complexes. Just up the street, the inn's Spa Vigne provides state-of-the-art pampering with treatments such as a Harvest Crush Body Polish. Fess and Marcella Parker developed and operate the inn as a team, and their civility and grace permeate the place. Each of the spacious guest rooms (Room 18 is 17 by 23 feet) has recently been redecorated by Marcella in fine fabrics and clear colors, down to different linens and towels chosen to fit each room's decor. Each has a fireplace, oversize bathroom (some have whirlpool tubs), wet bar, and cozy down comforter. Staying in the main building makes you feel more like a country-house guest, but the annex across the street has easier access to the heated outdoor swimming pool and whirlpool. A warm lobby/sitting room welcomes guests with its fire roaring in the main hearth; there's also a quiet cocktail lounge and a pretty back garden often used for weddings or small luncheons. The inn's restaurant, the Vintage Room, is open to the public and has a new chef, Kurt Alldredge, who insists on using local produce, which he hand-picks himself. The menu changes daily depending on what is at its peak, although the selection usually includes a few of the Parkers' favorite dishes, such as Marcella's Deviled Crab, and at breakfast, buttermilk pancakes, which Alldredge serves with a bit of vanilla whipped cream and a perfect small peach, in season. The restaurant's decor is elegant but comfortable, with soft pink padded chairs and a fire usually burning in the fireplace. The wine list features many local wines and of course the fine bottlings produced by the Fess Parker Winery and Vineyard; the restaurant has earned an Award of Excellence from *Wine Spectator* magazine. *2860 Grand*

Most large wineries have wine clubs whose members arrange for regular shipments of wine every few months. Members also usually get free tastings and discounts on any bottles bought at the tasting bar. But the Fess Parker Vineyard's wine club (805/688-1545; www.FessParker. com) has another special perk: a substantial discount on a room at the posh Fess Parker Los Olivos Inn.

Ave, Los Olivos; 805/688-7788 or 800/446-2455; $$$$; AE, MC, V; checks OK; www.FessParker.com; south of Alamo Pintado Ave. &

SANTA YNEZ

The center of cattle ranching in this valley since the 1880s, Santa Ynez remains a farm town whose centerpiece is the historic Santa Ynez Feed & Mill, which still supplies hay, grain, and tack to valley ranchers and cowboys. But don't be fooled; you'll also find cutting-edge decor and chic fashions in shops tucked behind Western storefronts. Spanning just two blocks, downtown Santa Ynez sports false-front Old West facades and down-home hospitality—notably illustrated by the local service station John's Chevron, where the family cheerfully washes your windshield and checks under your hood at the self-serve price.

ACTIVITIES

Wonderful Wagons. Using the words and tools of ordinary people, the Santa Ynez Valley Historical Society Museum and Parks–Janeway Carriage House give visitors a clear historical peek at the valley's past. In the museum, the exhibits of spurs and bits are explained in plainspoken but fascinating text by their makers, and a pioneer room shows a bed, crib, and stove in a simple room, the basics of a frontier life. For a look at wagons and buggies of yesteryear, step into the adjacent Carriage House. This small but exceptional museum holds the largest collection of horse-drawn vehicles west of the Mississippi, with rare examples of stagecoaches, covered wagons, a governess cart, a small package delivery wagon, a Sicilian donkey cart, personal surreys, and other conveyances once common in the valley. (Corner of Sagunto and Faraday Sts; 805/688-7889)

Camp in a yurt on a bluff overlooking the lake at the Cachuma Lake Recreation Area. A blend of tent and tepee, the yurts have platform beds to sleep four to six, a lockable door, and inside lighting. They cost $35 to $45 per night; call 805/686-5050 to book.

Chumash Casino. It's a surprise to see a casino out in the country like this, but it's not a mirage. The Chumash Casino is a gaming spot where high-stakes bingo, Las Vegas–style video gaming, and spirited card games entertain 24 hours a day (on certain days) while adhering to state guidelines that permit gaming on Native American lands. (On Hwy 246, Santa Ynez; 805/686-0855 or 800/728-9997; www.chumashcasino.com)

Eagle Cruise on Lake Cachuma. Follow Highway 154 south from Santa Ynez and you'll soon see picturesque Cachuma Lake (805/686-5054; www.sbparks.com). The reservoir, created in 1953 by damming the Santa Ynez River, is the primary water source for Santa Barbara County and the centerpiece of a 6,600-acre county park with a flourishing wildlife population and well-developed recreational facilities. Migratory birds—including bald eagles, rarely sighted in these parts—abound during the winter months, and full-time residents include blue herons, osprey, red-tailed hawks, golden eagles, deer, bobcats, and mountain lions. The best way to appreciate all this bounty is by taking a naturalist-led eagle cruise or wildlife cruise, offered year-round on the lake; call 805/686-5050 for reservations. Camping, boating, and fishing are all popular activities centered around the small marina.

The Littlest Library. Next to the Santa Ynez Valley Historical Society at the corner of Sagunto and Faraday Streets is the smallest library in California—the Santa Ynez Library, a branch of the Santa Barbara Public Library System. The cozy space in a small cottage is only open three hours a week, on Fridays from 2 to 5pm, but has a remarkable collection of current mysteries, novels, nonfiction, and children's books. Librarian Lynn Gilfry would love to have you drop in, and bring any good books you'd like to give a second home.

Glider Rides. Windhaven Glider Rides, based at the Santa Ynez Airport, offers several ways to glide silently above the beautiful Santa Ynez Valley. Among the most popular is the Scenic Flight ($75), which climbs to 2,500 feet above the lower ridges of the Santa Ynez coastal mountain range. Passengers see Lake Cachuma, the Santa Barbara coastline, and, by special request, the Reagan Ranch. Flight time is approximately 15 to 20 minutes. The Mountain Adventure Flight ($125) climbs above the highest peaks on the coastal mountain range. Be sure to bring your camera; at 4,000 feet you'll see some of the most breathtaking views available anywhere. This tour lasts approximately 25 to 30 minutes. (805/688-2517; www.glider rides.com)

Shopping. This may look like a backwater town, but open the door to one of the shops and you could be in Beverly Hills. Timbleweeds (3532 Sagunto St, 805/688-6404), a clothing boutique, is owned by the Spaulding family, which also owns the Santa Ynez Feed & Mill Company, but this is no hayseed operation. The stylish casual fashions for men and women are made in natural fabrics such as linen and cotton and would be just as appropriate in L.A. as here in ranch country. In 1993 Susanna Spaulding opened Sage of Santa Ynez (1095 Edison St; 805/688-6404), a home furnishings and accessories store that features pine furniture, baskets, elegant candles, and table linens. That cheery red barn you see at 3569 Sagunto Street (805/686-0842) is Dennee's, a sophisticated home interiors store selling custom-made cabinetry, rugs, custom bedding, linens, lighting, and gifts. The Victorian Gardens (3631 Sagunto St; 805/686-5442) are a cluster of Victorian buildings with shops in the midst of lovely gardens. The complex includes Coach House Antiques, offering estate jewelry, dolls, and collectible teddy bears, and Santa's Shoppe, selling holiday ornaments.

 Golf. The 18-hole Rancho San Marcos Golf Course (Hwy 154, south of the lake; 805/683-6334) was designed by Robert Trent Jones Jr. to wind scenically along the Santa Ynez River next to Los Padres National Forest.

RESTAURANTS

THE VINEYARD HOUSE ★

Until the 1980s, this lavish Victorian on Santa Ynez's main drag was a private residence. Now it serves as a welcome addition to the valley's interesting if limited dining scene. Though the food served here—a pleasant mix of American standards and lighter California-style dishes—isn't always competitive with that of other gourmet hot spots, the Vineyard House's utterly charming setting is a winner. Diners who choose a table on the wide front deck enjoy a bucolic view that has changed little since the house was built more than a century ago. Patrons inside are treated to the same picturesque vista through a giant picture window. Standout dishes include a soup like venison chili verde made with tomatillos and served with avocado salsa, a main-course salad topped with beer-battered fried chicken and creamy Gorgonzola cheese, and some inventive pastas. Other choices include rack of lamb, filet mignon, and salmon in an aromatic fennel sauce with spinach. The menu is complemented by a reasonably priced list of fine Central Coast wines and a worthy dessert list. *3631 Sagunto St, Santa Ynez; 805/688-2886; $$; AE, MC, V; local checks only; lunch, dinner Wed–Mon, brunch Sun; beer and wine; reservations recommended; 3 blocks from Hwy 246 via Edison St.* ᕕ

LODGINGS

SANTA YNEZ INN ★★

As this is written, owners Douglas and Christine Ziegler and manager John Martino are putting the finishing touches on their brand-new Santa Ynez Inn, a small European-style luxury bed-and-breakfast. The new two-story Victorian building has only 14 individually decorated rooms, all furnished with Victorian antiques. Each room has a whirlpool tub and

For the **Out of Africa** *set: luxury resort camping at the new El Capitan Canyon resort in the Santa Ynez Mountains includes deluxe safari tent, queen bed, linens, table, and chairs. Canyon cabins have all this and electricity and an eco-shower too. Massage is available, of course, for those tired hiking muscles. Rates start at $95 (805/685-3887 or 866/352-2729; www.elcapitan canyon.com).*

Nearly all area wineries now charge $3 to $8 for tastings, and by the end of the day these fees can add up. A tip: Visit the Curtis Winery in Foxen Canyon (5249 Foxen Canyon Rd; 805/686-8999), which is affiliated with the Firestone Vineyards (5000 Zaca Station Rd; 805/688-3940). Buy a Curtis tasting wineglass for $7, and you can taste all 15 to 20 wines offered both here and at Firestone at no extra charge.

steam shower, beds made with Frette 100 percent Egyptian cotton linens, two telephones, a dataport, and a balcony, and all but two have fireplaces. A full gourmet breakfast is served in the inn's dining room, and picnic lunches are available for wine touring. Afternoon tea and evening wine and hors d'oeuvres are also provided. A concierge will arrange wine tasting tours, golf, nature cruises, shopping, dining, flightseeing, and other activities. Martino worked as resident manager at El Alisal Resort for 20 years and knows how to pamper guests—with spa services such as facials and massages and by catering to people's whims. "If someone wants a tuna sandwich at 2am, they'll get it," he says. *3627 Sagunto St, Santa Ynez; 805/688-5588 or 800/643-5774; $$$$; AE, DIS, MC, V; checks accepted 30 days prior to arrival; info@santaynezinn.com; www.santaynezinn.com; on Sagunto St at Edison St.* &

SAN MARCOS PASS

California Highway 154 is a beautiful drive, and one we highly recommend as a scenic alternative to US 101, as it traverses the Santa Ynez Mountains on its way to Santa Barbara. After passing Cachuma Lake, the San Marcos Pass climbs to around 2,200 feet amid thick chaparral-covered hillsides, brightened each spring with blooming wildflowers. Whatever the time of year, a stellar ocean view comes into sight just as you reach the summit. This mountain pass has been used by people for centuries, including Colonel John Frémont, who sneaked through to surprise a band of Mexican soldiers during the American conquest of California in 1846. Stagecoach Road traces the original pathway through the pass, and until a bridge was built in 1963 this winding and rugged road served as the only way across 400-foot-deep Cold Spring Canyon near the top of the pass. Unfortunately, most drivers never appreciate the marvelous Cold Spring Arch Bridge, since its graceful, swooping arc (supporting the roadway in a single 700-foot span) cannot be seen as you cross it. For a glorious view of the bridge, turn off the main highway at Stagecoach Road and drive under it.

ACTIVITIES

Rancho Oso. You can live the life of the Old West by staying in a covered wagon or in a cabin built to look like a sheriff's office at Rancho Oso in the Santa Ynez River Valley. For this unvarnished Wild West camping/riding experience, turn off Highway 154 onto Paradise Road and drive for 5 miles along the river. You can

SANTA BARBARA REGION WINE COUNTRY

Like most renowned wine regions, the Santa Ynez and Santa Maria Valleys are bounded by transverse (west-to-east) mountain ranges, which allow ocean breezes to flow in and keep the climate temperate. White grapes flourish here, so everyone makes a Chardonnay, but several reds are also well regarded, including Cabernet Sauvignon, Syrah, and Viognier, a Rhône varietal that's gaining in popularity. A good way to familiarize yourself with the local wine country is by contacting the Santa Barbara County Vintners' Association (3669 Sagunto St, Unit 101, Santa Ynez; 805/688-0881 or 800/218-0881; www.sbcountywines.com). Be sure to pick up a copy of their Winery Touring Map, which is also available at hotels and the wineries themselves. If you'd like to sample wines without driving around, head to Los Olivos Tasting Room & Wine Shop (2905 Grand Ave, Los Olivos; 805/688-7406), located in the heart of town, or Los Olivos Wine & Spirits Emporium (2531 Grand Ave, Los Olivos; 805/688-4409; www.sbwines.com), a friendly barn in a field half a mile away. Both offer a wide selection, including wines from vintners that don't have their own tasting rooms.

The Fess Parker Winery & Vineyard *turns out some critically acclaimed Syrahs and Chardonnays. The winery buildings are beautiful; the tasting room building has an open stone porch fronted by perfect lawns. (6200 Foxen Canyon Rd, Los Olivos; 805/688-1545; www.FessParker.com)*

The Firestone Vineyard *was started by wine country pioneer Brooks Firestone of tire manufacturing fame; it's one of the county's largest producers. The tasting room and gift shop are a three-ring circus of merchandise, but Firestone offers a quick, worthwhile tour. (5000 Zaca Station Rd, Los Olivos; 805/688-3940; www.firestonewine.com)*

Zaca Mesa Winery *has an old barnlike tasting room shaded by oaks, set on a serene plateau. It offers the usual Syrahs and Chardonnays plus Rhône varietals such as Grenache, Roussanne, and Viognier. It's one of the few area wineries that doesn't charge for a tasting. (6905 Foxen Canyon Rd, Los Olivos; 805/688-9339 or 800/350-7972; www.zacamesa.com)*

The Gainey Vineyard *has a visitor-oriented winery with a large terra-cotta-tiled tasting room, plenty of logo merchandise, and a deli case for impromptu lunches at the garden tables. Gainey draws huge crowds thanks to a prime location on Highway 246 and the in-depth tours it offers seven days a week. (3950 E Hwy 246, Santa Ynez; 805/688-0558; www.gaineyvineyard.com)*

Sunstone Vineyards & Winery's *wisteria-wrapped stone tasting room and lavender-fringed picnic courtyard lie nestled in an oak grove overlooking the river. Don't be misled by the rambling dirt entrance road—this classy winery boasts a superior Merlot (its flagship varietal) and features a sophisticated gift shop with gourmet foods, cigars, and souvenirs. (125 N Refugio Rd, Santa Ynez; 805/688-WINE or 800/313-WINE; www.sunstonewinery.com)*

stay the night or just take one-hour Western trail rides on gentle horses in the back-country through foothills, valleys, and sagebrush with mountains looming overhead; you can even bring your own horse. Families, riding clubs, and other small groups especially like this place. The covered wagons (from $45) sleep four and are bare-bones tent affairs with a wooden floor and cots; the sheriff's office, assay office, and general store cabins (from $69) can sleep three and are simple wooden single-room cabins with small refrigerators, a coffeemaker, one double bed, one twin bed, and one top bunk. Cabins are heated, but there is no air-conditioning. Arrange for a day ride by calling 805/683-5110; to reserve for a custom-planned stay, call 805/683-5686. Most people bring their own groceries and cook out, but a chuck wagon, open on summer weekends, sells lunch items. Overnight guests can also use the pool and hot tub or eat in the historic Stone Lodge Kitchen, which serves breakfast and dinner. The web site (www.rancho-oso.com) offers good photos of this rustic retreat.

Painted Cave. The earliest evidence of inhabitants in the San Marcos Pass area can be seen at Chumash Painted Cave Historic Park, a worthwhile 10-minute detour from Highway 154. Turn off onto Painted Cave Road; after 2 miles, look for the small sign and parking turnout. On foot, follow the rocky path a few yards to the cave. It's dark inside, but not too dark to distinguish the vivid drawings; probably made by Chumash shamans, they include geometric and swirling designs, horned animals, human figures, and a sun drawing believed to represent a 17th-century eclipse.

RESTAURANTS

COLD SPRING TAVERN ★★

This charming moss-covered shingle cabin with gingham-draped windows and cozy fireplace nooks, nestled among the trees next to a babbling brook, is truly a testament to old-fashioned carnivorous dining. After 100-plus years, the former stagecoach stop is still a popular watering hole. The simple, hearty lunch menu features burgers of buffalo or beef, the famous house chili, sandwiches, salads, and barbecued pork baby back ribs. Dinner is more elegant than you might expect, with tequila chicken and game offerings such as stuffed pheasant breast, grilled venison tenderloin, and wild boar. All game meats are domestically raised. For dessert, you must have the Jack Daniels pecan pie. Trophy heads and photographs line the walls; a plaque reads, "God go with you, we haven't got time." Weekends and nights, especially during summer, the saloon-style bar next door is packed with revelers dancing to local bands; on Friday evenings and Sunday afternoons (known as "Biker Day") the grill is fired up outside and you can stomp to the beat and chew on ribs (or steak, chicken, and fish) at the same time. There are also bands on Saturday afternoons, when the only food served is chili dogs. It'll take you 20 minutes to drive here from downtown, but the incredible coastline views along the way make the trip worthwhile. *5995 Stagecoach Rd, between Santa Ynez and Santa Barbara; 805/967-0066; $; AE, MC, V; local checks only; breakfast Sat–Sun, lunch, dinner every day; full bar; reservations recommended at dinner; cst@silcom.com; on Stagecoach Rd off Hwy 154.*

SANTA BARBARA

With its sheltered bay and balmy weather, Santa Barbara, nestled in the foothills of the gentle Santa Ynez mountains, has drawn the rich and famous for almost 100 years, and this legacy has produced huge hidden mansions, luxurious gardens, grand public buildings, and well-funded museums. This self-proclaimed "American Riviera" and city of 90,000 residents is indeed breathtaking, from its red-tiled roofs to its picturesque hills to the wide sandy beaches and dolphin-filled Pacific waters. Adding to the area's natural beauty is the town itself, whose rich Spanish/Mexican history is evident in today's culture and architecture. The climate is near-perfect, with a year-round average temperature of 70 degrees.

ACCESS AND INFORMATION

Santa Barbara is 332 miles from San Francisco and 92 miles from Los Angeles on Highway 101. Highway 154, through the San Marcos Pass, joins 101 from the Santa Ynez Valley to the north. United Airlines (via United Express) and American Airlines offer the most flights daily to and from the Santa Barbara Municipal Airport, located in Goleta (15 minutes north of downtown Santa Barbara; 805/967-7111). Most major car rental companies are conveniently located at the airport, and the Superride (805/683-9636 or 800/977-1123) shuttle service provides passengers with advance-reservation rides to and from the airport, as well as custom tours of the city and the Santa Ynez wine country. The Airbus Coach (800/733-6354; www.sbairbus.com) offers seven trips a day to Santa Barbara from the Los Angeles airport (LAX). Amtrak (209 State St; 805/963-1015 or 800/872-7245; www. amtrack.com) makes several stops daily at State and Yanonaly Streets. Local trolleys and buses are easy to use and stop at most hotels and places of interest. The Santa Barbara Trolley Co. (805/965-0353) offers a round-town continuous tour from 10am to 4pm that stops at all major sites including the County Courthouse, Stearns Wharf, the mission, and other places, for a fare of $14 for adults and $8 for children. The MTD Shuttle Bus operates

Create your own rails-to-trails experience: take Amtrak (800/872-7245) to Santa Barbara from L.A., Oakland, or many cities in between, get off at the charming old Santa Barbara train station near the beach, cross the street to Cycles for Rent, and hit the town by bike, where a network of trails link the city and country. Amtrak also will check your own bike; ask when you make reservations.

every 10 minutes between downtown and Stearns Wharf and every 30 minutes between the harbor and the zoo (in the Santa Barbara Zoological Gardens), at a one-way cost of a quarter. For more information contact the Santa Barbara Visitors Bureau (1601 Anacapa St; 805/966-9222 or 800/927-4688; www.santabarbaraca.com).

ACTIVITIES

County Courthouse. If you have time for only one activity in Santa Barbara, take the elevator to the four-story clock tower of the outrageously beautiful Spanish Colonial Revival Santa Barbara County Courthouse, built in the late 1920s, with blue, yellow, and green tiles from Tunisia lining the stairs and ceilings. The view from the tower is magnificent: you can see from the mountains to the bay, and the good signage tells you which buildings and gardens you are eyeing in the distance. Downstairs, the Mural Room has soaring historical murals depicting important moments in Santa Barbara history, including John Frémont riding through the San Marcos Pass into the valley in 1846. Be sure to tour the sunken gardens and take time to simply wander the halls, where carvings and exotic woods create the feel of a European castle. (1100 Anacapa St; 805/962-6464)

Stearns Wharf. The second most important must-see stop in Santa Barbara is Stearns Wharf, built in 1872 by John Peck Stearns. The landmark wharf was the hub of cargo and passenger activity for many years; visitors now can walk or drive onto the wharf for fishing or dining. It's fun just to stroll the wharf, buy a snack, and watch the folks fishing and the pelicans soaring overhead. A free shuttle bus takes people back and forth every 10 minutes from the foot of the wharf. (foot of State St; 805/564-5518)

Only in Santa Barbara will you find a parking garage with a design inspired by a Spanish bullring: rounded parking garage number 7, across the street from the County Courthouse.

The Botanic Gardens. Santa Barbara could be called "Gardens R Us," since its cultured citizens have always loved the huge variety of plants that will grow in this balmy climate. At the 65-acre Santa Barbara Botanic Gardens (1212 Mission Canyon Rd; 805/682-4726; www.sbbg.org), flora, fauna, and weather come together perfectly—particularly in the spring and summer months, when most of the 1,300 indigenous and rare plants are in bloom. But the more than 5 miles of lovely trails are worth a rambling walk any time of year, winding through 1,000 examples of California plant life.

Mission Santa Barbara. In the foothills above Highway 101, up on a plateau, you'll find the majestic Mission Santa Barbara (2001 Laguna St at Los Olivos St; 805/682-4713), one of 21 Catholic missions founded by Spanish Franciscan friars. The present-day church was begun in 1815, built mostly by the local Chumash Indians. It is the only California mission to be continuously used and occupied since its founding. Be sure to take the self-guided walking tour ($4) and see the missionary bedroom and kitchen, complete with artifacts of the period. It's open daily from 9am to 5 pm. Visitors are welcome Sundays at Mass held in the majestic adobe church with its unusual double bell tower and rose garden.

The Natural History Museum. Also located out near the mission is a favorite with kids: the Santa Barbara Museum of Natural History (2559 Puesta del Sol Rd; 805/682-4711), which has a planetarium, lizard lounge, insect arena, and exhibits of everything from a 72-foot blue whale skeleton to a space lab to bears and mountain lions to outstanding Native American artifacts. Shows at the planetarium are well worth seeing. Call to check what temporary museum exhibits and learning experiences will be featured while you visit; one recent offering was a walk-through live butterfly environment.

Santa Barbara Botanic Garden. Roughly a mile and a half north of the Mission is the Santa Barbara Botanic Garden (1212 Mission Canyon Rd; 805/682-4726), 65 acres of native trees, wildflowers, and cacti in natural settings. It's open every day, but call ahead as times change with the seasons. The gentle nature trails can be managed by most everyone, and guided tours are available Saturday and Sunday at 10:30am and 2pm. Admission is $5 adults, $3 seniors and teens, $1 children 5–12.

Santa Barbara History Museum. The paintings, photographs, furniture, clothing, and artifacts at the Santa Barbara History Museum (136 E de la Guerra St; 805/966-1601) portray town life from the 1780s to the 1920s, with scenarios depicting the lives of the Spanish, Mexican, Chumash, Chinese, and American pioneers. The diverse collection of objects includes a magnificent Chinese altar, an original Pony Express saddle, an unusual Victorian hair wreath, and the beautiful 17th-century oil painting *Coronation of the Virgin* by Miguel Cabrera. It is open Tuesday to Saturday from 10am to 5pm, with docent-led tours Wednesday and Saturday at 11:30am and Sunday at 1:30pm. Across the courtyard is the Gledhill Library, a researcher's paradise where newspapers and periodicals dating back more than a hundred years are bound in huge leather volumes and available for your perusal; it is open

"Everybody's favorite parts of the Courthouse tour are the Mural Room, which shows the history of Santa Barbara in huge painted murals marching around the room—from native Indians to explorers to John Frémont coming through the pass—and the tower, where you can see so far, it's like having a bird's-eye view of almost the whole beautiful county."

—Marci Cox, docent, Santa Barbara County Courthouse

Astonishingly beautiful paintings in rich jewel colors suddenly appear on the broad plaza at the mission during the I Madonnari Italian Street Painting Festival each Memorial Day weekend (805/569-3873), then just as suddenly disappear when judging is over. Bring your camera to capture them!

Tuesday to Friday, 10am to 4pm. For more information or group tours, contact the Santa Barbara Historical Society (805/966-1601) or the Architectural Foundation of Santa Barbara (805/965-6307), which also offers informative walking tours of the city ($5) on Saturday and Sunday at 10am.

Santa Barbara Museum of Art. Santa Barbara boasts its own Santa Barbara Museum of Art, a soaring, elegant building with an impressive collection of 18th-, 19th-, and 20th-century American and European paintings and sculpture, as well as decorative arts from Asia. A pleasant informal restaurant is open during most museum hours. (1130 State St; 805/963-4364; www.sbmuseart.org; Tues–Sat 11am–5pm, Fri 11am–9pm, Sun noon–5pm)

Golf. Sandpiper Golf Course puts you on the edge of the Pacific Ocean. Recognized as one of the top 25 public golf courses in the nation, the seaside links layout of over 7,200 yards is a must-play for golfers visiting Santa Barbara. The course, which has hosted PGA, LPGA, and other events throughout the years, is at 7925 Hollister Avenue; 805/968-1541. River Course at the Alisal is another must-play course in the Santa Barbara area. Cut along the Santa Ynez River, just south of Solvang, it has great views and covers 6,830 yards. The clubhouse is a real treat. It was designed using native river rock, cypress, and glass. (Take Highway 101 to Highway 246 north of Solvang, and go south on Alisal Road; 805/688-6042)

The Zoo. The Santa Barbara Zoological Gardens consists of a quaint zoo on 30 acres of well-landscaped gardens on the grounds of a former estate, with a small but well-rounded collection of animals. Creatures range from African giraffes to white ruffled lemurs to American alligators. Situated on a knoll overlooking East Beach, the "zoo-with-a-view" is a great place for a picnic. Stroll its paths or tour the grounds in a bright-red miniature train. (500 Ninos Dr; information 805/962-6310; every day 10am–5pm; $8 adults, $6 children 2–12 and seniors)

Through Secret Courtyards to Treasures. The streets of Santa Barbara may not be paved with gold, but many of its sidewalks are adorned with terra-cotta, and surrounding walls and fountains are decorated with beautiful Spanish tile circa 1920. Though the town is steeped in Spanish heritage, the picture-perfect downtown landscape is actually a result of a massive earthquake that leveled much of State Street in 1925. As bizarre as it seems, the architectural commission of Santa Barbara saw the earthquake as a godsend of sorts, as they had been drawing up plans to rebuild the town to look more in keeping with its cultural roots. They had, in fact, already begun implementing the design concept a couple of years before with El Paseo (15 E de la Guerra St), which for years harbored a complex of shops and restaurants but today is mostly occupied by law and investment company offices. One block over is the remains of El Presidio (129 E Canon Perdido St; 805/966-9719), now a state park that commemorates the site where Santa Barbara was originally settled in 1782. The original fortress was one of four built in California by the Spanish as a seat of government and military headquarters (the other three are in San Diego, San Francisco, and Monterey). The Santa Barbara Trust (805/966-9719), which is painstakingly restoring all the buildings, offers guided tours.

Wheels along the Sand. For exploring on foot or wheels, hiking and biking trail maps are available at the Visitor Center main office (1 Garden St; 805/965-3021). Bikes and in-line skates are available for rent at Beach Rentals (22 State St; 805/966-6733). For vicarious thrills, stop at the skateboard park at the end of Stearns Wharf and watch the hotshots whoosh down the smooth cement curves and perform gravity-defying tricks as they roll.

Horseback Riding. If you'd rather travel by four-legged friend, call the people at Circle Bar B Guest Ranch and Stables (1800 Refugio Rd; 805/968-3901; www.circlebarb.com), who arrange all kinds of rides, including sunset and sunrise excursions. The usual rides last 1½ hours or half a day and wind along trails up into Refugio Canyon, where you will be treated to both ocean and island views in the distance.

On the Water. You can rent a sailboat, jet ski, kayak, or speedboat from the Sailing Center of Santa Barbara (at the breakwater, enter from Shoreline Dr; 800/350-9090; www.sbsailcom), or let someone else steer your craft with Sunset Kidd Sailing Charters (at the breakwater; 805/962-8222), which offers day tours, seasonal whale watches, and sunset cruises on a 41-foot Morgan. The *Condor* (board at SeaLanding at the harbor, 805/882-0088 or 888/77-WHALE), operated through the Natural History Museum, is an 88-foot boat that offers educational trips with knowledgeable volunteers (Feb–Apr only). For the more adventurous, Truth Aquatics (Sea Landing at the harbor; 805/962-1127) offers Channel Islands trips including kayaking, snorkeling, scuba diving, and hiking.

Shopping. Santa Barbara's shopping is excellent. There are specialty stores and boutiques in La Arcada (State St, above Figueroa St) and the beautiful modern mall Paseo Nuevo (State St at de la Guerra St), with Spanish colonial facades and faux balconies, which holds anchor stores Macy's and Nordstrom, boutiques, and a cinema. While State Street is the main shopping area and the prime destination for antiques and vintage clothing, some of the best shops are on side streets. For biblio-philes, the Book Den (11 E Anapamu St; 805/962-3321) has been the place to go for used books since 1979; Sullivan Goss Books (7 E Anapamu St; 805/730-1460) stocks art books and California art, old and new prints, photographs, and paintings such as those of revered local wine-label painter James Paul Brown. In the back in a charming courtyard is the Arts and Letters Cafe, a civilized place for dinner. A Walk in the Woods (15 E Anapamu St; 805/966-1331) has refinished and reproduction English furniture from the 1920s and 1930s. Browsing Tienda Ho (1105 State St; 805/962-3643) is like walking through a bazaar in a tropical rain forest: sarongs, masks, primitive wall hangings, and tribal rugs compete for space with flowing exotic women's clothes from Indonesia, India, and China. The Italian Pottery Outlet down near the beach (19 Helena St; 877/496-5599; www.italianpottery.com) has a huge selection of Italian serving dishes, plates, vases, and bowls for a third less than elsewhere.

Fiesta! August means it's time for Old Spanish Days Fiesta, five days of festiv-ities that include a historic parade with carriages and wagon from the Santa Barbara Carriage and Western Art museum, a rodeo, a festive market at De La Guerra Plaza in old downtown with Spanish/Mexican foods and outdoor dancing, a mariachi festival, an arts and crafts show, a symphony concert, and special luncheons and his-toric tours (805/962-8101; www.oldspanishdays-fiesta.org).

Memorial Garden. A hidden jewel of a park that most tourists never see is the Alice Keck Park Memorial Garden (1500 Santa Barbara St, between Arrellaga and Micheltorena Sts; 805/564-5418). This serene retreat has a meadow, a wandering stream, benches, lawns, lagoons with koi, a gazebo, bridges, lovely flower gardens, and lush trees such as jacarandas and rusty-leaf figs. Bring the family: it's across the street from a playground with wonderful play equipment.

Best Beaches. The broad, welcoming stretch of sand hugging the ocean from Stearns Wharf to Montecito is East Beach, the city's most popular beach; along it are places to fish, swim, and play volleyball, plus some grassy areas for sitting and a children's playground. Farther east is the more intimate (and clothing-optional) Butterfly Beach. The Cabrillo Pavilion Bathhouse (1118 Cabrillo Blvd; 805/897-2680) has showers, changing rooms and beach equipment for rent, plus lockers and use of the weight room for a minimal fee. West Beach, just west of Stearns Wharf, includes the Santa Barbara Harbor, where you can watch boats or launch your kayak. Gentle waves make it good for family swimming and wading, and there is a playground nearby. Leadbetter Beach, between West Beach and Shoreline Park, is sheltered by a high cliff and is good for swimming and beginning surfers. At Shoreline Park (Shore-line Dr, north of the harbor), take the steps down to the secluded white sand beach to escape the crowds, or for an even more remote spot head to Mesa Lane Beach (Mesa

Ln, off Cliff Dr), a very private strip of sand hidden by bluffs, which is also a good surf spot. Also off Cliff Drive is the beach locals refer to as Hendry's Beach, with good picnic areas, snack bars (such as the Brown Pelican), and excellent swimming, fishing, and surfing. Its official name is Arroyo Burro Nature Reserve (2981 Cliff Dr; 805/687-3714).

Nightlife. Beautiful people, many of them famous, drift up to Santa Barbara from L.A. for long weekends, and they come out at night in Santa Barbara to socialize, dine, and hear music. Most of the nightlife scene is centered in Old Town Santa Barbara, particularly on State Street. Q's Sushi a-Go-Go (409 State St; 805/966-9177) and Zelo (630 State St; 805/966-5792) are great for dancing to the latest sounds. Q's serves sushi and other dinners until midnight, and offers dancing nightly (or billiards if you don't dance) and action on three levels. The sound at SoHo (1221 State St; 805/962-7776) changes nightly, from jazz, blues, dance, funk, and reggae to Eastern European traditional folk. Also on State, in the Paseo Nuevo, is the popular Rocks (801 State St; 805/884-1190), where the food has an Asian twist, and lemon-drop martinis and cigars are practically mandatory. The nightclub upstairs has live jazz or R&B and the easygoing crowd is a mix of all ages, from 20s to 70s. A more sophisticated and consistently older set is drawn to the bar scene and upstairs lounge at Blue Agave (20 E Cota St; 805/899-4694), which serves a great margarita and has a porch for smoking cigars. It's not unusual to see celebrities at this cozy two-story restaurant/lounge.

Parking in the 12 city parking lots and garages that parallel State Street in or near downtown is free for the first 75 minutes, and only $1 per hour after that. Park in one and hop on the Downtown-Waterfront Shuttle, which costs only a quarter and comes every 10 minutes from 10am to 6pm. Call 805/963-1581 for a parking brochure/map and shuttle schedule.

RESTAURANTS

AFICIONADO EUROPEAN BAKERY ☆

No ordinary bakery, this. Here you'll find breadsticks in flavors such as chocolate walnut and lemon vanilla and Mediterranean flatbreads in pecan, lemon pepper, or ginger almond flavors. They make special breads and rolls served at Santa Barbara's finer tables (Simpson House, the Four Seasons Biltmore, bouchon, and Wine Cask, to name a few). But happily, there's plenty left over for all the folks who come here the rest of the week. Regional bread specials are featured and include herbed fougasse, levain boules (sourdough), onion focaccia, sweetly perfumed olive rolls, flatbreads, and Tuscan breadsticks. At lunchtime the breads become sandwiches: tuna with sesame-ginger mayonnaise, rosemary-marinated chicken, or roasted vegetable with crumbly feta. Start the day on a sweet note with a fruit-filled pastry or a lemon blueberry muffin and a foamy cappuccino, and savor it outside at a cafe table or inside perched on a stool. *10 E Carrillo St, Santa Barbara; 805/963-8404; $$; AE, DC, MC, V; checks OK; breakfast, lunch Mon–Sat; no alcohol; no reservations; on Carrillo St, just east of State St.* ♿

BOUCHON SANTA BARBARA ★★

Enter bouchon from the street through matching broken-stone fountains and stroll under the arbor created by lemon trees. Inside, the simple but dignified dining room has gold walls adorned with paintings by James Paul Brown (a respected local painter of wine labels), and the kitchen in view beyond beautiful etched glass panels. The garden patio is heated and in use year round. Although the name means "wine cork" in French, almost all of the corks are coming out of local bottles at this popular spot serving wine country cuisine. The roster of local wines by the glass is impressive, as is the wine list in general, including such selections as an excellent Sangiovese from the Cambria region and a Viognier from Santa Ynez. Owner Mitchell Sjerven and chef Charles Fredericks worked at many of the town's finer eating establishments before teaming up in 1998. The menu changes with each new season. Starters have included Ojai escargot as well as panzanella, a bread salad with basil, tomatoes, goat cheese, and organic field greens. Main courses might include pan-roasted bluefin tuna with roasted tomato tapenade, and lemon confit with Santa Barbara olives; lime-seared sea scallops with sweet corn risotto; or rosemary and garlic-marinated lamb loin with sweet potato gnocchi. Don't miss the Meyer lemon pudding cake or the warm chocolate cake with homemade banana ice cream. If you just want to drop in for the ambience and a glass of fine local wine, an adjoining wine bar is open on weekends. *9 W Victoria St, Santa Barbara; 805/730-1160; $$$; AE, DC, MC, V; checks OK; dinner every day; beer and wine; reservations recommended; www.bouchon-santabarbara.com; between State and Chapala Sts.* ♿

The Goleta Lemon Festival in October celebrates the fruit's golden history in that nearby seaside town, where several new varieties of lemons were introduced and a lemon packing plant once stood. You'll find demonstrations and food booths with everything from lemon chicken to lemonade to lemon meringue pie. Call 805/967-4618 for an events brochure, or consult www.lemonfestival.com.

THE BROWN PELICAN ★★

Come as you are to the Brown Pelican, a lone restaurant tucked perfectly into a cove on Hendry's Beach in the Arroyo Burro Nature Reserve. Sit on the patio and watch the waves roll in just a few yards away. It's possible that the view overlooking the vast expanse of ocean and surrounding cliffs makes the food taste better than it actually is. However, the fare here is actually quite good

A GOOD DAY IN SANTA BARBARA

8–9am: Have breakfast at Tupelo Junction Cafe.

9–10am: Rent a beach cycle and ride the beach path near Stearns Wharf.

10:30–11am: Climb the tower at the County Courthouse to see the surrounding scenery.

11am–noon: Wander the Paseo Nuevo and other mission-style arcades for shopping.

noon–1:15pm: Lunch in Montecito at Pane e Vino.

1:30–3:30 pm: Tour Lotusland by reservation.

4pm– 5pm: Tour Mission Santa Barbara or the Botanic Gardens.

6:30–7:30pm: Have a drink and oyster shooters at Brophy's at the harbor.

7:45–9:45pm: Slurp jambalaya and sing along on "What a Wonderful World" at the Palace Grill.

10pm–?: Dance at Q's Sushi-a-Go-Go.

if you stick to the fresh fish specials: fish and chips in an ale batter, light but hearty seafood linguine, crab cakes, or steamed local mussels. You can also slug back a few oyster shooters. The ahi tuna on focaccia and the grilled chicken sandwich are simple and tasty, and there's a children's menu to handle usual requests—grilled cheese, pasta, burger and fries. Breakfast is especially satisfying, with delectable offerings such as fluffy French toast, buttermilk pancakes, and ocean hash (poached eggs, crab cake, and a potato sauté). An even sweeter temptation is the heavenly chocolate chip pancakes. Don't worry: Afterward you can just step down onto the picture-perfect 2-mile stretch of beach to walk it off, along with a multitude of dogs walking their owners. *2981½ Cliff Dr, Santa Barbara; 805/687-4550; $; AE, MC, V; no checks; breakfast, lunch, dinner every day; full bar; reservations accepted for dinner only; on Cliff Dr in Arroyo Burro County Park (Hendry's Beach).*

BROPHY BROS. CLAM BAR & RESTAURANT ★★★

For local flavors of all kinds, from social to culinary, this is the place. Unrivaled harbor views and famous clam chowder are the main draws at this lively two-story restaurant where the air is full of banter and bonhomie. If you're alone, sit at the counter, where you're likely to fall into conversation with a local. The clam chowder and the cioppino are legendary; another good choice is the cold combo platter of shrimp, crab, oysters, clams, and ceviche or its hot counterpart with steamed clams, oysters Rockefeller, and beer-boiled shrimp. The fresh fish menu changes daily; you may find Hawaiian ahi breaded with roasted cashews, served with a tarragon mustard cream sauce; local grilled thresher shark marinated in olive oil, citrus, garlic, cilantro, and red onion; traditional lobster; fresh mahimahi; or succulent swordfish steak grilled and topped with tarragon-and-crab cream sauce. All entrees come with coleslaw and salad or chowder, and rice or french fries. You won't leave hungry. Meat eaters needn't be disappointed either; the burgers here aren't bad at all. Lunch outside on the balcony and absorb the sights and sounds (and sometimes smells) of the fisherman's world around you, or in the evening join regulars and yachtsmen at the inside bar as they trade tales of the sea over draft beer and steamers. Expect a wait, as this is one of Santa Barbara's well-known treasures. *119 Harbor Wy, Santa Barbara; 805/966-4418; $$; AE, MC, V; no checks; lunch, dinner every day; full bar; no reservations; enter the harbor wharf off Cabrillo Blvd and drive to the very back.*

CITRONELLE ★★

Michel Richard's name is well recognized by dedicated foodies, and they'll be grateful he is behind this elegant restaurant, after his successes on the Los Angeles restaurant scene. Citronelle sits on the third floor, atop the Santa Barbara Inn on Cabrillo Boulevard near the ocean, and has a 270-degree view of the coastline. Named one of the six best restaurants in the United States by the readers of *Conde Nast Traveler* magazine, as well as the Best Restaurant in Santa Barbara by the *L.A. Times*, it's no surprise it's sometimes packed. Since 1993 day-to-day chef duties have been under the capable direction of Felicien Cueff, who at one time cooked for former French President Francois Mitterrand at the Elysée Palace. Local seafood is always featured. For lunch try such appetizers as the avocado nest with fresh blue crab, saffron dressing, and flying fish roe, or opt for the Santa Barbara black mussels. Entrees include the Citronelle chicken salad, which combines sautéed chicken with shallot vinaigrette dressing. Dinner has starters such as the tuna tartare or cauliflower soup. For entrees the celery root–crusted chicken is popular, as is the Santa Barbara spiny lobster served with coconut corn sauce and vegetables. The decor is French Caribbean, with bright blue and yellow walls, white linens, and hardwood floors. The rotating artwork is by local artists. *901 E Cabrillo Blvd, Santa Barbara; 805/963-0111; $$$; AE, MC, V; no checks; breakfast, lunch, dinner every day, brunch Sun; full bar; reservations recommended; www.citronelle.com; Cabrillo Blvd across from the harbor.* ঙ

DOWNEY'S ★★★

A Santa Barbara classic, Downey's has become synonymous with great California food during its lengthy tenure on State Street, although its unassuming appearance inside and out offers no hint of its reputation. Inside the small dining room the tables are double-hung with champagne and white cloths, and the peach walls hold just a few oil paintings of California scenes. The result is a restrained, pure feeling. Chef John Downey, who honed his talents on that most royal of cruise liners, the *QE2*, has perfected the art of taste bud awakening with his simply prepared but unerringly conceived creations. The menu changes daily, so it's hard to predict what will be featured, but everything is guaranteed to be fresh and delicious. A sample appetizer might be Maine lobster with angel hair salad; sweet corn soup with red pepper salsa is a typical second plate. The main dish might be grilled duck with fresh peach chutney or veal chops with fresh morels. Indulge in the special house dessert—a rhapsody of white chocolate cream and raspberries sandwiched between two layers of buttery, sweet flaky pastry. *1305 State St, Santa Barbara; 805/966-5006; $$$; DIS, MC, V; local checks OK; dinner Tues–Sun; beer and wine; reservations recommended; between Sola and Victoria Sts.*

EL ENCANTO ★★

 The restaurant in the El Encanto Hotel and Garden Villas resort has the hands-down best view in the area. It's set in a section of Santa Barbara known locally as "the Riviera," and the mountain-to-ocean views from this restaurant's rambling perch are worth the drive. Whether you're enjoying lunch on a sunny afternoon or dinner under the stars, the food just makes the view seem even grander. Resort food and beverage manager Jim Craddock and chef Mark Kropczynski offer a fairly consistent menu that may include appetizers such as carrot and ginger cream soup or imported caviar served with buckwheat blinis; main courses might be paella with local black mussels, Manila clams, chorizo, rock shrimp, sea scallops, chicken, and cilantro, or grilled veal chop with braised endive and red wine cranberry sauce. Rack of lamb with provençal herbs, beef tenderloin with shallot morel sauce, and vegetarian entrees such as grilled asparagus risotto cakes are often listed, too. Don't miss one of the fabulous desserts, such as the floating island, served while the stars compete with the harbor lights. Plan to arrive here hungry, as there is a hefty service charge for splitting an entree or even an appetizer. *1900 Lasuen Rd, Santa Barbara; 805/687-5000; $$$; AE, DC, MC, V; no checks; breakfast, lunch, dinner every day, brunch Sun; full bar; reservations recommended; www.elencantohotel.com; from Mission St, go left on Laguna St and onto Los Olivos St, then veer right onto Alameda Padre Serra, and turn left on Laseun Rd up the hill.* ⅙

EMILIO'S RISTORANTE AND BAR ★★

At this romantic Italian restaurant, arched windows open to Pacific breezes on warm nights and candles provide the only light as evening sets in. As if that weren't enchanting enough, add whitewashed walls, exposed wood beams, and clinking wineglasses and you've got yourself one amorous dining room. Soulful dishes include oak-grilled salmon and the signature "Oscar's paella," created by longtime staff member Oscar Garcia and overflowing with mussels, clams, and spicy sausage. As you feast, enjoy the ever-changing display of works by local artists. Chef Max Hernandez also offers great vegetarian entrees such as capellini pomodoro or a crispy vegetarian roll with portobello mushrooms, truffle-sweet pea purée, braised spinach, sweet pepper salad, and whipped potatoes with curry sauce. Much of the organic produce served here comes from the restaurant's own organic farm. There is a good selection of Italian and local wines and imported grappas. Whatever your choice for dinner, come with a good appetite; the beautiful painted Italian plates bear hefty portions. *324 W Cabrillo Blvd, Santa Barbara; 805/966-4426; $$; AE, DC, DIS, MC, V; local checks only; dinner every day; full bar; reservations recommended; emailios@msn.com; between Bath and Castillo Sts; city parking across the street or reserved parking at Sambo's down the block.* &

EPIPHANY ★★

Kevin Costner is one of the partners (with husband-wife team Alberto and Michelle Mastrangelo) in this spare and elegant new restaurant just off State Street, but there is no Hollywood attitude here. Located in the former 1892 home and office of the first female doctor in Santa Barbara, it has a homey feel, with hardwood floors, and banquettes and couches in striped silk with lots of brushed silk pillows. There are some surprises on the menu, particularly the signature raw bar, made possible because all the fish is sushi-grade. Raw bar appetizers include crusted tuna, ceviche, and opa (moonfish) tartare. Entrees include vodka-cured salmon, cured in-house and served with Yukon gold potatoes; Atlantic salmon served with morels, braised leeks, and sauce foie gras; and amberjack (in the tuna family) with fingerling potatoes and heirloom tomatoes. Chef Michael Goodman also offers a roasted beet salad with citrus vinaigrette, quail egg, and brioche toast. The decor throughout is what Michelle calls "urban elegance," with the walls in the bar painted Ralph Lauren red behind the mahogany and marble counter, and the restaurant's walls in a khaki color. The welcoming foyer has a Victorian brick fireplace crowned with a stained glass window, and candles glow from every corner. *21 W Victoria St, Santa Barbara; 805/564-7100; $$$; AE, DIS, MC, V; no checks; dinner every day; full bar; reservations recommended; www.epiphanysb.com; half-block west of State St.* &

LA SUPER-RICA ★

This little roadside Mexican place is one of those finds you only know about if you have friends who live here, although its reputation has been burnished by the enthusiasm of a local resident and fan, Julia Child. The turquoise-trimmed white shack with its blackboard menu offers authentic and entirely unfussy south-of-the-border fare. Bite into your first soft taco filled with steak, pork, or chile and cheese—all with soft, buttery onions—and you'll be a believer. Try the sopes (corn tortillas filled with chicken, avocado, and cheese) or the chilaquiles (cheese and tortilla strips with a spicy tomato sauce). And if somehow you still have room, during the winter try the hot atole (a delicious milk drink laced with vanilla and cinnamon). Though most menu items cost less than $5, you're likely to end up spending more than you anticipated because the selections are too delicious to pass up and come in rather small portions. *622 N Milpas St, Santa Barbara; 805/963-4940; $; cash only; lunch, dinner Mon–Sat; beer only; no reservations; between Cota and Ortega Sts. & (but no restroom access)*

THE PALACE GRILL ★★

Let the good times roll whenever you plan an evening at the Palace Grill, a lively Cajun-Creole-Italian–style eatery where spicy temptation starts with the cocktails (the Cajun martini is served in a mason jar). Actually, the food here is flavorful but not necessarily spicy unless you request it. They serve up all kinds of dishes that originated in New Orleans, from jambalaya to crawfish etouffé to pan-cooked barbecue shrimp doused with rosemary, Dixie beer, Cajun spices, and butter. Any meal starts with a basket of muffins, in flavors such as blackstrap molasses with raisin and buttermilk with rosemary. Then it's a matter of choosing among blackened prime rib, Louisiana soft-shelled crabs, veal Acadiana in oyster-sherry cream sauce, steak, chicken, salmon, or Creole crawfish crab cakes. The king of fish here, though, is redfish, flown in from New Orleans. However, the food is only half the reason lines form out the door: don't plan to doze off after dinner here, because if the zydeco music or wheezing Cajun accordion don't keep you awake, the astounding feats of magician Mark Collier (on Friday nights) should do the trick. And limber up your vocal chords, because nightly (and sometimes several times a night) the staff leads diners in a sing-along, their repertoire including that perennial Louis Armstrong favorite, "What a Wonderful World." The interior is cozy with dark woods. There are lots of good places to eat in Santa Barbara, but for pure fun, this place is number one. Incidentally, the bread pudding soufflé with warm—and potent—whiskey cream sauce should not be missed. *8 E Cota St, Santa Barbara; 805/963-5000; $$–$$$; AE, MC, V; no checks; lunch, dinner every day; limited full bar (some hard liquors such as tequila, but not all liquors); limited reservations (taken only weekdays and for 5:30pm on weekends); www.palacegrill.com; Cota St, just off State St. &*

PARADISE CAFE ★★

The Paradise's secluded patio, shaded with market umbrellas and palm fronds, has been a local alfresco lunch favorite for over 15 years. People often come for a simple burger and end up ordering a $70 bottle of hard-to-find local wine and spending the afternoon. Equally appealing is the vintage diner-style interior, with its chrome bar stools and wide array of exotic tequilas, and where a retro mural of an Indian scout and his maiden is painted behind the bar. A small but creative wine list pairs well with the menu, which ranges from tasty local mussels, oak-grilled swordfish or fresh ahi tuna steak, and New York steak to the delectable teriyaki burger, Greek salad, rock shrimp and spinach salad, and an interesting penne with peppery sausage and onions. Their burgers (Paradise, bacon, teriyaki, chili, turkey, or garden) come with shoestring potatoes or green salad and are topped with cheddar cheese and wood-grilled onions on request. *702 Anacapa St, Santa Barbara; 805/962-4416; $$; AE, MC, V; local checks only; lunch, dinner every day, brunch Sun; full bar; reservations recommended for large groups; on the corner of Anacapa and Ortega Sts.*

STELLA MARE'S ★★

If you are looking for a romantic restaurant with a rustic European flair, this is it. The house now known as Stella Mare's was built by a sea captain in 1872 and moved a hundred years later from its original site in town to a charming and tranquil spot overlooking a pond that's a haven for birds. The friendly personalities of owners Eva Ein and Philippe and Kym Rousseau pervade this inviting country farmhouse with its painted pine chairs, distressed-wood fireplace mantels, and hand-painted Italian plates on the walls. The crowning glory is a restored greenhouse with a bar and cozy fire-front sofa sitting area, where every Wednesday night a jazz trio performs. Appetizers include foie gras with apricot confit and crab cakes with a tomato caper salsa. All entrees from the oak-fired grill (chicken, salmon, New York steak) are excellent, but the specialties are just that: special, including the smoked bacon-wrapped boneless quail stuffed with morels and served with an onion, blue cheese, and potato tart. Vegetarians will like the handmade spinach ravioli filled with mozzarella, ricotta, and Parmesan cheeses graced with a light sauce, complete with wild mushrooms, tomatoes, and artichoke hearts. Lunch favorites include croque monsieur (the classic French-style grilled ham and cheese sandwich) and a steak sandwich topped with caramelized onions. For dessert, try the crème brûlée of the day. *50 Los Patos Wy, Santa Barbara; 805/969-6705; $$; AE, DIS, MC, V; no checks; lunch, dinner Tues–Sun, brunch Sun; full bar; reservations recommended; www.stellamares.com; off Cabrillo Blvd.*

TUPELO JUNCTION CAFE ★

Tupelo Junction wins the prize as having the most creative menu in town. Order a tall iced tea and prepare to wait for your breakfast or lunch, as everything is made absolutely from scratch here and worth the delay. This cheerful Southern-style cafe has red linoleum floors, orange rate label art, light wood cafe tables, and a view of the traffic on Chapala Street. The breakfast menu offers buttermilk biscuits with chocolate gravy, vanilla-dipped French toast with homemade berry syrup, and a hash good enough to make you weep, full of chicken, andouille sausage, sweet corn, and potatoes, all of it supporting a couple of poached eggs and smothered in homemade barbecue sauce. Lunch offers homemade potato chips with caramelized shallot dip for starters, and for seconds, a salad tossed with caramelized pears, blue cheese, and candied pecans. Another outstanding salad is the fried chicken salad with cornbread and dried cranberries, pumpkin seeds, and herb buttermilk dressing. Like everything else on the menu, the BLT is made with a twist: it contains fried green tomatoes and avocado. Southern desserts rule here, including homemade praline pecan ice cream pie with sweet peach compote and chocolate beignets with white chocolate sauce. *739 Chapala St, Santa Barbara; 805/ 899 3100; $–$$; MC, V; no checks; breakfast, lunch, dinner Tues–Sat, brunch Sun; beer and wine; reservations recommended; on Chapala St across from the Paseo Nuevo shopping arcade entrance.*

WINE CASK ★★★

Informal elegance in the tradition of great European restaurants has been captured within these stucco walls, which are accented by a stunning hand-stenciled ceiling and a grand stone fireplace. Owner Doug Margerum, who has a small adjoining wine shop, now presides over a vast cellar of more than 2,000 labels. Former sous-chef Hector Martinez and Alex Castillo are chefs de cuisine. Appetizers include a Belgian endive, baby spinach, and apple salad; a crab cake with roasted corn–mango salsa; and grilled foie gras with apple risotto and blackberry sauce. Entrees range from peppercorn-crusted ahi, seared rare and served with ginger risotto and stir-fried vegetables, to roasted lamb sirloin with goat cheese–pancetta mashed potatoes and marinated vegetable slaw with Cabernet Sauvignon sauce and fresh mint infusion. The best dessert choice has to be the warm caramel pecan bread pudding. We recommend the Sunday or Monday prix-fixe tasting, which includes six courses and five wines paired with the savory items. The restaurant's general wine list is 60 pages long, with vintages from all over the world. An outdoor patio offers a charming alternative to the main room, especially on warmer nights. *813 Anacapa St, Santa Barbara; 805/966-9463; $$$; AE, DC, MC, V; checks OK; lunch Mon–Fri, dinner every day; full bar; reservations recommended; www.winecask.com; inside the El Paseo arcade.* &

YOUR PLACE ★★

Simple rattan furniture and bamboo paneling, traditional music, and wall hangings leave no question that this is a Thai restaurant. And framed awards on the walls testify to the accolades it has won for over a decade. You might want to start with a classic soup such as tom kah gai, laden with chunks of chicken and delicately flavored with lemongrass, or the grilled beef salad with spicy lime dressing, which is guaranteed to jump-start your taste buds. Choosing from the huge menu is the hardest thing you'll do here; go with a bunch of friends so you can order as many dishes as possible. Try the divine massamun, a beef curry with onions and peanuts in coconut milk. Eggplant tofu is an excellent vegetarian alternative. The deep-fried garlic-pepper spareribs are divine, as is the pra luck chicken, diced meat with spinach served in a peanut sauce. Along with the requisite satay (barbecued pork or beef on skewers with a peanut dipping sauce), honey duck, and phad thai, you can also find some more unusual items, including squid with mint leaves. *22 Milpas St, Santa Barbara; 805/966-5151; $; AE, MC, V; no checks; lunch, dinner Tues–Sun; beer and wine; reservations recommended for dinner only; Milpas St exit, 1 block north of Hwy 101.* &

LODGINGS

BACARA RESORT AND SPA ★★★

The newest resort in Santa Barbara for the sleek and chic is Bacara Resort & Spa, with more than 350 luxurious guest rooms and suites, all with stunning views from private patios or balconies, high-speed Internet access, 24-hour in-room dining, minibars, multiline telephones, and nightly rates starting at roughly $400 and soaring to $2,500. The resort was obviously built to appeal to the movie star and mogul crowd from L.A.—witness the 225-person screening room so no one will miss seeing the rushes of their latest film project. The lodgings are in one-, three-, and four-story Mediterranean villas, each graced with Frette linens, plush robes, and Spanish dark wood furniture with blue and white fabrics. Located five minutes from the Santa Barbara airport, it is suspended between the Pacific Ocean and the Santa Ynez mountains and has a 2-mile white sand beach. The resort is designed with a nod to Spanish Colonial and mission architecture in a villagelike setting, with tile roofs, splashing fountains, covered archways, and wooden trellises. Adjacent is the resort's own 1,000-acre Ranch of Bacara, a lemon and avocado ranch, where you can hike and ride mountain bikes or have a picnic. The three-level spa offers a full menu of treatments, including a citrus avocado body scrub, Thai massage, and an ultimate body blitz (if you have to ask, you don't need one). Three zero-edge swimming pools with cabanas keep you from being bored paddling in circles. There are also three restaurants: Miro, a fine dining restaurant on the bluff over the ocean; the Bistro, a relaxed cafe with Mediterranean food; and the informal Spa Cafe. *8301 Hollister Ave, Santa Barbara; 805/968-0100 or 877/422-4245; $$$$; AE, MC, V; checks OK, www.bacara resort.com; Winchester Canyon/Hollister Ave exit off Hwy 101.* &

THE BATH STREET INN ★★

This Queen Anne Victorian has a homey charm, with big comfortable chairs, fresh flowers, and a roaring fire on cool evenings. The friendly and comfortable bed-and-breakfast is set back from a quiet street in a well-kept, quaint area of old Santa Barbara. The 1890s house has eight rooms, including the Abigail Room, the original master bedroom, with a forest green print wallpaper and a rose comforter. Upstairs on the third floor is a library and sitting area with comfy chairs; downstairs there's another sitting room, with a fireplace and Victorian antiques. Breakfast and afternoon tea, wine, and cheese are served in the dining nook off the main room or, on warmer days, on pink linen-topped tables on the lovely trellised patio under a canopy of wisteria. In the Summer House behind the main house, and connected by a deck, are four more guest rooms: the Country Suite, the largest, boasts a canopy bed, fireplace, whirlpool tub, fully equipped kitchen, and mountain views. All the rooms are clean and comfortable, with their own unique features—a claw-footed tub in the Partridge Room, a window seat in the Wedgwood Room—and in the rose-patterned Tiffany, you can luxuriate in a bubble bath with mountain views. *1720 Bath St, Santa Barbara; 805/682-9680 or 800/549-2284 (within CA) or 800/341-2284 (outside CA); $$–$$$; MC, V; checks OK; between Valerio and Arrellaga Sts.* &

BAYBERRY INN ★★

The Bayberry Inn is a dignified blue-shingled 1894 Federal mansion that has been designated a Structure of Merit by the city of Santa Barbara. The formally decorated and restored inn has been featured on the city's historic home tour, and it is one of the more elegant inns in town. The inn's signature is its queen-size canopy beds (most with inset chandeliers overhead) complete with deluxe fabrics that cascade down around the bed to the floor. Kenneth Freeland and his wife, Jill, bought the inn in 2000 and with their family have worked hard to bring the house and its grounds back to their former glory, installing new wallpapers and carpets, enlarging decks, creating a new patio, and planting new roses, hedges, and orange trees. The inn is truly a family affair: Jill's Aunt Lillian

Santa Barbara sits on the U.S. West Coast's only east-to-west stretch of beach, which shelters it from wind and storms and makes for terrific sunsets.

Arechiga and her husband, Eddie, live on the premises; Lillian is the innkeeper and helps make the day's desserts; Eddie is the breakfast chef; and Jill's mother grows the flowers that grace every room. Each room is named for a berry: the Hollyberry is serene and elegant, a corner room shaded by a century-old oak. The queen bed has a forest green canopy, there's a fireplace, and the bath across the hall is private. The Cranberry on the first floor is drenched in burgundies, with a canopy bed, its own private deck, a private bath, a view of the garden, and a fireplace. Included in a stay are a gourmet breakfast, afternoon wine and cheese, and homemade dessert in the evening. Ask about the winter special, which offers the third night free. *111 W Valerio St, Santa Barbara; 805/569-3398; $$$; AE, DIS, M, V; checks OK; www.bayberryinnsantabarbara.com; on the corner of Chapala and Valerio Sts.*

EL ENCANTO HOTEL AND GARDEN VILLAS ★★★

View For those who want to revel in the old Santa Barbara resort style and also want the best views in town, this famous romantic retreat's 84 cottages are perched on 10 lushly landscaped acres high above town. Some of the cottages were originally built for faculty and students of the erstwhile nearby State Normal School (now UC Santa Barbara in Goleta), and others were added later for visiting artists and writers. Some were built as early as 1912 in the popular Craftsman style, and others have a Spanish Colonial sensibility, but all are set among 10 acres of grounds, tropical foliage, waterfalls, arbors, a Japanese garden, and lawns rolling down to views of the ocean beyond. By the 1920s El Encanto had opened as a resort hotel. In 1999 the hotel underwent a much-needed $10 million renovation. Many of the cottages have fireplaces, porches, and French doors and are furnished with Craftsman or contemporary furniture, wicker, and Oriental rugs; and some are ideal for families, with two bedrooms and two baths. The plantation-like main building houses a lounge and bar area with high-back wicker chairs, shutters, and colorful florals, and the award-winning El Encanto restaurant (see the review in the Restaurants section, above). *1900 Lasuen Rd, Santa Barbara; 805/687-5000 or 800/346-7039; $$$; AE, DC, MC, V; no checks; www.elencantohotel.com; from Mission St, turn left on Laguna St, right on Los Olivos St, right on Alameda Padre Serra, and left on Lasuen Rd to entrance.*

FRANCISCAN INN ★

Our nominee as one of the best lodging values in town, this appealing upscale motel/inn is in a pleasant neighborhood only a block from the beach. The inn has both regular rooms and suites, and all the bright and tidy accommodations have nicer furniture than most motels—more like inns usually offer, with fluffy, flowered spreads, white-painted iron beds, skirted tables, and armoires. The design of the red-roofed buildings is Spanish-Mediterranean, and there's a heated outdoor pool. The suites, good for stays of a week or longer, have kitchenettes, ovens, stoves, fully-stocked fridges, and every utensil you'll need. All rooms and suites have direct-dial phones with free local calls and TV/video players with cable. Daily, weekly, midweek, and seasonal rates are available. You can easily walk to the harbor or Stearns Wharf for dinner. A complimentary continental breakfast of muffins, croissants, juice, and coffee is served by a staff person in the cozy lobby. Winter and midweek rates can be a real bargain. *109 Bath St, Santa Barbara; 805/963-8845; $–$$; AE, DC, MC, V; checks OK; franciscan inn@att.net; www.franciscaninn.com; corner of Mason and Bath Sts.* &

SIMPSON HOUSE INN ★★★★

If you were very rich and had a very good houseman, life would be like this. The Simpson House is the only B&B in North America that has been given a 5-diamond rating by AAA, and it's well deserved. The superlative B&B experience begins the moment your car comes to a stop at the end of the driveway leading to this imposing Victorian gem, fenced into its own world. A staff member will greet you, show you around the estate, and offer you a refreshment. If you have chosen accommodations in the main house, you won't be disappointed; period detailing on the painted ceilings is color-coordinated with the Oriental rugs and plush upholstery and complemented with brass beds, European goose-down comforters, and elegant antiques. In back, beyond the stone patio and lawn (the domain of Bella, the most petted black Lab in town), guests can enjoy more privacy in old barn suites and two-story cottages with private courtyards and stone fountains, tucked between tall oaks and magnolias. Each is stylishly modern country-cottage in decor, with open-beam ceiling, river-stone fireplace, whirlpool tub, and wet bar. A complete gourmet breakfast—with china and silver—is delivered to your room. A European facial, warm herbal oil massage, or manicure can be arranged in your room. Local Santa Barbara wines and a lavish array of hors d'oeuvres are served nightly in the sitting area. Bicycles and beach equipment are also offered, along with an extensive collection of videos. *121 E Arrellaga St, Santa Barbara; 805/963-7067 or 800/676-1280; $$$–$$$$; AE, DIS, MC, V; checks OK; reservations@simpsonhouseinn.com; www.simpsonhouseinn.com; between Anacapa and Santa Barbara Sts.* &

THE UPHAM HOTEL AND COUNTRY HOUSE ★★

The Upham is the oldest continually operating hotel in Southern California. Unlike many local bed-and-breakfasts, this one didn't begin life as a private home, but was built in 1871 as a hotel; its main hotel building and garden cottages house 50 rooms. Still, feather duvets, botanical prints, plush settees, wooden louvered shutters, and armoires make this feel more like a country house than a hotel. Furnishings echo the period architecture, which works particularly well in Rose Cottage rooms 28 and 31, with their four-poster beds and mahogany desks overlooking the main garden area. The ultimate in luxury here is the secluded Sycamore master suite, which has a large enclosed patio with a cafe table and chairs and a hammock, plus a double whirlpool tub in the bathroom. A walkway with trellised arches and a gazebo weaves its way around the pretty garden and into the main building, where continental breakfast, afternoon cheese and wine, and evening milk and cookies are served. The Upham also boasts its own highly regarded bistro-style eatery, Louie's, which serves lunch and dinner Monday through Friday and dinner only on Saturday and Sunday. It fills up with more than just hotel guests, so be sure to make a reservation. The Upham also owns the Tiffany Country House Bed & Breakfast lodging across the street, which has recently undergone a complete renovation. Lodging there is even more like staying in someone's elegant antique-filled country home, very private and cozy. Call to ask for rates and availability. *Upham: 1404 De la Vina St, Santa Barbara; 805/963-2283 or 800/999-5672; Tiffany: 1323 De la Vina St, Santa Barbara; 805/962-0058 or 800/727-0876; $$$–$$$$; AE, DC, MC, V; no checks; on the corner of Sola St, 2 blocks west of State St.*

VILLA ROSA ★★

In the boutique hotel tradition of London and Paris, the Villa Rosa is sparsely but tastefully decorated: soft desert and ocean hues, simple carved furniture that gives a nod to Santa Barbara's Spanish and Mexican heritage. The beautiful building with its red-tiled roof and scrolled iron detail wraps around a secluded pool and spa. Some of the rooms overlook the pool, while others have ocean, harbor, or mountain views. Some have tiled adobe fireplaces and sitting areas, and all have beamed ceilings and louvered doors and windows. The location, near the harbor, is convenient yet quiet. In-room continental breakfast and a newspaper are included in the price, as are afternoon and evening aperitifs. The affable staff have good knowledge of the local scene. Day membership at the nearby athletic club and massage, available on request, adds to the appeal of this small inn with big value. *15 Chapala St, Santa Barbara; 805/966-0851; $$–$$$; AE, MC, V; checks OK 2 weeks in advance; Cabrillo Blvd to Chapala St.*

MONTECITO

Driving through the lush byways of Montecito is like motoring through a private park or along the Mediterranean coast. The home of two of California's top-notch accommodations (San Ysidro Ranch and the Four Seasons Biltmore), this exclusive pastoral community of country lanes and gated multimillion-dollar haciendas is an idyllic retreat for the moneyed few who can afford to live in relative privacy among the shady oaks and the jasmine-scented air. Visitors (and residents) who venture beyond their glamorous digs meander to the town's charming main street, Coast Village Road, the central village area and gathering spot.

ACTIVITIES

Our Lady of Mount Carmel Church. Drive west on East Valley Road to where it meets Hot Springs Road, and you will stumble onto the beautiful adobe Mount Carmel Church, set in a contemplative desert garden with a soaring religious statue, a likeness of the church's namesake. The primitive painted interior has teal and coral walls behind the altar, wood carved beams, and naif wainscoting painted in waves. Overhead are Mexican silver chandeliers. This is a wonderful place to retreat and take a quiet moment for reflection.

Lotusland. One of the best-kept secrets of the Santa Barbara/Montecito area is this stunning private estate garden with lush plantings so exotic they are seldom seen all in one place. Lotusland was named for the lotus water plant, which was first grown on this property in 1882. More elaborate gardens were designed in 1918, when the property was called Cuesta Linda. In 1941 a Polish opera star named Ganna Walska bought the 37-acre estate as a spiritual refuge and poured her passion into finding the most rare and far-flung plants in the world to furnish its garden landscape—including the thick grove of dragon trees visitors can still enjoy today. Ponds and waterfalls lace the property, and on the tour you will wander a labyrinth of separate garden "rooms" that feature only aloes, or succulents, or water garden plants, or ferns or cacti or topiaries. A Japanese garden, an Australian area, and a water garden with the famous lotus flowers keep the stroller enchanted. Bromeliads and cycads (known as sago palms) were Walska's special love, and she was known to spend thousands of dollars on a single rare plant. You will definitely see plants here that you've never seen before: there are shaving brush palms, Chilean wine palms, and Bunya Bunya trees, which have big warts and bear 40-pound cones. The gardens don't just look good, they smell good, which Walska planned, particularly with the Breath of Heaven trees. This is not a place you drop in; you must call months ahead for an appointment (805/969-9990; www.lotusland.org) and directions (they do not reveal the location until you book a reservation). You will be assigned a particular time to take a tour led by a well-trained docent. (Tours offered Weds–Sat mid-Feb–mid-Nov, 10am and 1:30pm; $15 per person)

Shopping. Kim International Furnishings is a treasure trove of Asian artifacts, antiques, and contemporary furnishing and accessories. Owned by Kim

Mascheroni-Kieler, this gallery (1273 Coast Village Rd; 805/565-2999) has themed traveling "shows" of artifacts as well as regularly stocked items. Another branch is located in downtown Santa Barbara. At 516 San Ysidro Road are several shops of interest. Wendy Foster Clothing (Wendy is Pierre La Fond's wife) has chic and wearable clothes in fine fabrics (805/565-1506), and on the same ground level is Pierre La Fond and Wendy Foster Sportswear (805/565-1505). Upstairs over the Pierre La Fond Deli is a gift shop (surprise!) called Upstairs at Pierre La Fond (805/565-1503), which has a bath section and bedding, women's loungewear, tabletop, and garden departments, plus some sophisticated furniture pieces and many trendy household items.

Beaches. Since as far back as the 1920s, Montecito has been known for its fine homes, which today range from $500,000 to $5 million on up. But visitors can still access its beautiful beaches without having to swing for a hefty mortgage. Miramar Beach fronts the former Miramar Resort Hotel (1555 S Jamison Ln), which is now a fenced construction site, but you can still drive to the beach via South Jamison Lane. Butterfly Beach (Butterfly Ln and Channel Dr) fronts the Four Seasons Biltmore Santa Barbara; adjacent is Hammonds Beach, a public access beach—connected to Butterfly via walking trails. To reach Hammonds, park at the end of Eucalyptus Lane in Montecito and take the path to the beach. There's a free parking lot, no lifeguards, and the beach is open 8am to sunset. For more information contact the Santa Barbara County Parks Department (805/568-2460; www.sbparks.org).

RESTAURANTS

LITTLE ALEX'S ★

Tucked away in a busy local shopping center that also houses everything from a barber to a gas station, you'll find a small but very busy Mexican eatery that makes up for in taste what it lacks in charm. Whatever your choice from the variety of enchiladas, burritos, tacos, or chimichangas, know that the portions are huge (even the ones that are purportedly small), so come here with an appetite. From the popular primo burrito, chile verde, and chile relleno to the house-special arroz con pollo (chicken breast simmered in ranchera sauce), you won't be disappointed. Phone ahead for to-go orders to take to the beach. The perfect picnic item is the "burrito-on-the-run," a hand-held burrito full of beans, rice, cheese, and sauce that comes in large or small and can be ordered with chicken, carnitas (lightly fried seasoned pork), chile colorado (beef), veggies, or other fillings. *1024A Coast Village Rd, Montecito; 805/969-2297; $; checks OK; breakfast, lunch, dinner every day; beer and wine; no reservations; at the junction of Coast Village Rd and Hot Springs Rd in the far rear corner of the Vons Shopping Center.*

LUCKY'S ★★

One of the newest restaurants in town is this hip retro steak house, with its clean lines of stucco and wood in a structure very near the Montecito Inn on Coast Village Road. Vegetarians should just pass on by, as they would be aghast at the 22-ounce Porterhouse or the enormous rack of lamb for one. The New York pepper steak with Cognac gets raves, as does the New York strip steak with Roquefort. Seafood is not neglected: you'll find a salmon fillet, grilled or poached; a Maine lobster, steamed or grilled; and daily fish specials. Other old-fashioned dishes include creamed spinach, jumbo shrimp cocktails, and wilted spinach salad. The sauces alone are more reminiscent of 1960s France than America in the new millennium: rich béarnaises and hollandaises and another with red wine and shallots. Chef James Sly seems to know what diners want; it is often packed here and can be hard to get a reservation, especially on weekends. You can always sit at the bar, where they serve the full menu. Decor is restrained, with plush seating. *1279 Coast Village Rd, Montecito; 805/565-7540; $$; AE, DIS, MC, V; no checks; dinner every day, brunch Sat–Sun; full bar; reservations recommended; luckys@west.net; south end of Coast Village Rd, next to the Montecito Inn.*

PANE E VINO ★★★

Good luck finding this terrific but nearly hidden restaurant with a red-tiled roof and ivy-covered patio, tucked into the corner of a quiet shopping center. However, at this popular Italian trattoria (part of a chain based in San Francisco), it's the patrons who are truly lucky. The authentic country fare attracts quiet power brokers, well-heeled locals, and many local restaurateurs, who rave about the fresh pasta (Thursday-night gnocchi is legendary), risotto, simple grilled fish, bistecca alla fiorentina (beefsteak with spinach), bresaola con rucola (dried cured beef with arugula, sweet onions, and vinaigrette dressing), and juicy veal chops. Daily specials—which sometimes outnumber regular menu items—include seasonal items such as local mussels in garlic sauce or spaghetti with rock shrimp and radicchio. The wine list is largely Italian; desserts include classically good tiramisu, crème caramel, and an assortment of gelati. The outdoor patio, especially appealing on balmy summer nights, provides the largest seating area, but the more intimate interior, which evokes Old World charm and comfort, is equally coveted, charmingly adorned with a shelf of assorted plates, bowls, and children's soccer trophies. *1482 E Valley Rd, Montecito; 805/969-9274; $$–$$$; AE, MC, V; no checks; lunch Mon–Sat, dinner every day; beer and wine; reservations recommended; San Ysidro Rd to Montecito Village.* &

PIERRE LA FOND DELI ★

Suppose you wake up at 5:30am on your trip and want a cup of gourmet coffee. Not to worry, just head for this gourmet deli in Montecito, where they open extra early because their neighbors in nearby mansions are early risers. While you're there pick up a delicious pastry or bagel to be savored on the vine-covered patio. When lunchtime rolls around try the famous chicken or black bean enchiladas or a roll filled with crab cake, or try the Caesar chicken wrap, individual quiche, or salad bar. You might want to pair a cappuccino or chai tea with one of their famous farmcakes—a dense and decadent chocolate muffin swirled with cream cheese and chocolate chips. They sell beer and wine but do not serve it; if you buy a bottle you can take it out to enjoy on the patio. There is also a downtown Santa Barbara branch at 516 State Street between Cota and Gutierrez Streets, and one in the Paseo Nuevo Shopping Center. *516 San Ysidro Rd, Montecito (and branches); 805/565-1502; $–$$; AE, MC, V; local checks only; breakfast (downtown only), lunch, dinner every day; beer and wine (for purchase); no reservations; www.pierrelafond.com; in Plaza del Sol Center.*

LODGINGS

FOUR SEASONS BILTMORE ★★★★

This is where you stay if you will be arriving in a Jaguar. The elegant 234-room property, loaded with the luxury associated with the Four Seasons chain, is one of the state's most beautiful Old World–style hotels. The regal main Spanish Revival building, built in 1927, stands amid towering palms overlooking the Pacific. Magnificent wrought-iron gates lead into a pale-hued lobby with hand-decorated archways, bowls of orchids, and polished antiques resting on waxed terra-cotta tiles. Rooms are tastefully furnished in soft tones with beds of the utmost comfort, plantation shutters, botanical prints, and marble bathrooms with big fluffy towels and robes. Heat lamps, hair dryers, book lights, and bowls of candy are some of the extra amenities, and at the touch of a button, earplugs, hot water bottles, nonallergenic soap, and even that toothbrush you forgot will magically appear. For more privacy book one of the green-trimmed California bungalows, many of which have fireplaces and patios with wrought-iron lounge chairs. In addition to the pool and tennis courts, the expansive lawn area behind the main building is home to croquet, shuffleboard, and an 18-hole putting green. The gym is fully equipped and bikes are at the ready along with a map of local bike paths. The Patio restaurant, with its retractable glass roof, offers casual fare and also hosts a famous Sunday brunch where chefs man a multitude of food stations serving everything from roast beef to custom omelets. La Marina is an elegant, timber-beamed dining room that serves an array of continental and American cuisine such as truffled brie-and-cauliflower soup, lobster, salmon, and beef tenderloin. (Try to reserve the table by the arched ocean-view window.) At the La Sala lounge, afternoon tea, served cozily by the fire, gives way to live jazz nightly, with dancing on Friday and Saturday. *1260 Channel Dr, Montecito; 805/969-2261 or 800/332-3442; $$$$; AE, DC, DIS, MC, V; checks OK; www.fshr. com; Olive Mill Rd exit from Hwy 101, to Channel Dr.* &

MONTECITO INN ★★

This is the hotel about which Richard Rodgers wrote the love song "There's a Small Hotel." While the wishing well immortalized in the song is unfortunately long gone, the hotel retains its romantic charm. The Mediterranean-style red-tiled stucco establishment was once owned by actors Fatty Arbuckle and Charlie Chaplin (whose image is everywhere, from the etched glass doors to the vintage movie posters lining the hallways). It also seems fair to note that the 101 freeway runs directly alongside, whereas formerly only Coast Village Road offered access, but windows now have double glass and the sound is muted. The hotel is as popular now as when it opened in 1928 and hosted Hollywood royalty from Norma Shearer to Marion Davies. The hotel owes its popularity partly to its prime location in Montecito village, within walking distance of a beautiful beach shared with the nearby Biltmore. The 61 rooms with their Provençal blue-and-yellow prints and wooden shutters remind one of the south of France. The seven one-bedroom luxury suites have hand-painted designs, whirlpool tubs set in marble, fireplaces, French doors, and arched windows. The much-sought-after Tower Suite has an upstairs bedroom and downstairs sitting room, both with ocean and mountain vistas. The original 1927 Otis elevator still brings guests up handily. California cuisine is served daily in the casual cafe. A central sitting area leads to a modest heated pool, where piped-in music mutes the moderate traffic noise from 101 below; there is an attached gym. A video library that includes all of Chaplin's film work is available to guests. When you call for weeknight reservations be sure to ask specifically for the midweek special rate, which is a remarkable value. *1295 Coast Village Rd, Montecito; 805/969-7854; $$–$$$$; AE, DC, DIS, MC, V; no checks; info@montecitoinn.com; www.montecitoinn.com; Olive Mill Rd exit from Hwy 101.* &*(new suites)*

SAN YSIDRO RANCH ★★★★

At first glance this casual scattering of modest cottages in the foothills of the Santa Ynez Mountains looks like a comfortable family-style resort. But don't be fooled: Vivien Leigh and Laurence Olivier married here and Jackie and John F. Kennedy honeymooned in one of the cottages. You can, too—just be prepared for a serious bill: although the Canyon Room is only $375 per night, the Kennedy Suite runs $1,850 per night and the Eucalyptus Cottage, with its own pool, spa, and kitchen, is $3,950. At least you won't feel constricted—there is plenty of room to roam on this 540-acre resort. From the moment you find which white cottage has your name by the door (and your dog's name is registered in the special canine guest book at the desk) luxury awaits you in the form of carefully selected antiques, Frette bed linens, goose-down-filled comforters on beds high enough that some offer a stepping stool, toiletries worth taking home, and robes you can buy. You are also guaranteed a view of beautiful landscaped terraced gardens, mountains, canyons, or ocean from your private porch or outdoor hot tub. The pool, gym, and tennis courts are grouped at the top of the property. Within easy walking distance of all rooms is the casual Plow & Angel bistro, complete with fireplace and bar, which serves tasty pub grub. On weekends they host Neighbor Nights with comfort food such as baby back ribs served as part of a complete meal at a fixed price. Upstairs is the renowned Stonehouse restaurant, where Chef Jamie West, who has been named as Southern California's Chef of the Year by the American Tasting Institute, draws heavily on his ranch kitchen garden to create fresh regional cuisine. If you want to see how he does it, just flip on the TV on Friday mornings, turn to the local ABC affiliate KEYT, and enjoy his regular cooking segment. Entrees include peppercorn-seared rare ahi tuna with shrimp dumplings, jasmine rice, and watercress pesto; butter-braised Maine lobster; and Asian-spiced Muscovy duck breast in port wine sauce. The Stonehouse also has peaceful, country-formal surroundings, a fine wine list, and professional service; dinner here is definitely an event. While it's wonderful to stay at the ranch, you can also lodge elsewhere and come for a meal at the Plow & Angel or the Stonehouse, soaking up the ambience without breaking the bank. *900 San Ysidro Ln, Montecito; 805/969-5046 or 800/368-6788; $$$–$$$$; AE, MC, V; checks OK; reservations@sanysidroranch.com, www.sanysidroranch.com; from Hwy 101 take the San Ysidro exit, drive north, and turn right on San Ysidro Lane.* &

THE CHANNEL ISLANDS

These lonely islands off the Central Coast are called California's Galapagos, thanks to their isolation and its effect on the plant and animal species that thrive there. The city of Ventura is the best departure point for visiting the Santa Barbara Channel Islands National Park, consisting of five unspoiled islands that sit 14 to 55 miles offshore. Remote and wild, the islands are said to closely resemble what Southern California's landscape looked like hundreds of years ago when Native Americans were the only inhabitants. Facilities are few—just primitive campgrounds and ranger stations—so visitors are usually hikers, divers, kayakers, and wildlife watchers. Relative isolation has led to the development of distinct species like the island fox. The rocky shorelines are home to sea lions and seals and provide nesting areas for dozens of species of seabirds. The many coves make for colorful scuba diving and snorkeling. During the annual gray-whale migration in winter and early spring, pods of the graceful mammals pass close to the islands with their newly born young in tow. The unpredictable climate on the islands adds to the wildness; though breezy, clear days with strong, hot sun are the norm, thick fog banks or howling windstorms can often descend suddenly.

GETTING THERE

The park's official concessionaire for boat transportation is Island Packers (1867 Spinnaker Dr; 805/642-7688 or 805/642-1393; www.islandpackers.com), next door to the Visitors Center, which offers marine transport to the islands from Ventura Harbor and Channel Islands Harbor in Oxnard. They recently put into service a larger and faster boat than formerly available, a catamaran that shaves nearly an hour off the usual trip. Their web site lists what island tours are offered on days you plan to visit. Regularly scheduled boat excursions range from 3½-hour, nonlanding tours to full-day naturalist-led trips.

The Visitors Center has information on scuba, kayak, and whale-watching tours. There are a few boat tours that leave from Santa Barbara's harbor and others from Oxnard, but the Ventura Visitors Center is the most extensive, and Island Packers offers the largest menu of tours and the most frequent departures from here. Each island has a distinct personality.

Truth Aquatics (805/962-1127) provides boat travel from Santa Barbara Harbor to all the islands. And Channel Islands Aviation (805/987-1301) furnishes air travel to Santa Rosa Island.

"After we landed on Anacapa Island, a ranger led us through flocks of hundreds of adult sea gulls caring for their fledglings, which were in the process of learning to fly. We were surprised when he told us that Anacapa is their only place to hatch and that this tiny, shrub-covered island is absolutely crucial to their existence."
—Malei Jessee Weir, Ventura resident

Fares and schedules vary. Boat ride fees vary according to which island you choose to visit.

Visiting the Channel Islands requires some planning. Your first step should be to contact the Channel Islands National Park Visitors Center (1901 Spinnaker Dr; 805/658-5700; www.nps. gov/chis) in Ventura Harbor, where you can get maps, weather reports, and individual guidance. In the same location, the Robert J. Lagomarsino Visitors Center in Ventura has interpretive programs, a movie about Channel Islands National Park, a tide pool display, a native plant garden, a bookstore, and island exhibits. There's also a great picnic area overlooking Ventura Harbor (1901 Spinnaker Dr, Ventura; 805/658-5730).

ANACAPA

Anacapa Island is the closest to shore (14 miles). Ninety minutes or less is all it takes to reach this tiny (1.1 square miles) isle, whose principal appeal is a network of easy hiking trails that lead to scenic overlooks. Ocean waves along its perimeter have created sea cliffs, lava tubes, and sea caves. This most accessible of the five islands is really three small islands in one, totaling 5 miles long and covering 1 square mile of land. East Anacapa is 14½ miles from Ventura, and it takes about an hour and 15 minutes to get there by boat. Be ready for an immediate trek when you arrive; there are 154 steps waiting for you at Landing Cove that lead to the top of the bluff and the Anacapa Island Lighthouse. The national park has a visitor center here. West Anacapa is the largest and westernmost of the three islets, but it's off-limits for the protection of brown pelicans that use it as a prime nesting area. Middle Anacapa, with a landing spot at East Fish Camp, has a grove of eucalyptus trees and steep cliffs that tower hundreds of feet high, showing volcanic origins of air pockets, lava tubes, and sea caves. The 40-foot-high Arch Rock (and its image) is an official trademark of Anacapa and the Channel Islands National Park. Island Packers offers a day trip and a half-day Express Trip.

SANTA CRUZ

Trips to Santa Cruz Island are the most popular Channel Island excursions, according to the folks at Island Packers, who take visitors there for hiking, snorkeling, kayaking, or bird-watching. Santa Cruz, 24 miles long and nearly 100 miles square, is the largest in the chain and has a diverse landscape, with huge canyons, beaches, cliffs, Chumash village sites, and a copious variety of flora and fauna. Roughly three-quarters of the island has been protected by the Nature Conservancy since 2000. The central valley's north slope is marked by a rugged ridge, but the older south slope is more weathered. The island's Picacho Diablo peak, at 2,434 feet, is the highest point of the Channel Islands. Santa Cruz also has the chain's greatest total length of sandy beaches, a wide variety of terrain, and the greatest number of plant and animal species—650 plant species in 10 plant communities, and 140 species of bird. Channel Islands Aviation (805/987-1301) offers day trips, transportation to and from the island for campers, and surf fishing excursions as well. Trips depart from the Camarillo airport; flights take roughly 25 minutes.

SANTA ROSA

Windy Santa Rosa also has a strong ranching past, but the cows are all gone now. Ranger-led tours explore the island's canyons, beaches, and unique endangered plant species. The second-largest of the Channel Islands at 15 miles long, 10 miles wide, and 53,000 acres, Santa Rosa offers the best overnight camping and a number of very good hiking trails that explore mountains, canyons, a large marsh, and stretches of sandy beach. The island is a favorite for bird-watchers, hikers, photographers, beach-combers, and kayakers. It's covered with grasslands and has canyons lined with oak trees and ironwood. Torrey pines, which only grow naturally here and off La Jolla, can be found at Beecher's Bay. More than 180 archaeological sites have been mapped on the island; the most noted paleontological find was the exciting 1994 discovery of the world's most complete skeleton of a pygmy mammoth, which lived more than 13,000 years ago.

SAN MIGUEL

Westernmost San Miguel Island is also the wildest, and constant howling winds can't drown out the barking from its crowded seal and sea lion breeding grounds. San Miguel is also the farthest Channel Island from the mainland, 55 miles off the coast from Ventura, and is considered the most primitive in the chain. It can be a harsh, windswept place to visit and is notorious for rain and fog, but there are lots of incredible natural and cultural features worth seeing. (It's best to stay overnight here: the boat ride alone from Ventura is about five hours.) The Channel Islands' best examples of caliche, a mineral sand casting, are here, and there are 500 archaeological sites, some dating back thousands of years. The U.S. Navy bombed the area from the mid-1940s to the mid-

A special undersea viewing program is offered on Anacapa every Tuesday and Thursday from Memorial Day through Labor Day. Rangers conduct a unique live underwater video program: a diver from the national park system videotapes the forest underwater, and sends back pictures of the diverse ecosystem. For information on this program at Anacapa Island Landing Cove, call 805/658-5730. Island Packers boat company also makes day trips to Anacapa; call 805/642-7688.

1950s, and sometimes live ordnance is still uncovered by shifting sands, so it's crucial to stay on designated trails. The island's Point Bennett is the only place in the world where you can spot up to six different species of sea lions and seals—and in the winter, as many as 20,000 of the creatures can be seen at one time. From December through August there's breeding, birthing, and a whole lot of carrying on by these noisy and smelly sea mammals.

SANTA BARBARA

Grass-blanketed Santa Barbara Island sits alone to the southeast, an isolated isle out of visual range of the other islands, and often of the mainland as well. Other than the landing cove, the island has no boat access, since it is rimmed with rocky cliffs inhabited by elephant seals, sea lions, and abundant seabirds. Santa Barbara is the smallest of the islands at 640 acres and is also the farthest south. It takes a long, 3½-hour boat ride to get there, so plan on staying overnight. The island was named by Sebastian Vizcaino, who landed here on December 4, 1602—Saint Barbara's Day.

The islands are named for the deep marine troughs that separate them from the mainland. They are home to 2,000 species of animals and plants—145 of which are found nowhere else on earth.

ACTIVITIES

 Hiking. The Anacapa Island Loop Trail (easy; 2-mile loop) circles Anacapa Island and includes sea caves, sea cliffs, and spectacular bluff-top views. The nature trail heads out from the visitor center to explore a campground and several areas for picnicking and sightseeing.

Santa Cruz Island's Prisoners Harbor Trail (easy; 6 miles round trip) passes among old oak trees and through eucalyptus groves on a fennel-lined ranch road. On San Miguel, the Island Trail from Cuyler Harbor to Lester Ranch (easy; 3 miles round trip) offers great views and a chance to see as many as 15,000 marine mammals such as sea lions, northern elephant seals, harbor seals, and Guadalupe fur seals. Santa Rosa Island's East Point Trail (easy; 1 mile round trip) visits a rare stand of Torrey pines and a freshwater marsh that attracts a variety of shorebirds and waterfowl. The trail extends to a great beach. The Cherry Canyon Trail (easy; 3 miles round trip) leads to plants and animals unique to the Channel Islands, including the coastal scrub and Catalina cherry, along with the island fox and island spotted skunk, two extremely rare creatures. The trail traverses a steep canyon to an oak grove, where you might spot some Roosevelt elk, mule deer, and other critters, and ends at the island's historic ranch. Santa Barbara Island's Signal Peak Loop Trail (easy; 3.2 miles round trip) includes a spur trail to an overlook of a sea lion rookery. The visitor center and camping area south of the Landing Cove is a good place to start. Get an interpretive brochure and take the Canyon View Nature Trail there.

The Channel Islands National Park has a fine brochure/map describing the islands and their environment with beautiful artwork and explanatory text. Native animals, plants, and their habitats are depicted with an opaque watercolor technique. For a copy, call the Ventura Visitors and Convention Bureau (800/333-2989).

 Camping. Camping is permitted on all five islands in campgrounds managed by the National Park Service. But no camping is allowed on the Nature Conservancy's western 75 percent of Santa Cruz Island. The first thing you must do is secure transportation to one of the five islands (see information above). If you go by private boat, you must have the required camping permit. Protected anchorages are few, and no moorings are available. For camping reservations on San Miguel, Santa Rosa, east Santa Cruz, Anacapa, and Santa Barbara Islands, call 800/365-2267. Camping on the beaches of Santa Rosa Island is available for experienced kayakers and boaters on a seasonal basis. A free permit is required and can be obtained by calling 805/658-5711. A free backcountry permit to hike unescorted beyond the ranger station on San Miguel Island is required and can be obtained by calling 805/658-5711. Camping reservations are required for all the island campgrounds. The camping fee for all islands is $10 per night.

Wildlife Watching. The foxes on each of the Channel Islands are genetically different, but none are large—they're generally about the size of a house cat. Anacapa Island offers an opportunity to see migrating gray whales from the bluff near the lighthouse. Anacapa's west side has the largest breeding colony of the endangered California brown pelican, and the island's rocky shore is a favorite resting and breeding area for California sea lions and harbor seals. The boat ride to Santa Cruz Island from Ventura Harbor is a good way to see dolphins, migrating whales, sea lions, and seals. Hikes along Cherry Canyon Trail on Santa Rosa Island offer chances for sightings of Roosevelt elk and mule deer, as well as the rare island fox and spotted skunk. San Miguel Island, the best for birding, offers a chance to spot three different species of cormorants, storm petrels, Cassin's auklets, and pigeon guillemot, all of which nest on the island. The island also is home at times to many California sea lions, northern elephant seals, Steller sea lions, harbor seals, and Guadalupe fur seals. Santa Barbara Island offers some great chances to see seabirds such as gulls, cormorants, pelicans, and black oystercatchers. Rare birds include the black storm petrel and the Xantus' murrelet. The island night lizard, a threatened species, is also on the island but rarely seen.

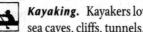 **Marine Wildlife Tours.** Wildlife-focused "sanctuary cruises" (in the waters around the islands) are occasionally offered by the Channel Islands National Marine Sanctuary and the Sea Center in Santa Barbara. The full-day excursions leave from Santa Barbara Harbor and explore the waters for whales, dolphins, and other marine mammals. These trips often include sightings of blue whales and humpback whales as well as sea lions, harbor seals, and seabirds. Trips are aboard the 88-foot *Condor* each summer. There's also a small-boat tour to the Painted Cave of Santa Cruz Island, one of the world's largest sea caves, which extends some 1,250 feet under the island. Cruise operators include Captain Don's Whale Watching and Charters (805/969-5217); Condor Whale Watching at Sea Landing (805/963-3564), which now has a new high-speed catamaran; the *Double Dolphin* (805/962-2826), usually a cocktail cruise; the *Varuna* (805/963-0068), Santa Barbara's own tall ship, which offers 2-hour sunset or coastal sails; and Paddle Sports of Santa Barbara (805/899-4925) which provides kayak rentals, island trips, and lessons.

The island deer mouse is abundant on all the Channel Islands. They are carriers of the hanta virus and will jump on you if you let them, so be very careful. Do not touch them, seal your food in tight containers, and zip your tent securely.

 Kayaking. Kayakers love to explore the Channel Islands' sea caves, cliffs, tunnels, arches, grottoes, and blowholes. Most paddlers prefer to transport their kayaks on one of concessionaire Island Packers' boats, as it is a difficult and strenuous trip from the mainland even to the closest island, Anacapa. Guided kayak experiences suitable even for beginning kayakers are given by Aquasports (800/773-2309; www.islandkayaking.com) and include single or tandem kayaks, instruction, and a guide. One-, two-, and three-day trips are offered, and 99 percent of them go to Santa Cruz Island, which offers a wide range of wildlife, the most sea caves of any island, and also a good sand beach from which to launch. The best time of year to kayak is August through November: as the water becomes cooler, it also becomes clearer.

Swimming/Scuba Diving/Snorkeling. Landing Cove on Anacapa Island has a dock with ladders from which

All the campgrounds have pit toilets and picnic tables, but except for on Santa Rosa Island, water isn't available, so you must take it with you. On Santa Rosa and Santa Cruz there is some well water to wash with that is also technically potable, but not very pleasant tasting, so bring your own to drink. The islands are subject to campfire closures during dry times, so check on that. Beach fires may be allowed seasonally (bring manufactured logs only) but they must be only on cobbled areas or a sand beach. You may take enclosed camp stoves. There's no trash service, so all campers must pack out what they pack in. Because of the potential for bad weather or transportation delays, always pack supplies for an extra day on an island. Call the Channel Islands National Park at 805/658-5730 for more information.

you can go swimming or snorkeling, but there is no beach. Local rangers call this area the "aquarium," as snorkelers will see spiny lobster, garibaldis (the state's official marine fish), calico bass, California sheephead, and much more in these National Marine Sanctuary waters. The water warms up enough for swimming in late summer and early fall. Cathedral Cove, along the north shore of Anacapa Island, is a very good place to dive. The island has caves, coves, and shipwrecks. The steamer *Winfield Scott* grounded and sank off Middle Anacapa in 1853, and there are remnants of the wreck still on the ocean floor. West Anacapa's Frenchy Cove has a beach and a snorkeling area.

Picnicking. Robert J. Lagomarisino Visitors Center has a great picnic area overlooking Ventura Harbor (1901 Spinnaker Dr, Ventura; 805/658-5730). Anacapa Island has an excellent picnic area. Santa Cruz Island has tables for day-use at both Scorpion Ranch and Smugglers Cove.

BEST PLACES
DESTINATIONS
CENTRAL CALIFORNIA COAST
REPORT FORM

Based on my personal experience, I wish to nominate the following restaurant or place of lodging; or confirm/correct/disagree with the current review.

_____

_____

_____

_____

(Please include address and telephone number of establishment, if convenient.)

REPORT

Please describe food, service, style, comfort, value, date of visit, and other aspects of your experience; continue on another piece of paper if necessary.

_____

_____

_____

_____

_____

_____

_____

I am not concerned, directly or indirectly, with the management or ownership of this establishment.

_____
SIGNED

_____
ADDRESS

_____

_____

_____
PHONE   DATE

Please address to Best Places Destinations and send to:

SASQUATCH BOOKS
615 Second Avenue, Suite 260
Seattle, WA 98104
Feel free to email feedback as well: books@sasquatchbooks.com

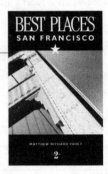